LANCASTER

A HISTORY

Andrew White

LANCASTER

A HISTORY

Andrew White

Phillimore

2003

Published by
PHILLIMORE & CO. LTD,
Shopwyke Manor Barn, Chichester, West Sussex, England

© Dr Andrew White, 2003

ISBN 1 86077 244 7

Printed and bound in Great Britain by
MPG BOOKS LTD
Bodmin, Cornwall

Contents

List of Illustrations vii

Acknowledgements x

Introduction xi

One   Where do you come from? 1

Two   Development of the Townscape 13

Three   House and Home 25

Four   Lancaster on the Map 45

Five   Working for a Living 57

Six   Entertainment 76

Seven   Getting There 90

Eight   Alarums and Excursions 115

Nine   Priory and Castle 125

Ten   The Majesty of the Law 145

Notes 156

Index 161

List of Illustrations

Frontispiece:'Engraving of Lancaster from the south east by W. Westall, 1829'.

1   The North East Prospect of Lancaster, 1728 xii
2   Roman altars from Burrow-in-Lonsdale and Folly Farm 2
3   Drawing of the tombstone of Lucius Julius Apollinaris 3
4   Drawing of Roman bronze forceps 3
5   Anglo-Saxon Cross with a Latin inscription 4
6   Anglo-Saxon Cross with an inscription in Anglian runes 4
7   Grave of Sambo at Sunderland Point 7
8   Grave of John Dixon 7
9   Painting of ship being built at Brockbanks yard 8
10 Cartoon of German band from *Punch* magazine 9
11 Mosque in Fenton Street 11
12 Advertisement for Luneside Engineering, Halton, 1964 12
13 Fragment of the Wery Wall 14
14 Reconstruction of Roman Lancaster from the Moor 15
15 The Roman fort and distribution map of Roman finds 15
16 Marsh Enclosure, 1796 16
17 Location of main fields 17
18 Villas on the Greaves, from Harrison & Hall's map of 1877 19
19 Anchor Lane under excavation, 1999 21
20 Aerial photo of Castle Hill, *c*.1973 22
21 Reconstruction of the Dominican Friary 23
22 A typical yard: Ross Yard off Cheapside 24
23 Excavation of 65 Church Street in 1973-4 26
24 Reconstruction of Sir Robert de Holand's 1314 house 27
25 Detail of 1684 map – Great Bonifont Hall and Stewp Hall 28
26 Three of four pairs of re-used oak crucks found at Mitchell's Brewery 29
27 View of Stonewell in 1810 by Gideon Yates 30
28 View of the Market Place *c*.1770 31
29 Seventeenth-century stone houses in Church Street 32
30 Drawing of Church Street with old houses surviving 34
31 Reed and plaster wall at 11 Chapel Street 35
32 Reconstruction of the building of St George's Quay in 1751 35
33 Plan of lots for leasing in Dalton Square 36
34 Detail from Clark's map of 1807 36
35 The Albert Terrace, East Road, seen from St Peter's spire, *c*.1890 37
36 St George's Quay terrace 38
37 Plan of area around Town Hall *c*.1910 39
38 Moorlands estate, seen *c*.1900 from the spire of St Peter's 40
39 Council Houses, Denny Avenue, Ryelands, *c*.1932-3 41
40 Scale Hall developments, 1930s 42
41 Pre-fabs at Ashton Road 43

42 1960s high-rise at Skerton 44
43 Speed's map of 1610 46
44 Map of 1684 48
45 Detail of Market Place from 1684 map 49
46 Map of 1778 by Stephen Mackreth 51
47 Binns' map of 1821 53
48 Cartouche to Harrison & Hall's map of 1877 54
49 Detail of Freehold Estate from Harrison & Hall 1877 55
50 Detail of the Military Barracks from Harrison & Hall 1877 56
51 John Lawson's farthing token 58
52 Portrait of William Stout 59
53 Clay tobacco pipe with John Holland's mark 61
54 Robert Gillow in the Freemen's Rolls 62
55 Portrait of Dodshon Foster by William Tate 63
56 Handbill for Richard Dilworth, tallow-chandler 65
57 Centre of Moor Hospital 66
58 Handbill for Jane Noon 68
59 Watercolour of 'Lancaster from the East' 69
60 Houses at Golgotha 72
61 A Victorian washerwoman, from *Punch* magazine 72
62 Thornfield, Ashton Road 74
63 The 1993 boundary walk 78
64 Theatre bill, 1772 79
65 The Circus comes to town in the 1890s 80
66 Pencil sketch of Mr Green's balloon attempt, 1832 81
67 Racecourse on the Marsh, from Yates' map of Lancashire, 1786 82
68 Handbill for a 'long main' of cocks 83
69 Detail of Mackreth's map showing the bowling green at the *Sun Inn* 85
70 Portrait of S. Dawson, cycling pioneer 86
71 Williamson Park Cycling Club, *c*.1895 87
72 Scene from the Pageant, 1913 89
73 Roman roads in Lunesdale 91
74 Reconstruction of Cockersand Abbey by David Vale 92
75 Road map by Ogilby, 1698 93
76 Detail of coal cart and horses from a Wray estate map of 1773 96
77 *Waterwitch II* 97
78 Oversands travellers 98
79 Fowler Hill toll bar 100
80 Handbill for coaches running from the *Old Sir Simon's Inn* 104
81 The old *King's Arms Inn* 105
82 Drawing of the locomotive *John O'Gaunt* 107
83 Local cartoon of *c*.1842 108
84 Reconstruction of Penny Street station by David Vale 108
85 Battery bus in Market Square during the First World War 112
86 Single-deck Lancaster Corporation buses at Scotforth Square 113
87 The M6 motorway under construction, *c*.1959 114
88 Charter of 1193 and wrapper 117
89 Detail of Church Street from 1684 map 119
90 Fred Kirk Shaw's pageant painting of Bonnie Prince Charlie 122
91 Reconstruction of a seventh-century chieftain's house and church 126
92 Hubert Austin's plan of discoveries in the Priory church, 1911 127
93 Reconstruction of the Priory in the 12th century 128
94 Reconstruction of the Priory church in the late 15th century 130
95 Plan of the Priory church in 1819 130

 96 Engraving of the Priory church looking east as it was in the 1840s 132
 97 The medieval choirstalls 132
 98 Engraving of the Priory church looking east in about 1864 133
 99 Engraving of the Priory church after 1864 133
100 'Empty Stalls or The Mare and the Manger' by Emily Sharpe 135
101 St Joseph's Catholic church, Skerton 136
102 Reconstruction of Castle in Norman times by David Vale 137
103 Plan of Castle prior to 1788, with the names of towers. P. Lee 138
104 Interior of the Well Tower, showing a window seat 139
105 The great Gatehouse of the Castle 140
106 Vertue's engraving after the 1562 drawing of Lancaster Castle 141
107 Watercolour by Thomas Hearne showing the rear of the Castle 142
108 Watercolour by Robert Freebairn showing the Shire Hall 143
109 Drawing by J. S. Slinger showing the lock-ups in the old Town Hall 145
110 The High Sheriff and javelin men ready to meet the Judge at the Castle 146
111 Title page of Potts' 'Wonderfull Discoverie' 147
112 Engraving of life in the debtors' prison by Edward Slack, c.1836 149
113 'The Castle and Arrival of Prisoners' 150
114 Hanging Corner 153
115 Portrait of Rev. J. Rowley in 1856, aged 86 153
116 Bill for hanging John Heyes in 1834 154

Acknowledgements

I would like to acknowledge the help of a great many people in bringing this book to publication. First of all to Noel Osborne and the staff at Phillimore, who encouraged and assisted at every stage. Then my colleagues at Lancaster City Museums, especially Susan Ashworth, Paul Thompson, Ivan Frontani and Wendy Moore, for information and technical help with illustrations. Then there were the staffs at Lancaster Library, especially Jenny Loveridge and Susan Wilson, at the Lancashire Record Office, especially Bruce Jackson and Andrew Thynne, and at the Whitworth Art Gallery, especially Charles Nugent. I am most grateful to David Vale for his reconstruction drawings; those in this book and others are the fruit of a long collaboration between us at Lincoln and Lancaster. Deborah Dobby and Ruth Shaw are credited separately in sections for which their research was most helpful. I am also grateful to Dr Michael Winstanley and to other members of the Wray History Group for many useful insights, and to Mike Derbyshire for discussions on Lancaster's fields.

Finally I acknowledge the support and forbearance of my wife Janette as I headed off to my study each evening in the winter of 2001-2 to write the text.

Picture Acknowledgements

Nos. 16, 68, 80, 83 Lancaster Central Library; nos. 10, 61 Punch Magazine; no. 28 Whitworth Art Gallery; nos. 56, 58 Soulby Collection, Cumbria Record Office, Barrow-in-Furness; no. 34 Binns' Collection, Liverpool Library. All the remainder are courtesy of Lancaster City Museums.

Introduction

Today Lancaster has the dignity of a city. But this rank only dates from 1937, which surprises many people. Lancaster and York are often referred to together as historic cities, largely because of the mistaken view that the two medieval royal houses of Lancaster and York actually stemmed from those places. In truth the two could not be more different in origins. York was a Roman legionary fortress, a colony of Roman citizens and, later on, capital of one of the provinces of Britain. It became the seat of one of the two medieval archbishoprics in England, a walled city with a great minster church, and *de facto* medieval capital of the north. Lancaster was a Roman auxiliary fort with a cluster of civilian buildings around it which probably felt more like a village than a town. In the Middle Ages it had a single large parish church, not a cathedral, and no walls. It was the county town of a far-from-prosperous and thinly populated county and what power it had was mainly vested in the royal castle which dominated the town. Any resemblances between the two places are of more recent origin and little more than skin-deep.

I have not gone on at such length to do down the merits of Lancaster; it is a city of great charms and much historical interest. But it is as well to start out with a clear idea of what it is not, and why. The north west was until the Industrial Revolution a poor and often backward area. Its archaeological remains from almost every period before the 18th century are more exiguous than those of any comparable area on the east coast. In the Middle Ages the region could support only two cities, Chester and Carlisle. It lay close to the Scottish border and for centuries a very real threat hung over the region, breaking out at intervals into outright warfare and invasion. This in turn cast a blight over many material developments, such as architecture and agriculture. Great changes do not tend to occur under an ever-present threat of raid and ruin. Lancaster was for many centuries typical of its region, a modest town in a very modest environment. Only with the rise of overseas trade in the Georgian period did it make much of a mark. Even this was short-lived and eclipsed by the much greater rise of Liverpool, with which it competed as a port, and of Manchester as a great manufacturing town.

It has, however, a remarkable history and one which has been established in considerable detail. The town is of a manageable scale even today, and it has kept to a remarkable degree evidence of its early layout and topography, two factors alone which make it a rewarding place to study. Its position as county town and its possession of a significant royal castle have given it an importance beyond that to be predicted from its size in the medieval period. Its geographical location, so poorly placed for trade and influence when Europe was the main target, suddenly became a great advantage in the late 17th century following the opening up of trade with the West Indian and American colonies.

With the coming of the Industrial Revolution Lancashire, too, was suddenly catapulted into prominence. From being a poor and backward area the county rapidly grew to become one of the most densely-populated in western Europe. Unfortunately, institutions such as the law and the parochial systems failed to keep pace. Consequently the county overstretched the available resources. Its county town gained a huge accession of

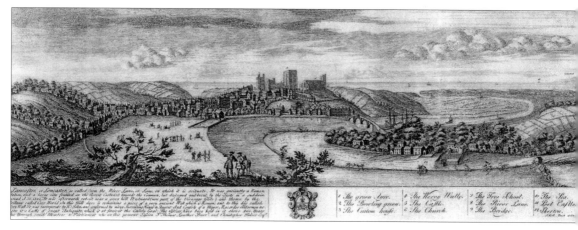

1 The North East Prospect of Lancaster by Samuel and Nathaniel Buck, 1728, one of a series illustrating all the major cities and county towns of England and Wales. The view takes in Skerton village, with its mill, to the right, the S-bend of the river Lune, and St Leonardgate, Moor Lane and Penny Street respectively to the left. In the foreground is the main reach of the river around Green Ayre, the open ground to the left of centre. In the centre are the Castle, still partially demilitarised after the Civil War and the Priory church still with its medieval tower. Below is the late medieval bridge and shipping. Despite the somewhat sketchy nature of the view and the conventionalised buildings, it seems quite accurate in its main details and equates well with the Towneley Hall map of 1684.

legal business at the Assizes held twice each year. While the failure of the parochial system here is less marked because of its widespread impact in the north, Lancaster still remains a good example of the huge undivided parishes left over from the Middle Ages to more expansive times.

Because the town was on the main road to the north and was the seat of the Assizes it attracted a disproportionate number of visitors. From the 18th century this was enhanced by the growth of the Picturesque movement. Travellers to the Lake District from the south and east habitually used Lancaster as a stepping off point for the Lake District via Lancaster Sands, a route which had the sanction of no less a guide than Wordsworth.

In the 18th and 19th centuries Lancaster was often out of step with the rest of its county, experiencing boom when others experienced bust, and vice versa. Its industrial base was established later, and dependency on textiles only followed the decay of a mercantile empire. Its position as county town led to an accumulation of facilities here, some of which still survive. In the 20th century its historic nature, different from other Lancashire towns, was a plus when it bid for one of the new universities in the 1960s. The University which was established here in 1963-4 immediately took an interest in its environs, leading to the creation of a Centre for North West Regional Studies, which in turn has fostered many studies of Lancaster and its region. The decay of traditional industry and of Morecambe's status as a resort, has led to an increasing reliance upon tourism as a source of income. This in turn has bred a policy over the last fifteen years or so of promoting the 'historic city', as well as the beautiful countryside of North Lancashire, a policy which has been extremely effective and pursued by some very talented individuals.

It is difficult to predict the future of the city, but it is clear that many people find it a very attractive place to live and undoubtedly its rich history, its setting and its natural advantages will continue to be factors in its favour for many years to come.

One

Where do you come from?

There is a tendency among local historians to assume that until very recent times the population of most provincial towns and cities was homogenous and largely home-grown. This is manifestly untrue, as even a quick glance at our history will show. There seem to have been periods when local society was very varied in origin, and times when it was more uniform. In recent centuries prosperity has encouraged inward migration from less affluent parts of the countryside, from European persecution (Flemings, Huguenots and Jews) and latterly from countries of the former British Empire, while slump has led to emigration to other towns and cities, or to other countries where opportunity seemed to present itself, especially America, Canada, Australia and New Zealand. In all this Lancaster is a microcosm of national behaviour, although it has experienced neither the range nor the quantity of inward and outward migration that some of its larger neighbours, such as Manchester and Liverpool or the cotton towns of East Lancashire, have experienced.

Many different peoples have lived on the banks of the river Lune, including those whose Neolithic pottery was found under a Roman building in Church Street. We have no evidence, direct or indirect, for their cultural affiliations or language until we meet the Celtic Iron-Age tribesmen of the Brigantes or, more probably, one of its more localised sub-tribes, who occupied the area on the eve of the Roman conquest. Whether they were native to the land or incomers we cannot tell. Celtic was not the first language in Britain, for traces of earlier language appear in place-names, perhaps even in the name 'Lune', but language and race are not synonymous. The Celtic language spread across Europe with an aristocratic warrior-culture and the use of iron, but the people who used it may not have been genetically uniform.

We know from Roman sources that the Brigantes were a very large and loosely organised tribe occupying most of northern England and southern Scotland. The Romans exploited their fatal weakness, disunity, to split them and ultimately to force them into direct conflict and inevitable defeat. The lower Lune valley may have been a distinct area known as 'Contrebis', if inscriptions at Burrow and at Folly Farm just north of Lancaster record an area name. North Lancashire may have been on the fringes of two tribes, but throughout the Roman occupation, from about A.D. 70 to A.D. *c.*450, and beyond, the majority of inhabitants of this region were Celtic-speakers.

From about A.D. 70 the dominant, as opposed to majority, language would have been Latin. The Roman invaders themselves, represented first by the army and administrators and then later by merchants and adventurers, were far from uniform. Some administrators and army officers may have been of Italian origin, but the ordinary soldiers were probably mainly Gaulish in origin, from modern France and Germany.

2   Roman altars from Burrow-in-Lonsdale and Folly Farm near Lancaster. Both of these record the name of 'Contrebis', which may be the epithet of a local god or even the name for the lower part of the Lune valley.

It was standard practice to raise auxiliary troops on the fringes of the empire, and the principal regiment in garrison at the fort was the *Ala Sebosiana*, raised in Gaul. Its soldiers were not even Roman citizens until they retired from the army, usually after 25 years' service. Another soldier, whose tombstone was discovered in Cheapside in the 18th century, was Lucius Julius Apollinaris, a trooper of the *Ala Augusta*, who died aged 30 and whose place of birth was Trier, now in Germany.

While few military tombstones have been found here, depriving us of a useful source of knowledge for ethnic origin, we can make several assumptions based on more general evidence. All Roman forts had a hospital, and these were often staffed by Greeks. The island of Kos was particularly famous for supplying doctors. Greek doctors are recorded at Chester and elsewhere, while Burrow-in-Lonsdale has an inscription to the gods of healing in their Greek form, suggesting that Julius Saturninus, the dedicator, was a Greek. The only evidence of a hospital at Lancaster is a pair of bronze forceps from Vicarage Field, but it is a fair assumption that Greeks may have been here too. The merchants who thronged the streets and markets of the civil settlements outside the forts included many of more distant origin, including the eastern Mediterranean and north Africa. In fact Italian Romans would have been in a minority.

Many of these men, whatever their origin, will have arrived without dependents and a high proportion will have married local women. Within a few generations the racial mix is likely to have been complex, but all will have felt themselves in some way 'Romans'. It was one of the secrets of Roman success that their culture, while apparently dominant, was also inclusive and allowed them to incorporate many other cultures into their own.

This area was settled late by Anglo-Saxon people. From the fourth century A.D. they had been colonising eastern England and gradually becoming the dominant culture, but their movement into the north-west via the Pennine passes was delayed by nearly two centuries. Lancaster must have been a mixture of resurgent Celtic and residual Roman influences at this time, lying at a crossroads between the vibrant Christian churches of Rome and of the Irish Celtic world, which were widely divergent in practice. The Celtic church brought missionaries and monks. The church of Rome maintained economic links with the Mediterranean world, and sites of this period in Wales and the south-west often have a distinctive archaeology, with imported Mediterranean pottery. Lancaster has not produced archaeological evidence for this period, but may yet do so.

The first Germanic Anglo-Saxon settlers started to arrive just before A.D. 600. This area of North Lancashire, perhaps a petty kingdom in its own right, was gradually absorbed into the great kingdoms of Northumbria and of Mercia. These two powers were mortal enemies in the seventh century, Northumbria having been converted to Christianity under King Edwin while Mercia under King Penda was pagan. What is now Lancashire was thinly populated and a border region of little importance, the prize of battles fought elsewhere. It is likely that the colonisation process here was slow, more one of intermarriage than of conquest and replacement. However, by degrees the dominant culture and language became Anglo-Saxon.

People with Anglo-Saxon names are recorded on the few inscriptions of the next three centuries or so. Stone memorial crosses found at Lancaster ask us in Latin to pray for the souls of Cynibad and Hardwine, while one in Anglian runes asks us to pray for Cynibald, son of Cuthberect. In this period many of our towns and villages were named. Unlike Celtic place-names, which tend

3 Drawing of the tombstone of Lucius Julius Apollinaris, a Roman soldier from Trier in Germany. Apollinaris died aged 30, presumably while on active service. The tombstone was found in Cheapside in 1772. From its position it may already have been moved from the Roman cemetery for re-use as a building stone. The only cemetery so far known was at the southern end of Penny Street and adjacent areas.

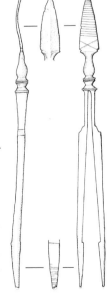

4 Drawing of Roman bronze forceps. These forceps were found during excavations in the Vicarage Field in 1927 and indicate the presence of a hospital and doctor in the fort. Burrow-in-Lonsdale has produced an inscription (now in Tunstall church) to the gods of healing, Asclepius and Hygeia. Many Roman doctors were of Greek origin.

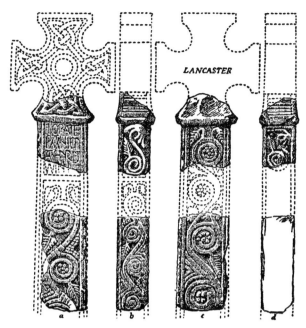

5 Anglo-Saxon Cross with a Latin inscription found in 1903 built into the medieval walls of the Priory church. This invites the onlooker to pray for the soul of Hardwine ('Orate pro anima Hardwini'). It dates from the ninth century A.D. Another fragment found more recently names a man called Cynibad. Both are Old English names.

6 Anglo-Saxon Cross with an inscription in Anglian runes. The inscription reads 'pray for the soul of Cynibald, son of Cuthberect'. It was found in the Priory churchyard in 1807 and is now in the British Museum.

to be purely descriptive, many of the Anglo-Saxon place-names incorporate personal names, presumably those of leaders and landowners. Names such as Melling, Gressingham, Heysham, Heaton or Caton are typical, the latter meaning the 'tun' (village) of a man called 'Kati'. Some place-names, however, despite their modern form, are descriptive. Among these are Wray ['village in the corner'] or Arkholme ['at the shielings', an Old English dative plural form].

The Anglo-Saxons, a great deal naturalised after four hundred years of stability and intermarriage, were now to be the target for Viking raiders and settlers. The Vikings, of Danish origin, were genetically not unlike the Angles and Jutes, who came from the same area several centuries earlier. Some of these Danish-Vikings found their way across to the west coast. Place-names ending in '-by', indicating 'farm', are their hall-mark, and the Lune valley has 'Hornby' right at its heart, perhaps indicating that the settlers' route was via the river valleys. Most of the other Viking names are given by Norse settlers who came by way of Shetland, Orkney, the Isle of Man and Ireland. They arrived quite a long time later, in the 10th and 11th centuries. Some of their place-names include Irish elements which they had picked up on the way. Among these are particles such as 'argh' or 'ergh', which form the endings of farm names and possibly indicate some form of transhumance, although this is still a matter of disagreement among place-name scholars. 'Holme', 'Thwaite' and 'Dale' for 'meadow', 'clearing' and 'valley' are typical, the latter giving rise to 'Lunesdale'.

While Danish Vikings in eastern England seem to have renamed large tracts of countryside and the majority of village names, the Norse do not seem to have had such an easy task in the west. The landscape may have been more settled when they came, or they may have been content with what the natives regarded as more marginal land. At all events, they named the higher farms on the fell-edge, and those on the low clay islands in the coastal marshes such as Cockersand Moss, like Norbreck, Kendal Hill and Thursland Hill. Many villages with Anglo-Saxon names have fields with pure Norse names, so their impact may have been greater than we think. Fields are likely to have been named by their users, rather than their owners. Impact was greatest in the Lake District and across Morecambe Bay, in Furness, where the place-names of this period are dense and where Old Norse may have been spoken into the 13th century. Norse names can be found in a number of Lancaster's fields, such as 'Edenbreck' or 'Haverbreaks', and even in the town centre, where 'Calkeld' Lane refers to the cold spring which until recently emerged in a cellar.

Within a couple of centuries these settlers were overtaken by another group, the Normans, probably smaller in number but even more dominant in spite of this. Conquering the royal army and killing the king in 1066 had given them sway over the whole country, ironically because of the very centralised nature of the English administration. But they still had to earn their prize, and hold it. The Normans were another branch of the Viking raiders, who had settled in Normandy and absorbed some French culture, including the language. Their hold on English lands was fierce and based upon military might. Lords like Roger de Poitou, who took Lancaster as his portion some time before Domesday, probably felt little affinity with his new lands, preferring to give its ecclesiastical wealth to the abbey of his home-town, Seez. The Normans ultimately provided our legal system, part of our complex language, and many of our institutions, but in terms of influence on the landscape they had little effect. In the area around Lancaster only 'Beaumont', now part of Skerton, can be identified as a new place-name. Essentially, the small Norman ruling class left others to farm the land. On the other hand, their passion for order and information led to the first catalogue of land and its owners, Domesday Book, and hence the first record of our local place-names. By such means the names began to be fixed, coverage of large geographical areas leading to introductions such as '-le-' to distinguish Bolton-le-Moors from Bolton-le-Sands, problems which had never troubled the essentially local Anglo-Saxon administration.

The Middle Ages are not a period in which we would expect many foreigners to make Lancaster their home. Most of the trade was focused on the south and east coasts, facing Europe. Nonetheless French pottery found its way to Lancaster, and was found in some quantity on the site of Mitchell's Brewery in Church Street. Such pottery, from the Saintonge area, is thought to be a marker for the more-or-less invisible wine trade, so some French ships may have been involved and certainly the royal connections of the Castle would have meant access to a wider range of foreign goods and visitors than was the case with lower-status sites. The Priory, too, housed French monks between 1094 and 1414, drawn from the mother house of Seez. The names of some 21 priors are known, such as Emery de Argenteles (1337-42), John de Coudray (1344-5), John des Loges (d.1399) and Giles Louvel (1399-1414).

From the late 17th century at least, when Apprenticeship Rolls begin, Lancaster was drawing on areas such as Furness and the Fylde for its new blood. Young men who sought a good trade, or whose families sought one for them, came to Lancaster to be apprenticed. Sons of yeomen and rural labourers expected to give themselves an edge by gaining this experience, while Lancaster was also a closed shop, literally, due to its retention of Freeman status and the exclusive rights which went with this. Even into the 19th century the poorer rural areas, and those with fewer prospects, such as the Lake District, provided Lancaster with some of its most entrepreneurial spirits. Robert Gillow was the son of a poor widow from the Fylde, while the two manufacturing houses of Storeys and Williamsons were founded by incomers from Bardsea, in Furness, and Keswick respectively.

The movement was not all inwards. In the 17th and 18th centuries Virginia called on many without prospects in this country, who set out to make their fortune in a new land. Among these were a few recorded in the Borough Records:

> 1682 Francis [sic] Robinson, of Gosforth, near Ravenglass, spinster, agrees with Robert Pearson of Lancaster, mariner, to serve four years in Virginia according to the custom of the country. (Pearson to pay her passage.)

> 6th Jan 1709 Mem. that John Fell and James Fell sons of James Fell sometime of Lancaster of free will and volition have consented before Mayor and Baylives of the said Corporation to goe to Virginia by the first opportunity and there to serve Mr Robert Carter of Lancaster and Mr Joshua Lawson of the same merchants and their or either of their orders for the Terme according to the Custom of the Country.

Many younger sons also set out for the West Indies as factors to merchant fathers, acting as local agents. Some made their fortunes and came back as nabobs. Many never returned, either through bankruptcy or early death.

Because of the slave trade the parish registers of Lancaster and several surrounding villages, such as Warton and Heysham, record the baptisms of black servants, presumably former slaves. What was probably the first black face ever seen in Lancaster belonged to 'Richard Nigroe, son of Peter a Blacamore', baptised at Lancaster in 1602. His arrival dates from long before the Lancaster slave trade had got under way. A more typical entry is that at Heysham in 1738:

> Thomas A Negro Servant to Captain Peeter Woodhouse of Lancaster bapt. May the twenty first being upon Whitsunday.

Another entry in 1800, at Warton, records;

> Edwin a Negro boy servant to Mr Law of the Island of Barbadoes baptised at Mr Bishop of Y[ealand] about 13 yrs old.

Black servants were very fashionable in high society in the early 18th century and were often given fancy names, but most of these servants must have returned with members of ships' crews, whose family names they seem to have taken. Indeed, other than these particular church records, we could not distinguish by name alone most of the later black incomers from other individuals of local origin. We know in all of about forty black men and women who appear in the Parish Registers because they were baptised or buried here. Baptism seems to have been taken at the time as an acknowledgment of freedom.

Two are better known than the rest. These are the man known only as 'Sambo', whose grave can be seen on the western shore at Sunderland Point, and John Dixon,

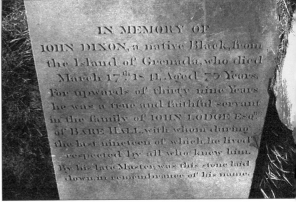

7 Grave of Sambo at Sunderland Point. 'Sambo' is reputed to have died in 1736. Sixty years later a brass plate with verses by Rev. James Watson, master of the Free School in Lancaster, was set on his grave.

8 Grave of John Dixon. Dixon, a 'native Black from the Island of Grenada', was a household servant for many years at Bare Hall and was buried in Morecambe churchyard in 1841.

a servant of the Lodge family at Bare Hall, 'a native Black, from the Island of Grenada', whose tombstone of 1841 stands in Morecambe churchyard. Their lives were very different. The former, so legend tells, died of grief in the 1730s when he thought his master had abandoned him. The latter died aged 79 following over 39 years in honoured domestic service and was commemorated by a tombstone at a time when many servants lay in unmarked graves. Frances Elisabeth Johnson, aged 27 in 1778, who worked for Mr Satterthwaite at 20 Castle Park, is one of only three black women to be recorded.

From the Registers of the Priory Church, Lancaster:

Baptisms

Thomas John, a negroe, Jan. 3 1759
William York, a negroe, Jan. 27 1759
John Lancaster, a negroe, Feb. 2 1760
Henry Hind, an adult negroe, May 3 1761
John Thompson, an adult negroe, Aug. 23 1761
Richard Peters, an adult negroe, Nov. 10 1761
William London, an adult negroe, Jan. 20 1762
Rebecca Thorn, an adult negroe, Oct. 27 1763
George Stuart, an adult negroe, May 20, 1764
John White, an adult negroe, June 10 1764
William Trasier, an adult negro, Oct. 21 1764
Molly, an adult negroe, Nov. 6 1764 [burial recorded Dec. 1 in the same year]
William Leuthwaite, an adult negroe, Feb. 3 1768
Stephen Millers, an adult negroe, May 15 or after, 1768

9 Painting of a ship being built at Brockbanks yard. Attributed to John Emery (1772-1822), this shows Brockbank's shipyard on the Green Ayre and St George's Quay in the background in about 1806. On the right a ship's hull is nearing completion – the date and the admiral figurehead make it almost certain that this is *Trafalgar*, a ship of 267 tons built for William & Samuel Hinde of Liverpool 'for the Guinea Trade'. To the left is a pair of studded timber wheels, used for manoeuvring large baulks and tree trunks around the yard, while further left again a man is caulking a smaller vessel with hot pitch. In the background is the ruin of the old bridge with one arch missing (it was bought and demolished in 1802 by Brockbank to make it easier for his ships easier to get through) and the warehouses and shipping at St George's Quay.

Benjamin Johnson, an adult negroe, May 28 1769
Jeremiah Skerton, a black man, an adult, Nov. 17 1773
Benjamin Kenton, a black man, in the service of Capt. Copeland, Mar. 5 1774
John Chance, a black, aged 22 years & upwards in the service of Mr Lindow, Sept. 12 1777 [burial recorded on Oct. 8 1783]
Frances Elisabeth Johnson, a black woman servant to Mr John Satterthwaite, an adult aged 27 years, Apr. 2 1778
Thomas Burrow, a black, an adult, Feb. 15 1779
George John, a negro and adult, Jan. 22 1783
Isaac Rawlinson, a negro and adult, Feb. 3 1783
William Dilworth, an adult negro, Oct. 6 1783
Thomas Etherington, an adult negro, aged 22 years, Oct. 13 1785

There are also the following burials, for which less information is forthcoming:

A negroe, Nov. 14 1755
A negroe, Nov. 17 1755
John Bolton, a black, Nov. 20 1756
A Negroe Boy, Nov. 6 1762
Samuel Powers, a Negroe, Apr. 10 1765
Robert [ ], a black Man, Mar. 25 1778

French prisoners-of-war were held in Lancaster Castle during the Napoleonic Wars. A Yorkshireman, Richard Holden, saw them here in 1808, '… Many French prisoners in the body of the Castle now'.

German nationals of various description seem to have made up an important part of Lancaster's 19th-century immigrants. Two, at least, were associated with the running of the sugar house in St Leonardgate, and perhaps another one in Cable Street. This business, set up by Robert Lawson in the early 18th century, was still running in the early 19th under George Crosfield & Co. It is clear that large numbers of Germans from the Hanover and Hamburg areas were involved in many of the British sugar-refineries, and this possibly accounts for Heartwick Grippenhearl and Johann Hinrich Holthusen. The former became a Freeman of Lancaster in 1748-9, while the latter died aged 38 in 1824, although a directory of 1834 lists him at a second sugar house in Cable Street, as well as the one run by Crosfield in St Leonardgate.

"PREVENTION'S BETTER THAN CURE."

10   Cartoon of German band from *Punch* magazine. So-called 'German' bands were very common on the roads of late 19th-century England as they walked from place to place, playing in towns and villages and just scraping a living. Many of them were actually from Austria or Czechoslovakia.

We know of two or three other groups of 19th-century German immigrants. The 1881 census returns provide us with three interesting examples. At 103 Penny Street was the Kuhnle family, pork butchers on the New Market. George and Mary, both aged 29, are merely noted as 'born Germany', but their eldest three children were born in Sheffield, while the youngest two were born in Lancaster. It seems therefore that George and Mary had moved from Sheffield where perhaps they formed part of a German colony. Were they like the Yorkshire Schulz family described by Hartley & Ingilby, escapees from military service in an increasingly militaristic 1870s Germany? We may never know. With them lived John Speidal, aged 16, also born in Germany. At the same time a lodging–house at 11 China Lane offered overnight accommodation to nine members of a German band. No names or ages were recorded, although they had managed to indicate that they came from Bavaria; perhaps there was mutual incomprehension between the band and the owners of the lodging-house. German bands were very popular at this time. Wearing a rudimentary uniform they walked from town to town, playing wherever they could find an audience and collecting what money they could. Not all 'German' bands were German. The name covered a wide range of Czechs, Austrians and other nationalities. Finally, there was Laurenz Schmitz, born in the Rhineland and a teacher of music. The presence of a 'Rheinheimer' lodging-house on China Lane in around 1890 suggests other Germans may have been here. Germanic, Russian and Polish names may also disguise Jewish refugees from the many pogroms and other scares to which European Jews were subjected in the 19th century. There seems little earlier evidence for Jewish people in Lancaster, although a gradual return to England had been possible since the 17th century. However, the recent intriguing discovery in America of a 'Book of Nikodemus' published in Lancaster by Rabbi Jacob Bailen in 1784 must surely suggest the existence of a settled community.

Signor Rodolphe Pandolfini was a rather mysterious character, born in Rome in 1832 and said to be both a Count and, at one time, influential in diplomatic circles. He had come to Lancaster in about 1874 on the invitation of Edmund Sharpe to help with some architectural work. He stayed on after Sharpe's death, using his skills as a linguist to act as correspondent for Messrs Storey Bros and teach languages at the Storey Institute. He was also an artist and a photographer, and had he not died in his darkroom in 1897, thus precipitating an inquest, we might never have heard of him at all. The inquest showed that he died of natural causes.

From 1801 Ireland had been part of the United Kingdom and, as well as the huge outflow of Irish people following the disastrous Potato Famine of 1846-7, there was a regular flow of seasonal workers, usually men, to work the land and send most of the proceeds to families at home. Many of these labourers lodged in barns and outbuildings, happy to find cheap or free accommodation and make the most of their earnings. In arable areas much of the labour was only needed at harvest time, but there was a longer season in the potato-growing areas such as the Fylde and Pilling for both planting and lifting. Such was the Irish influence here that the local word for potatoes was 'praties'.

There were also many Irish people living in Lancashire. It was close to the ferry ports and had a strong surviving Catholic element, which meant there was already a support system supplied with churches and priests. Many lodging-house keepers in Lancaster were Irish, and the building trade thrived upon the loose arrangements of casual Irish labour. A disproportionate number of Irish people were taken into custody, according to the Police Photograph Book of the 1890s, a sort of rough justice in which local drunkards were seen home while those without friends or relations spent the night in the cells.

In Lancaster today there are, apart from the somewhat artificial and short-term gatherings of representatives of many nations (currently some 120) at the University and the Royal Lancaster Infirmary, three main minority ethnic groups, Germans, Indians and Poles. The census of 1991 provides a general breakdown of numbers under 'country of birth'. The categories are unsatisfactory for historians, but the census is not carried out for their

11 Mosque in Fenton Street. The Mosque lies behind the old Friends' Hall, built in 1902-4 to house the Quaker Adult School and designed by the architect Spencer Barrow.

benefit! From a district total of 123,856, Germany provided 368, India 365 (but there are almost as many ethnic Indians who were born in this country) and Poland 166. These are really tiny figures, but still larger by a considerable amount than those for any other group, and the last two remain distinctive through custom, language and even costume, retaining their own church and mosque. They also need to be seen against the 3,291 Scots or 1,058 natives of Ulster or 754 natives of the Irish Republic, who can merge much more easily in the background population. A further breakdown of some groups is possible. Of the 563 whose 'ethnicity' rather than birth is Indian, almost half (277) were actually born in this country, demonstrating that this is a group made up of families. Of those of Polish birth, 98 were men and 68 women, the disproportion perhaps explained by their displacement by war and, in particular, the role of Polish men in the armed services.

The Indian community is made up largely of Moslem families from the Gujarat area of western India who came as economic migrants to this country in the early 1960s when there was a shortage of labour in the textile mills. It is likely that few came specifically to Lancaster but rather to Bolton, Blackburn or Preston first, especially the latter, and then onwards to Lancaster where Bath Mill was offering jobs at the time. The community acquired houses initially in Blades Street and Dallas Road where large houses were relatively cheap and ideal for extended families. Later some moved to Bulk – Green Street and Hinde Street – and to the large houses of Dale Street. The community has succeeded through sheer hard work and traditional family support, and has managed to integrate very well into the local population, while still retaining a distinctive cultural tradition. There is a mosque in Fenton Street and several shops, as well as the very popular Sultan Restaurant in Brock Street, and many other businesses. There is also, since 1996, a 'Jamea' or Moslem school in Lancaster, based in the former Royal Albert Hospital. It was only the third of its kind in Britain. Most of the girl pupils are from elsewhere, and board there. Many 'ethnic' Indians in

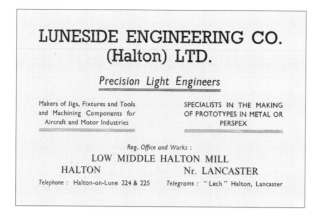

LUNESIDE ENGINEERING CO. (Halton) LTD.

Precision Light Engineers

Makers of Jigs, Fixtures and Tools and Machining Components for Aircraft and Motor Industries

SPECIALISTS IN THE MAKING OF PROTOTYPES IN METAL OR PERSPEX

Reg. Office and Works :
LOW MIDDLE HALTON MILL
HALTON   Nr. LANCASTER
Telephone : Halton-on-Lune 224 & 225   Telegrams : " Lech " Halton, Lancaster

12 Advertisement for Luneside Engineering, Halton, 1964. Under the leadership of Col. Teodor Benirski, a group of Polish engineers was established here in 1948, initially taking on almost any job that was offered, but later specialising in complex defence contracts.

Lancaster are now of the second or even third generation to be born in this country; their cultural distinctiveness may well be diluted as time goes on. A recent study by Kusminder Chahal has increased our knowledge of the issues facing the Indian community and, to a lesser extent, the Black, Chinese and Traveller communities.

Lancaster had no particular significance to start with for the Polish community, but became a focus for ex-servicemen who could not go home after the war, either for political reasons or because eastern Poland had been annexed to the Ukraine. There were also women and children who had been sent to a series of transit camps or forced to labour by the USSR or Germany and had ended up in Britain. Among these were 15 girls of Polish origin housed at Aldcliffe Hall in 1947, with others from Latvia, Hungary and the Ukraine. By degrees a Polish community of some 500 developed here. The presence of compatriots, with the chance to share the familiar language and culture, was a magnet to others. In addition the opportunity to work was offered by places such as Luneside Engineering at Halton, established in 1948 by Col. Teodor Benirski, who offered many of his compatriots jobs. Initially the works took on any contract it could gain, simply to keep going, but soon it started to specialise in defence contracts. Numbers have now shrunk again. The community, being strongly Catholic, initially used Lancaster Cathedral but in 1984 acquired its own church in Nelson Street (Our Lady Queen of Poland). The church serves as a focus and there is a community centre adjacent. There is also a section of the cemetery on Lancaster Moor which contains graves with the stones inscribed in Polish.

What is true of most of the incoming groups throughout history is that they rarely had Lancaster in mind as their original destination. Many came here via other places. They sought at different times land, peace, security, work and new opportunities. Many initially met hostility in word or deed, especially if they seemed 'different', but this hostility decreased with familiarity, and now, thankfully, is a thing of the past. To incomers with nothing in the way of possessions the support of family or community was crucial. No-one else was going to favour them, lend money or offer jobs. A strong family or community network provided most of those things which the rest of us take for granted. Finally, there is a natural tendency to group together and share support, religion, language and a familiar culture in a strange land. Such things are very important in giving a sense of purpose and in defining personality, and should not be bulldozed out of the way in the search for multiculturalism.

Two

Development of the Townscape

Lancaster is unusual among towns of its size in that its topography shows traces of its Roman ancestry. Such features are commoner among walled cities where elements such as roads are often constrained by the presence of gates. So, cities such as Lincoln, Chester or York, which originated as Roman legionary fortresses, retained the lines of their walls substantially into the Middle Ages. They also contain some relics of the original street pattern, although these are often rather distorted. It is much less common for those towns based upon smaller forts and their civilian settlements to show evidence of Roman layout. Yet Lancaster does, with at least two streets appearing to follow ancient lines.

Early visitors to Lancaster were clearly struck by what traces of antiquity they saw. One of the first, *c.*1535, was John Leland:

> Lancastre Castel on a hille strongly builded and wel repaired. Ruines of an old place (as I remember of the Catfields) by the castel hille. The new toune (as thei ther say) builded hard by yn the descent from the castel, having one paroch chirch wher sumtime the priori of monkes alienis was put doune by King Henry the v. and given to Syon Abbay.
>
> The old waul of the circuite of the priory cummith almost to Lune bridge. Sum have thereby supposid that it was a peace of a waul of the toune. But yn deade I espyd in no place that the toune was ever waullid.
>
> The old toune (as they say ther) was almost al burnid and stoode partely beyounde the Blak Freres.
>
> In thos partes in the feeldes and fundations hath ben found much Romayne coyne.

And later he adds, 'The ruines of old walles about the bridg were onely of the suppressid priory.' Later in the same century (*c.*1580) came William Camden, gathering material for his *Britannia*:

> ... yet for proofe of Romane antiquity, they finde otherwhiles peeces of the Emperours coine, especially where the Friery stood: for there, they say, was the plot upon which the ancient City was planted, which the Scots ... in ... 1322 set on fire and burnt. Since which time they have begunne to build nearer unto a greene hill by the river side, on which standeth the castle ... And hard by it standeth upon the height of the hill, the onely Church they have ... A little beneath which, by a faire bridge over Lone, in the descent and side of the hill where it is steepest hangeth a peece of a most ancient wall of Romane work, seeming ready to reele; Wery wall they call it, after a later British name, as it should seeme, of this towne. For they called it Caer Werid, as one would say, The Greene City, happely of that fresh greene hill. But I leave this to others.

Camden's conjecture about the rebuilding of the town on a new site after 1322 was quite erroneous, as even the swiftest glance at the evidence of the street-pattern would show, but it has been remarkably popular and is still repeated today.

13 Fragment of the Wery Wall. The last remains of a corner bastion of the fourth-century fort walls. Seen in 1973 against the masonry of an 18th-century garden wall, since removed, the Wery Wall is represented by the mass of stone with pale mortar. When Stukeley visited Lancaster much more of it was to be seen.

The antiquary William Stukeley described the Roman remains visible in his time (1724) thus:

> Where the castle and church stand is a high and steep hill, length east and west; this was the Roman castrum.
>
> I found a great piece of the wall at the north-east, in the garden of Clement Townsend; and so to Mr Harrison's summer-house, which stands upon it; it is made of the white stone of the county, and with very hard mortar, and still very thick, though the facing on both sides is peeled off for the sake of the squared stone, which they used in building. A year or two ago a great parcel of it was destroyed with much labour. This reached quite to the bridge-lane and hung over the street at the head of the precipice in a dreadful manner; it went round the verge of the close north of the church, and took in the whole circuit of the hill. The ditch on the north side of it is now to be seen. I suppose it enclosed the whole top of the hill where the church and castle stand, which is steep on all sides, and half enclosed by the river Lune; so that it is an excellent guard to this part of the sea-coast, and commands a very great prospect both by sea and land. Here was this great convenience too in the situation; that on the south side of the castle walls, under the tower, is a spring. All the space of ground north of the church is full of foundations of stone buildings, Roman, I believe; and much stone has been taken up there. To the west of the church is part of a partition wall left of that time …

Lancaster shows another uncharacteristic feature. Streets which are first recorded in the 12th or 13th century seem to survive largely intact, with very few losses. Elsewhere the demands of 20th-century traffic have often cut a swathe through the older townscape – Lancaster's neighbour Preston is such a case – but a glance at the earliest plan of Lancaster (Speed 1610) shows a layout of streets in its centre which is still quite recognisable after four centuries. Moreover, there is evidence that this same layout would have been quite recognisable even some four centuries before that. The anciently-established core of streets contains some which owe their origin to Roman roads and others either to late Saxon urban development or to the effects of the earliest borough charters in the late 12th century. In addition, there are a number of 18th-century

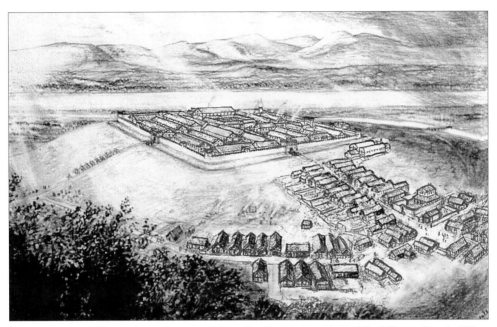

14 Reconstruction of Roman Lancaster from the Moor by David Vale. The hilltop of Castle Hill is crowned by the Roman fort and partly ringed by the river Lune flowing ultimately into Morecambe Bay, seen in the middle distance backed by the mountains of the Lake District. To the right is part of the civilian settlement lining the roads outside the east gate of the fort. Closest to the fort is its military bath-house, found when Mitre House was constructed.

15 The Roman fort and distribution map of Roman finds demonstrating where the main part of the civilian settlement lay. The picture may become more complex as more finds are made. Recently traces of a considerable Roman burial ground have been found at the southern end of Penny Street, suggesting that this was the limit of the settlement. (P. Lee)

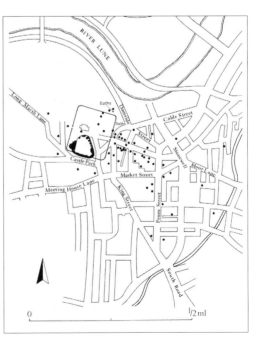

additions such as New Street and New Road which cut through ancient burgage plots, but the majority of new roads resulting from the burst of activity in Georgian times lie on the edges of the medieval town and represent some modest growth.

Of course, ancient lines may be preserved but functions changed. That is only what one should expect. The Roman layout was influenced by the presence of the north and east gates of the fort. These may have gone by the mid-fourth century A.D. when the fort was rebuilt on different lines, and had certainly gone by the 12th century. Nonetheless the line of Church Street survived, perhaps because it enshrined old property boundaries. These were very potent and long-lived. There is further evidence in Lancaster for the survival of ancient boundaries between plots, from the excavated Mitchell's Brewery site, between Church Street and Market Street.

The Fields

Much of the later development took place on former fields. Some field names are thus preserved, while others, now lost, occur in property deeds of the 18th and 19th centuries. Anyone able to return to the town as it was until the late 17th century would remark upon how small it was, how low the density of buildings and how close the ring of common fields and small private enclosures to the centre.

In the Middle Ages the town had been surrounded by common fields, although it was quite constrained by the closeness of some of its neighbours. Scotforth township,

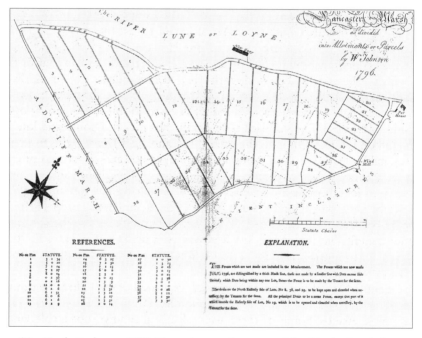

16 Marsh Enclosure, 1796. The unimproved pasture of the Marsh, shared since time immemorial by the Freemen of Lancaster, was finally enclosed in 1796. The rents, known as 'Marsh Grasses', went to the oldest surviving Freemen. From about the 1870s the Corporation started to develop the edge of the Marsh for housing.

for instance, hemmed the borough in to the south, and the river demarcated its northern and western sides. Of course, Lancastrians could and did own land in neighbouring townships, but the rights and privileges of the borough, possessed by all freemen, did not extend this far. On the west the valuable Marsh, not enclosed until 1796, offered pasture to Freemen. On the east the less well-defined boundaries with Quernmore were to cause problems and disputes for centuries. The first charter of 1193, allowing Freemen to graze their cattle on Lancaster Moor, probably does no more than

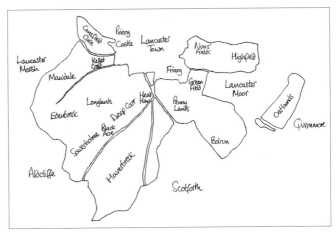

17   Location of main fields

regularise an existing custom. Moor Lane and Ridge Lane both reflect the ancient routes up on to the unenclosed Moor from the infields around the town.

Medieval sources are limited for Lancaster's common fields and so, apart from monastic charters, we have little to go on but backwards extrapolation of the evidence. It is sad, too, that Lancaster has no large-scale Tithe Award map of the 1830s or 1840s, other than for a handful of fields above Moor Lane, because the issue of tithes had been resolved by a private Act several years before. It is clear from later field shapes and positions, and confirmed by the charter evidence, that Lancaster had four or five large open fields in the medieval period, each divided into bundles of strips, divided by headlands on which the plough turned, in the usual manner of the period.

Strips were held by burgesses in a complicated relationship depending upon their ownership of a house. The standard relationship was that the house and long narrow strip of land on which it stood in the street ('toft and croft') gave rights to strips in the common arable fields, access to common pasture, woods and water, and often special benefits like summer pasture on nearby high ground and perhaps pannage for pigs on beech-mast in local woodland. The key to all was the original 'toft and croft', usually now described as a 'burgage plot'. Such plots still determine many property boundaries and can be best seen in Penny Street. The relationship with land in the common fields and other benefits has long been lost, and was even being lost in the Middle Ages as land was given to monasteries and as townsfolk became more urban in character and less tied to their rural roots.

The identifiable fields within the borough consisted of the following, from west to east: Edenbreck, Mawdale, Head Haw, Sowerholme, Haverbreaks, Greenfield, Highfield, Bolrum and Oatlands. Some of these were clearly meadows, not arable land. There were also a number of smaller fields and what were clearly private enclosures. The classic 'three-field' system appears only in the text book; reality was usually much more complex. Some of the names give an indication of common crops. Both Haverbreaks and Oatlands indicate the growing of oats, from Old Norse and Anglo-Saxon linguistic roots respectively. Oats were well adapted to this wet northern climate and replaced the wheat of the south and east. They served as food for both men and horses, the former often eating them in the form of oatbread, a flat, pancake-like form, made on a very hot 'backstone', which had good keeping qualities. Crop returns for the Diocese of Chester in 1801 show the township of Lancaster having only 201 acres under wheat but 1,617 acres under oats.

The roots of Sowerholme seem to suggest that this field had acid soil. Deep Carr and Lancaster Marsh represented common grazing land. North Lancashire is now very green, being almost entirely under pasture, but a hundred and fifty years and more ago the picture was quite different, with much more arable land. The area had to be largely self-sufficient until better transport brought in grain from elsewhere, and particularly from the prairies of America and Canada as these were opened up.

As well as the common fields there were from very early times numerous private enclosures, wrested from the lower slopes of the Moor. The common fields, too, must have been largely enclosed by consent long before the enclosure movement. By the late 18th century their fossilised shapes and names, such as the ancient meadows of Deep Carr, Usher's Meadow and Fenham Carr, were still identifiable but they had long been broken up into smaller units. Most of the Moor was also enclosed by the early 19th century, while the Marsh was enclosed and partly drained in 1796 but retained as a common asset of the borough, the income from letting of the stinted pasture going to the oldest Freemen, the so-called 'Marsh Grasses'.

Many of these smaller enclosures became valuable building land in the expansive days of the 18th and 19th centuries. Many of their names are inscribed on property deeds such as those of Dr Marton recording, amongst others, Town End Close, Corless Close, Wheat Cake, Little Longlands, Little Haverbreak and Yoke o' the Egg (presumably a field with very rich soil). Another useful insight is gained from a property list of 1796. Some of the fields are described as 'in' another field. Presumably these larger units were the older common fields, the areas within them either bundles of former strips or else newer enclosures named for their location, quality or encloser's surname. Thus many enclosures appear 'in Sowerholme' or 'in Haverbricks'.

Inner fields and closes must have been very prone to changes of name. When they changed hands the new owner's name might be applied to them, although there was also a degree of conservatism which held on to the old name. Newer features, like the theatre of 1782, gave their name to a group of fields known as 'Playhouse Fields', later the site of Edward Street and Alfred Street, developed in the 1850s. Binns' map of 1821 shows Usher's Meadow, Kendal Fields and Kellet Croft lying to the west of the town, all now built upon – Kellet Croft became the site of Castle Station in 1846. Usher's Meadow is named after the Usher, or junior master of the Free School, for whose salary it provided. Some of the oldest open land in the city, at least demonstrably so, is the pair of fields to the north of the Priory church, the east and west Vicarage Fields, glebeland until 1947. This roughly triangular area of open land, truncated slightly to the north by the building of St George's Quay in 1751, can be traced right back to the original land grant of the Priory church in 1094, so it has been open land for over 900 years. It also helps to preserve the outline of the Roman fort, whose northern side underlies it.

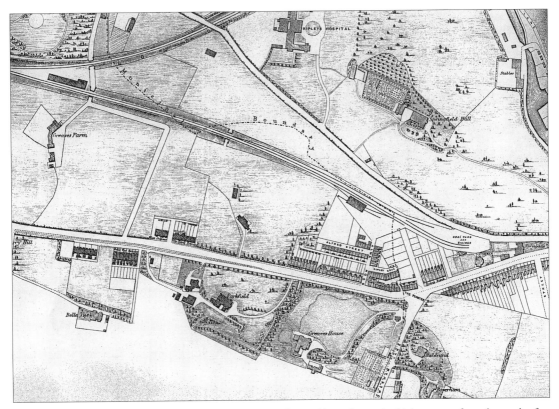

18 Villas on the Greaves, from Harrison & Hall's map of 1877. Along the road which emerges from the south of the town a series of large detached houses such as The Greaves, Belle Vue and Parkfield have been built. They serve the professional and trade élite of the town. At the same time substantial terraced housing is making an appearance as ribbon development at Belle Vue Terrace and Halcyon Terrace, while smaller terraced houses are being built near the Pointer.

In the Georgian period the town grew outwards to a small extent with new streets, especially eastwards with the Dalton Square development from 1783. It thus finally escaped the stranglehold which the medieval Blackfriars' precinct had placed upon development in this direction. Queen Street and High Street also extended onto former fields, as did Green Ayre to the north, but much of the Georgian development consisted of rebuilding existing streets and infilling low-density occupation.

Early and mid-18th-century visitors were struck by the rebuilding and the thriving nature of the town. Among these were an anonymous visitor from Wiltshire in 1747:

> Lancaster has the appearance of being in a flourishing state from the many Houses lately built there, it is clean but not very large, the Castle is the great ornament of the Town.... The river ... runs just below the Castle wch brings vessels to the Town from the sea about a mile distant ...

Dr Richard Pococke, successively Bishop of Meath and Ossory, was also impressed:

> Lancaster is of late become a very thriving town, much improved in trade and buildings, for which they have the convenience of a very good light yellow free stone ...

A Cheshire visitor 'W. M.' in 1817 described the buildings thus:

> The town of Lancaster is situated on the south bank of the river Lune. Although its streets are narrow, there are several good buildings in it. The town is built with a light-coloured free stone & the houses generally covered with blue slate which gives the town a handsome appearance.

The medieval townscape must have been quite sparsely built, with many gaps and also with large open spaces between streets. It was the medieval pattern of burgage plots which gave rise to the building of smaller houses on the backland during the 18th and 19th centuries, when demand increased for rentable property. Initially these rows of speculative cottages behind the street frontages may have been reasonably healthy and acceptable, but as the town centre grew ever more densely populated by the mid-19th century so the pressure on inadequate water-supply and in particular on a non-existent clearance of privies and middens led to serious health problems. Richard Owen singled out many of these yards and courts for particular censure in his report on 'The Sanatory Condition of Lancaster' in 1845. What had proved adequate for a small population had become quite unacceptable with a much larger one.

The immediate consequence was that those who could escape the squalor of the town centre did. The middle class increasingly lived in more salubrious houses on the outskirts; either in suburban villas, or, for those of lesser means, in terraces along the main roads leading out. The centre was left to lock-up shops and to the poor. Respectable working-class people were also on the move, to areas like Primrose in the 1880s or to Moorlands in the 1890s. It was easier to control the quality of new build than to find the money and energy to pull down slums. This work was left to the period between the wars, when demolition went hand in hand with the building of new council housing.

The pressure to expand has continued. By the end of the 19th century Lancaster had taken in the villages of Scotforth and Skerton. In the period between the wars it started to grow north and west towards the resort of Morecambe, which was already doing the same thing in reverse. They met on Morecambe Road/Lancaster Road and at Scale Hall and Cross Hill. The Lancaster boundary has not moved significantly in the last century, but a tide of housing has welled up to it on all sides and it is now difficult to see where Lancaster starts and Morecambe ends. The rural green belt is particularly under threat and it will probably not be long before Caton and Halton are overwhelmed by urbanism. At present the M6 motorway, in the unintended and unaccountable way these things happen, acts as a barrier to eastwards development, but, like a sandcastle facing a rising tide, its days as a barrier are numbered.

Central Streets

Lancaster still retains an ancient core of central streets which with very few exceptions existed before Speed (1610) and can still be recognised today.

It is easiest in some ways to consider groups of streets. Church Street (formerly St Marygate) is one of the oldest streets or at least street-lines in the town. Roman in origin, it was probably the principal street of the pre-Norman settlement and has remained significant since, although a good deal of its former trade has moved away.

19   Anchor Lane under excavation, 1999. This narrow lane between medieval burgage plots links the two main streets of Market Street and Church Street. Since the 18th century buildings have stood on both sides of the lane, and of Chancery Lane, to the right of the picture. There was some evidence of Roman plot boundaries coinciding with these later ones. The area was cleared for development, although the lanes will survive in some form.

Beyond Lower Church Street, Moor Lane once straggled up towards the unenclosed Moor and was a natural route for driving the townsfolk's cattle out to pasture. From its south side there was access to the Dominican Friars' precinct.

Although Market Street is now one of the principal thoroughfares and effectively the centre of the town it seems to have been the creation of the early charters granting market rights as it is not named before *c*.1220. How much else was created at this time is unknown. Market Square clearly also once incorporated the area now known as New Street Square, the old Town Hall site now forming an island between the two. At its lower end the street joined St Nicholas Street. This was lost in 1967 following the building of a new shopping centre, now St Nicholas Arcades. At its upper end Market Street becomes Meeting House Lane, which originally ran out into the fields. It was named no earlier than the building of the Friends' Meeting House in 1677.

Joining these main streets in a north–south direction are Anchor Lane and Chancery Lane. Both are passages between burgage plots. Excavation on the former in 1999 shows that it may even have origins in Roman property boundaries. Linking Church Street with the mill-dam (Damside Street) is Calkeld Lane, one of the oldest named streets in the town, meaning, in Old Norse, 'the cold spring'.

20 Aerial photo of Castle Hill, *c.*1973. The view is from slightly north of east and shows the site of Mitre House, cleared and ready for construction work to start, at the lower right. Immediately to the west lie the two Vicarage Fields, divided by the tree-lined Vicarage Lane. Earthworks in the fields include the north-west angle of the Roman fort, the line of the medieval precinct wall of the Priory, and a hollow way for leading clay down to the Summer Pasture, where St George's Quay stands. The southern limit of the fort seems to be marked by the line of Castle Park, immediately south of the Castle.

One road leading in from the south is King Street (formerly Back Lane and Kemps Lane). This was not a particularly important street in the pre-modern layout and seems in fact to have been a sequence of narrow lanes until the 18th century, offering an alternative route from the south. This accounts for its odd kinks. Beyond Market Street it becomes China Street (formerly China Lane), which was originally just eight feet. It gives every indication of arising from a passage between burgage plots, as early plans show burgage plots lying parallel to, not at right angles, this street – in other words, aligned to the east-west street pattern. Perhaps it was a convenient bypass to the steep climb over the shoulder of Castle Hill. It was widened in 1896, on its western side only. Beyond Church Street it joined Bridge Lane, which it matched in width. Both formed one of the rookeries of 19th-century Lancaster, characterised by lodging houses and densely packed, overcrowded houses. Bridge Lane was demolished in 1938-9 to create a new approach to the Bus Station. A curve to the east was

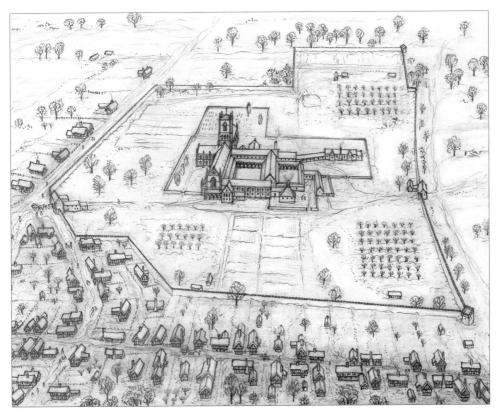

21 Reconstruction of the Dominican Friary by David Vale. The Dominican Friars or Blackfriars came to Lancaster in the 13th century and gradually acquired 12 acres of land on the eastern side of the town on which they built a large church dedicated to the Holy Trinity. The Friars were great preachers and it became popular among wealthy citizens to be buried in their church, bringing the Friars and the Priory into conflict. The massive precinct wall saved the Friary from destruction in 1322 and its line was determined by existing burgage plots in Penny Street. The site passed into the hands of the Dalton family and became Dalton Square in the late 18th century.

created, but the old line has been preserved and can still be seen passing the front of the *Three Mariners*.

Penny Street is one of the oldest streets of the town. The presence of plentiful Roman remains along its length and the alignment of some Roman features suggest it may be the main Roman road from the south. It was certainly here in the early 13th century and the building of the Dominican Friary and its precinct wall respected the line of its medieval burgage plots. Beyond Market Street it becomes Cheapside (formerly Pudding Lane and Butcher Lane).

Linking the two roads in from the south are Common Garden Street and Spring Garden Street, both of 18th-century origin. The latter was originally called Mackarell Street after the landowner.

Damside Street is named after the old mill-dam which turned a corn mill near the foot of Calkeld Lane. The curved line of the street represents fairly faithfully the line

22 A typical yard: Ross Yard off Cheapside. Until about 1927 a large part of the poorest population of Lancaster lived in yards such as these. A programme of gradual clearance then took place. Some yards were demolished outright; this one ceased to be lived in, but became shop storage until cleared for new building in the 1970s.

of the dam, which lay open until the 18th century and which is still in a culvert. The mill-dam itself appears to fossilise the line of an earlier, perhaps Roman, river channel, left behind as an ox-bow by later movement of the river. In between the two lines lies the island of Green Ayre. ('Ayre' means 'island'.) This was for centuries open land, but began to be developed on its river-ward side by enterprising merchants in the late 17th century for quays and warehouses and then for housing from the 1740s. It is now entirely built up, but the ancient shape can still be made out.

Stonewell was originally a widening where a number of roads met. This formed the end of the town to the east, leading to the straggling St Leonardgate and Moor Lane and to the precinct of the Dominican Friars. A well on the northern side gave it the name. Beyond it runs St Leonardgate, a street of low-density occupation until the 18th century. Originally it led to the Leper House of St Leonard, which lay beyond the borough boundary, hence its name. The 'gate' element of the name, like that in St Marygate, comes from the Old English *gata* for a street.

Three

House and Home

The narrative of how Lancastrians lived in the past has many gaps in it. From a modest knowledge of how the Roman population lived we pass on to a long period for which we still lack archaeological evidence. We pick up the thread again in the Middle Ages, although it is a very thin thread indeed. From the 17th century we find the research progressively easier, largely because buildings survive in ever greater quantities, until in the 18th and 19th centuries we can even hazard some generalisations based on factual evidence. The later 19th and early 20th centuries bring an associated photographic record, while the planning process has produced a most useful record of deposited specifications and plans from the 1880s to date. As an archaeologist I am constantly in search of the physical and practical explanation: how big was it?; what did it look like?; how did people use it? I have to admit to frustration with much of the evidence before the 17th century, because it is simply too patchy. Just once in a while, however, the evidence is sufficient to allow buildings to be visualised. It is thus with the remarkable building accounts of 1314 for Sir Robert de Holand's new house, as we shall see.

To judge from the scanty evidence we have, Roman houses in the civilian settlement outside the fort were laid out on long strips, gable end to the roadway. Most of them probably had dual functions, with a shop on the street frontage and living accommodation behind, or possibly workshops behind the living quarters. They were of timber, with stone or tile roofs. Passages between the buildings gave access to the sides for maintenance and to the rear for servicing. Several fragments of such buildings have been found on Church Street, at nos 41 and 65 for instance.

While only archaeological evidence survives for Roman buildings in Lancaster, there is so far only documentary evidence for medieval houses. No single medieval burgage house has yet been excavated, partly because of the very widespread cellaring of the town in the 17th and 18th centuries, which has cut away later deposits on the street frontages, leaving in some cases only parts of the underlying Roman ones.

Medieval houses in Lancaster were chiefly, if not exclusively, timber-framed, with thatched roofs. Timber was plentiful in the neighbourhood, although the existence of royal forest rights in Quernmore made the relationship uneasy; like many medieval rights it was probably exerted in a patchy fashion, with occasional exemplary punishment, an element of licence, marked by payment of fines, and a large degree of laissez-faire. We would not know of the building of a house in Penny Street in 1297 if timber had not been obtained illegally for the solar (private living room) from Quernmore Forest. In 1338 a lease of a burgage in St Mary's Street by Stephen Lemeyngs and his wife specifies details of a house to be built by them, with a solar, garderobe (privy) and chamber of new timber.

23 Excavation of 65 Church Street in 1973-4. Roman remains were found under the floor of the cellar and were subsequently excavated. Although all the later Roman levels had been removed by the digging of the cellar, the outer wall and part of the interior of a food-shop were found, dating from the second century A.D. When the stones of this outer wall were removed, the foundation trench, marked on this photograph by a lighter colour, was found to contain fragments of a Neolithic bowl, itself already some three thousand years old, which had been broken and scattered by the Roman builders.

The cartularies of Lancaster Priory, Cockersand and Furness Abbeys all carry references to burgage plots with houses and other buildings upon them, such as those of Nicholas of Lindsey, Garner, son of William de Lancastre, or Robert, son of Iva de Lancastre in St Leonardgate, all 13th-century benefactors of Lancaster Priory. Occasionally there is more detail. Simon of Lancaster, chaplain, refers to his burgage, garden, etc. in St Mary's Street, lying between the burgages of Hugh, son of Adam Crud, and of Garner Sutor (the tailor?). In some other towns and cities this kind of evidence can allow us to map whole streets, but in Lancaster the evidence is far too thin.

The Cockersand cartulary records a toft in 'Markahastrete' (Market Hall Street?) on the east side by the booths ('juxta bohas'), perhaps meaning facing onto the Market Square. This would approximate to the present site of the *Blue Anchor*. Another toft, belonging to Gerard of Lancaster in 1225-35, unfortunately not closely located, is recorded as measuring 20 perches by three. As we know from later documents that the perch measured seven yards by local custom, this usefully gives us a depth of 140 yards and a frontage of 21 yards for a toft or burgage plot. Whether this was characteristic we cannot tell. It seems much wider than most plots which have survived in the city centre, which seem on average to be about one perch (6.4 metres) wide or less.

The names of a number of medieval inhabitants come out of the Furness cartulary. Two burgages are held by Hardoll and Dilekoch in 1210-30, while another burgage is recorded between those of John Podioch and Nicholas the Dyer. Another burgage, in Penny Street, appears in a series of charters running from *c*.1280-1393. In 1280 it lies between those of Robert son of Mawe and of William Matte. By 1300 the names have become Robert de Bolleron (Bowerham) and William de Sclene (Slyne). Are

24 Reconstruction of Sir Robert de Holand's 1314 house by David Vale. This shows the raising into place of the main timber trusses of the house, referred to in the documents as 'levatio'. The wagon belonging to the Abbot of Furness has just brought prefabricated timbers to the site. Once the main structure is up the walls can be infilled with timber-framed panels and the floors and roofing fitted. All the load bearing is done by these main trusses.

these different people or is this just a different way of referring to the same people? In the Middle Ages, before surnames became fixed, people could be known by their patronymic, by their job, by their place of origin or even by a nickname. This does not make it any easier to demonstrate continuity of ownership.

In 1314 we have a most interesting account for the building of a house for Sir Robert de Holand, which probably stood on the site of the present Judges Lodging. The house cost the amazingly large sum of over £91. We can follow the work in its various stages. First the site had to be 'cleaned' ('mundare'), by which we should probably understand 'cleared and levelled'. Timber including planks for the ceiling of the solar had to be sawn. Most of the framing may well have been prepared off-site since a wagon had to be hired, with two wagoners, from the Abbot of Furness for 28 weeks for bringing timber and roofing to the site. Over £2 was spent on the carpenters and others on the 'levatio' or rearing of the individual trusses. Wooden shingles for the roof and 14,500 special nails for fixing them show that the end of the work was at hand. The Receiver had to travel to Pontefract and back (the seat of Earl Thomas, who was funding the work) at a cost of £1 7s. It is sad, all things considered, that this building may have had a life of no more than eight years; it almost certainly became a casualty of the Scots raid of 1322, although re-used timbers have been noted in the roof of the Judges Lodging which may derive from it.

After the Scottish raid in 1322 many of the burgages were worth a fraction of their former selves, as is recorded in several successive years of rentals of the former lands of Thomas, Earl of Lancaster, who was executed after the battle of Boroughbridge in 1322. This raid, and another in 1389, must have destroyed many of the earlier timber

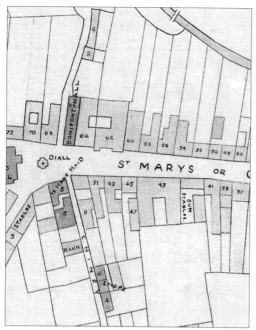

25 Detail of 1684 map – Great Bonifont Hall and Stewp Hall. St Marygate or Church Street was the most important street in the 17th century. It contained houses of both rich and poor and some houses of greater distinction which were let out to tenants or subdivided. Bonifont Hall, on the corner of Bridge Lane, appears in a survey of Hornby Castle estates in 1581-2 as 'Great Bamfant Hall', at this time divided into three quite large tenements. Stewp Hall (43) was owned by the powerful Molyneux family and tenanted by George Foxcroft in the early 18th century. Both houses are candidates for late medieval survivals which had fallen on hard times.

houses and may well account for much of the lack of surviving medieval domestic architecture in present-day Lancaster.

Timber-framed buildings continued to be constructed over the next three centuries, although there is a lack of documentary evidence for the period. Herber House, probably originally built as a chantry priests' house at the southern extremity of Penny Street, was repaired in 1504 in 'Walls Timber Thatch and Dawbe' (daub was clay applied to laths between the timber frames). This is clearly the traditional medieval timber-framing technique.

The survey of Hornby Castle estates in the 1580s shows from its many references to 'bays of buildings and onsetts' that the tradition in the area was still a timber one. In Lancaster one of the properties was Great Bamfant (or Bonifont) Hall on the north side of St Marygate. It was at this time divided into three tenements, which must have been the fate of many formerly grand houses of this period. Stewp or Stoop Hall lower down Church Street and on the south side must have been another such. It belonged to the Molyneux of Sefton, who never used it but let it out to tenants. It seems to be referred to in the description by Captain Howard of the Norwich Garrison in 1634: 'The situation of this towne is is [sic] more pleasant than the buildings, onely one I can remember of note [the Ld. Molineux's] …'

By the early 18th century at least part of it housed the *Sun Inn*. Built around a courtyard and with columns ('stoops' in dialect) on its street frontage, it may well have been a late medieval survival, modernised in the 17th century. Others, such as the Old Hall/New Hall complex on the site of the Judges Lodging, probably grew up between the damage or destruction of Sir Robert de Holand's house and the building of the new house in about 1631 by Thomas Covell.

26 Three of four pairs of re-used oak crucks found at Mitchell's Brewery in 1988. The great rebuilding of Lancaster in the 17th century changed it from a town of timber to a town of stone. Cruck buildings must have been very common here in the 16th century and before, but now the evidence mainly comes from finds like this and from sawn-up segments of crucks and other structural timbers, re-used in later buildings.

By the 17th century, then, we can imagine a town still of timber and thatch, with some medieval buildings which had survived all the hazards of fire and destruction but mainly newer ones of the Tudor period. The streets were still not completely built up; there were gaps between houses and a low density of building by modern standards. Many of the houses and shops presented gable ends to the street, running back into stables, workshops and living accommodation behind, with access to the rear via an archway from the street. Here and there would have stood something more substantial, perhaps built by the monasteries on the land they had acquired: priests' houses, chantries and town houses to accommodate the abbots and senior office-holders of the monasteries on business and during the Assizes. Some of these will have survived the dissolution of the monasteries in the 1530s.

A very few of the wealthier citizens had started building in stone, though, and to more fashionable standards. Several houses belonged to distant gentry families, who would use them when they needed to transact business at the courts in Lancaster. Thomas Covell, governor of the Castle, built his own new house in stone in the 1630s, a house which still survives. There are traces of others, too. When work was in progress on the site of the *New Inn* in 2000, in preparation for the new cinema, a carved stone door-head was found reused in a cellar wall. It was quite wide, with a shallow arch at the head, of a type current in about 1600. It may possibly have stood over the street

27   View of Stonewell in 1810 by Gideon Yates. This poor part of the town still retained a number of older buildings and thatched roofs at a time when the rest had been largely rebuilt and re-roofed in slate.

entrance to the yard of a substantial stone house. While such houses were rare in the early 17th century, before the century was out they had become common.

When I describe houses as 'timber-framed' I am referring in general to cruck construction, which was common in the countryside, although the more sophisticated box construction may have been more prevalent in the town. However, we are beset with a great lack of evidence. There is little to suggest sophisticated timber-framing of the South Lancashire pattern. Even most of the evidence for crucks – paired angled timbers, usually cut from a single tree to form individual trusses – has gone. One re-used set of four crucks was found in 1988 on the site of Mitchell's Brewery behind Market Street, while others have been recognised among re-used and shortened timbers in roofs, such as that of the *New Inn*. Cruck construction was not necessarily visible from the outside of a building, although the steepness of the resulting roof angle was well adapted to thatch, which would thus be a potential sign. Since the walls of cruck houses are not load-bearing they can be constructed of close timbering, wide timbering with infill of lath or wattle and clay, of clay alone, or even of stone. It is quite possible that many Lancaster houses had timber frames but stone walling. If the whole surface was then rendered, or lime-washed, it would be very difficult to identify the method of construction. The evidence of the spread of fire, such as the one in 1698, suggests, however, that at least some timbering was exposed at that date.

28 View of the Market Place *c.*1770 by an anonymous artist. Recently recognised as the earliest known view of Lancaster's Market Square, this image is of great interest. The view, from the south, shows the then Town Hall, various houses and shops on the north and east sides of the square, including three inns, and various structures in the foreground. These include, from the left, the stocks, the Market Cross (taken down in 1782), the pump and the Fish Stones, all approximately where the fountain now stands. In the background is, from left to right, the old Town Hall of 1671, predecessor of the City Museum building, which was the Town Hall from 1783 until 1910. Its three main storeys were carried over an open space containing shops, supported on columns. Next to it is a group of buildings around a yard, which, with part of the site of the large building in the centre left of the picture, became the *Commercial Inn* in 1799 and now forms the site of the Central Library. The large building is 'Mr Hornby's Great House', which at this time seems to have been divided up. Next to that is the *Royal Oak*, with the name of Wm. Sharp, the landlord, over the door. Sharp's will was proved in December 1765, so the view cannot date from much later. Next to this is the *George and Dragon*, apparently a 17th-century building, with a mounting block outside. It appears that part of its frontage may have formed a lock-up shop. From 1766 to 1799 its landlord was James Bland. Next to this is a house or shop with, on its right, the entrance to Anchor Lane. Next to this, on the east side, is the *Blue Anchor*, very much as it is today, with a shop next to it now part of the premises. In 1766 this inn paid duty on 18 windows. Judging by the long shadows to the west and the awnings on several buildings, the view is taken quite early on a summer's morning.

The change from timber to stone in Lancaster was gradual, but had a large effect on the appearance of the town. Relatively few 17th-century houses remain, although quite a few have been merely refronted, like the Masonic Hall, which retains its rear wall, staircase and windows, or the nearby 76 Church Street, whose typically Georgian frontage belies its earlier side and rear walls and many interior features. One of the factors leading to the changeover was undoubtedly the risk of fire. The great fire of 1698, covered elsewhere, must have had a profound influence, since many timber buildings were destroyed but two stone buildings were unharmed. However, we should

29 Seventeenth-century stone houses in Church Street. These two houses stood on the site of the Masonic Hall extension. The one on the left has a dated lintel of 1684 and, with its mullioned and transomed windows, is typical of a generation of substantial 17th-century stone houses which were largely superseded by Georgian or later buildings. It is possible that these two stone houses were the ones which escaped burning in Stout's account of the great fire of 1698.

not overestimate the speed of change. Datestones over doors of many buildings in North Lancashire show the progress of the 'great rebuilding' in both rural and urban areas. It is too easy to generalise. People had many different reasons for rebuilding: family pride, desire to be in fashion, security of tenure, surplus income, fear of fire or even prudent capital investment. William Stout, the ironmonger and merchant, was responsible for several rebuildings as he became in law or by default an executor for dead or failed business colleagues.

The rebuilding was patchy, however, and in drawings and paintings of Lancaster in the 18th or even early 19th centuries many timber and thatched houses can still be seen, mainly in poorer areas such as Moor Lane and Stonewell, alongside houses of the first stone rebuilding, themselves to be rebuilt in the Georgian period. 'Mr Hornby's Great House' in Market Square, seen in an anonymous watercolour of about 1770 in the Whitworth Art Gallery, is a representative of an earlier generation of quite sophisticated building, replaced by the Georgian *Commercial Inn*.

Many of the 17th-century stone houses may have echoed the ground plan and layout of their medieval predecessors, just in another material. There is some evidence from old photographs for stone houses with a gable end to the street and a cross wing striding over an access passage to the rear. The pattern of burgage plots was very pervasive and led to considerable conservatism. Even in the 18th century rebuilding tended to respect the ancient plots, as these of course represented property boundaries, and it was rare for anyone to be able to collect enough contiguous plots to change the layout.

Even outside the ancient core, whenever new developments were built on former fields, such as Queen Street of the 1770s, or even more particularly in Dalton Square of 1783 and later, sites similar in proportion to burgage plots were let out. It is striking that in Dalton Square the plots were generally regarded as too wide, resulting in failure to let and subsequent sub-division of a number of them, usually two into three. The scale of burgage plots seems to have been about right. However, Georgian rebuilding tended to produce a different and distinctive house plan, and the long narrow sites had a further effect in the 19th century in producing the yards lined with cheap cottages for rent which were later to become slums.

The 18th century was a period of rapid change and development for Lancaster. The growth of trade with the West Indies, America and the Baltic from a faltering start in the last quarter of the 17th century completely altered the face of the town. Slavery played a part also, particularly in the mid-18th century, although by the end of the century the slave trade had concentrated on certain ports such as Bristol and Liverpool. Many Lancaster slavers moved their base of operations to Liverpool in a manner followed a generation later by more conventional traders and merchants, seeking a larger infrastructure for their business. In the meantime the outward sign of prosperity was a fever of rebuilding within the older streets and a rapid development out into the former fringes of the countryside. Some two hundred Georgian houses substantially survive and give the modern city centre much of its character.

The new building was all of stone. Brick was only used where it was not seen. The huge resource of timber locked up in older buildings that were being replaced was itself valuable. Being mainly oak it had the tendency to harden with age, while the larger timbers were relatively fireproof, since they merely charred on the outside unless

Old Red Lion & John Threlfall's Old House, Church St. Lancaster

30 Drawing of Church Street with old houses surviving in the early 19th century. The scene is Lower Church Street, the south side adjacent to the corner of Cheapside, now lost under the buildings of St Nicholas Arcades. It shows the old *Red Lion Inn*, clearly of 17th-century date with mullioned windows, and 'John Threlfall's old house' next to it. This building has the steep gable, outshuts and jettying which suggest a surviving timber structure, perhaps of 16th-century date or earlier.

subjected to fierce and continuing heat. All the evidence suggests that house-carpenters were re-using 17th-century and earlier timbers for roofing, floor joists, window and door lintels (behind stonework), and as levelling pieces in the core of walls, well into the 18th century. Often referred to as 'ships' timbers', these have nothing at all to do with ships, the requirements of which were utterly different. Just occasionally, however, sections of re-used or rejected softwood spars (masts and yards of ships) may have found their way into buildings, forming such things as the newel-post on a spiral stair in the Old Town Hall or a pillar in the cellar of 7 Friar Street. New timber increasingly consisted of Baltic softwoods as oak became scarce. Many of Lancaster's Georgian houses have stone outer walls and timber-framing for internal partition walls.

Apart from rebuilding in such areas as Market Street and Church Street, the infilling of gaps and the creation of new streets like Common Garden Street and Spring Garden Street, the earliest deliberate development was by the Corporation on the former open space of the Green Ayre in 1743. Although it took some time to build, and some lots were probably still unoccupied twenty years later, the evidence can still be seen in Chapel Street, many other houses having disappeared in the building of the

31 Reed and plaster wall at 11 Chapel Street. This is typical of many internal walls of Georgian stone-built houses in Lancaster. The carpenter's work is often concealed. A timber frame would be set up, into which were inserted either reeds, thin laths or woven wattle panels. Over this clay or plaster would be thickly applied. The presence of such walls can usually be detected by tapping on them.

32 Reconstruction by David Vale of the building of St George's Quay in 1751. The quay was built quite rapidly by constructing a retaining wall in the river and then backfilling behind it. Lots were then let out for warehouses and houses. The field on which it lies was called the 'Summer Pasture' and was glebe land, belonging to the vicar.

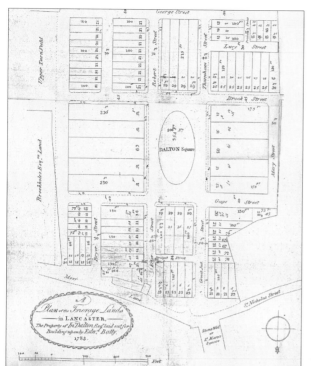

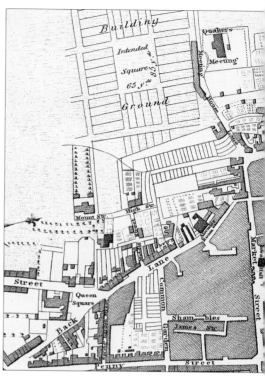

33 Plan of lots for leasing in Dalton Square. This plan accompanied all the deeds drawn up between John Dalton and those who acquired leasehold property in the 'Fryerage' development of 1783. The plan was the work of Edward Batty, architect. The Square was still not complete in 1820, although what was built was elegant and to a high standard. Lancaster could not sustain so much high-quality development and many of the plots were subdivided before 1800 to produce houses of a more manageable size.

34 Detail from Clark's map of 1807. The map shows intended streets and squares to the north, east and west of the town. This detail envisages a whole series of streets and a square to the south of Meeting House Lane. In fact, this map appeared at nearly the high-water mark of building optimism and little was added in the next thirty years to the existing, shaded, portions. When building recommenced in this area in the last quarter of the century it was to a very different scale and for a very different market.

bus station in 1938-9. St John's Church was constructed here in 1755 to serve the growing population, Lancaster's first new church since the medieval Priory church. Other developments soon followed: New Street in around 1747, New Road in 1752 and Cable Street from around 1759. The biggest development, however, was connected with the port. St George's Quay was created as a result of the Act of Parliament bringing into being the Port Commissioners. The quay was developed by the sale of lots, in three phases between 1750 and 1780, occupying a strip of former glebeland bordering the river Lune – the Summer Pasture – leased from the vicar. Upon these lots merchant speculators built a variety of houses, public houses and warehouses.

By the 1770s the former Head Haugh Fields to the south-west of the centre had been sold for a development which became High Street and Middle Street, while further south Queen Square and Queen Street appeared. The Corporation had big plans for the riverside area at the end of Cable Street in the 1780s, a project intended to complement the new bridge being built there, now Skerton Bridge. A dispute with Squire Bradshaw of Halton, who had an alternative claim, put paid to this, but a private development by John Dalton of Thurnham in 1783-4 led to the building of Dalton Square, Lancaster's only claim to a London-type development. The Square and its surrounding streets were never completed, probably due to a lack of demand and capital, but it also came at a difficult time, towards the end of the century, when general prosperity began to slip as an effect of the Napoleonic Wars. Enough was built, however, to show us what might have been.

In the early 19th century building work was pursued cautiously, the state of war not encouraging much speculative development. In general the growth of the town slowed, and a plan published in Clark's *History of Lancaster* in 1807 shows many streets and squares proposed but never built. In 1822 and 1826 the two local banks (Thomas Worswick, Sons & Co. and Dilworth, Arthington & Birkett) both crashed, the second taking with it much of the credit which had survived the first. The effect was devastating. Although the result was the almost immediate creation of a joint stock bank on

35 The Albert Terrace, East Road, seen from St Peter's spire, *c.*1890. Although this terrace of the 1860s is no longer known by this name, it indicates a Victorian sense of solidity and respectability. This was on the edge of the country and in an area of trees and open spaces, including the Cemetery and Williamson Park. Soon the large working-class development of Moorlands would be under way to the right of the picture, below Christ Church. More recently several of these houses have served as boarding-houses for the Grammar School.

36 St George's Quay terrace. This terrace of 11 houses was built before 1856 by a co-operative of building trades workers to replace an earlier terrace demolished to make way for the railway line. Houses of this date in Lancaster are relatively uncommon. They pre-date the bye-laws controlling housing and had, for instance, shared and unenclosed privies and drying grounds behind them, where most later houses have individual yards.

the Scottish model, the Lancaster Banking Company, the horse had, metaphorically, bolted. For the next twenty years or so no building of any substantial sort took place unless it was financed from outside, such as railways, churches, etc. When domestic building recommenced it was on a different scale and for a different market. Lancaster had in the interim lost its mercantile mentality and become a town of textile workers.

Early Victorian developments are few in Lancaster, but what there is showed what was to come. They took place at both ends of the social spectrum: semi-rural villas and terraces for the middle class; small and in many cases back-to-back developments for rent to the poorest workers. Examples of the former can be seen in West Place, in 'the Albert Terrace' (not now identified as such) in East Road, and in the earliest part of Belle Vue Terrace on the Greaves. Much of the latter type has gone, but was represented by dense housing around the Marton Street/George Street area and east of Dalton Square in Monmouth and Plumb Streets. Some early housing for millworkers appeared in Bath Mill Lane, put up by the employers in 1837, but this was to be uncommon in Lancaster. Most workers' housing was privately rented; there were probably fewer than forty houses built by employers in the town for their workers at any time in the 19th century.

The 1850s also saw extension of the town eastwards, firstly into the former Play-house Fields, south-east of St Leonardgate, for Edward Street, Lodge Street and Alfred Street, and then again for entirely different reasons on four fields off Moor Lane, the

37 Plan of area around Town Hall *c.*1910 showing back-to-backs. Back-to-back housing was by no means common in Lancaster. It involved building two rows of houses under a single roof, with no rear access, and it was outlawed by bye-laws quite early in the Victorian period. Here, however, can be seen a number of rows built in the 1840s, some of which are back-to-backs and some conventional houses. It gave rise to a very high density of occupation and a very unhealthy environment with shared privies and no proper place to deposit rubbish.

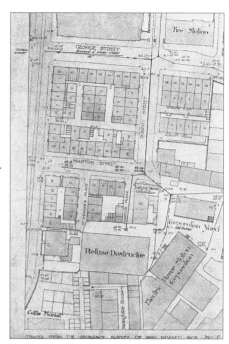

Freehold Estate. This was politically inspired, designed to supplement the Liberal vote by increasing holders of the necessary property qualifications. It was a remarkable social experiment but not a success since there was not enough demand for housing of this scale and the plots were sold slowly, the idea eventually being compromised by the building of terraced houses for rent. The very large gardens and the grid plan of the estate survive, however, as a relic of its origins.

Pre bye-law housing is rare in Lancaster and distinctive. The first terrace on St George's Quay is a good example. While the frontage looks normal, the land behind is not divided into separate yards. Originally the grouped privies and the undivided drying grounds each served several houses. Other such houses at the junction of Aldcliffe Lane and Queen Street, now demolished, are remembered by one of Dr Elizabeth Roberts' oral history correspondents. The lady, born in 1888, remembered that her grandmother took in washing but had no tap, no range, a shared privy in a common yard and no bath. The family bathed in a bowl and took any of their food which could not be cooked over the fire to a common bakehouse in Penny Street. Another lady from a poor family, born in 1889, lived as a child in Albert Place behind the Town Hall, an area of back-to-back houses. She, too, shared an outside privy, but its seat was scoured with soap and soda. The children sat on stools and shared one large plate at table.

Most Victorian housing in Lancaster was terraced and was built after 1870, in contrast to many other Lancashire towns. As a consequence most of it was built to the various bye-law standards of 1858 and 1877 and, substantially, of stone. As a result a high proportion survives, and is still in demand. The bye-laws controlled density of building, road widths, privacy and drainage. They tended in practice to produce a series of standard designs which were graded according to the rent they would fetch per week, with the plainest design flush to the street at one end of the spectrum and front gardens, bay windows, extra bedrooms, etc. at the other. All houses built thus had a private yard to the rear and, more importantly, their own privy and drying space for clothes. Indoor lavatories were not a feature and, indeed, were thought to be a health risk. Bathrooms were also unknown, except in the larger middle-class terraced houses. Many current occupants of traditional working-class terrace houses have sacrificed a bedroom to provide modern amenities.

38   Moorlands estate, seen *c.*1900 from the spire of St Peter's. Moorlands represents one of the last large-scale Victorian developments in Lancaster. Formerly the site of a gentleman's villa (the Gregson family lived here), the land was put up for sale in 17 lots in 1893. A consortium of local builders acquired it and developed it as a unit – until then an unusual move because the unit of development had been more usually a street or even a small group of houses. Fourteen streets were built in a few years and provided standardised housing for 2,000-2,500 people. The Scottish names of most of the streets are probably a result of the Scottish holiday habit of Mr Dowthwaite, one of the principal builders! Primrose estate can be seen in the background.

Discrete groups of streets were built on the Dry Dock estate, on the former Woodville Gardens, in Bowerham and along the road to the south, on the Greaves. The biggest developments, however, were on Primrose Hill and at Moorlands, both as it happened on the sites of former semi-rural villas. The 14 streets of Moorlands, all built within about seven years, totalled by 1901 some 460 houses and housed a new population of some 2,000 people. The social effect, on a relatively low population base, must have been startling at the time. As the 19th century wore on the capacity to build such large numbers of houses at a time increased, culminating with the former Greaves and Dallas estates, to the south and west respectively, at the turn of the 20th century. Further work went on in Westbourne Road, on the Wingate Saul property, but here a dramatic collapse in the property market led to houses standing untenanted after about 1904 and indeed little building of any kind occurred until after the First World War.

Two main effects stemmed from the war. One was an expectation that housing for working people should become better. People wanted more space and facilities, but this could not be achieved without subsidy. The other was the idea that the worst of the unhealthy slums should be demolished. Despite opposition from private landlords,

39   Council Houses, Denny Avenue, Ryelands, *c*.1932-3. The quality and spaciousness of these houses compared with what had been available to working people before must have been staggering to their first occupants. Although built to a price and with little in the way of frills, these houses contained inside loos, bathroom and hot water, as well as a small garden.

council housing, subsidised by central government, became a reality. The first council houses in Lancaster were built in 1921, and the process has continued since, but the sale of council houses from 1979, the reduction in demand and the growth of housing associations which have taken on former council functions have changed the picture radically. Ten main estates were built before the Second World War, beginning with Bowerham in 1921. They were all on the outskirts of the built-up area at the time and contributed to the geographical growth of the town. Estates at Newton and Beaumont extended along the main Caton and Halton roads while the new Ryelands estate, between Lancaster and Morecambe, mirrored private housing development around Scale Hall that was taking place in the 1930s.

The new housing was larger, airier, more spacious and had more facilities than anything tenants were used to. It is not surprising that two of Dr Roberts' oral correspondents were full of admiration for the new houses. One who moved in in the 1920s said, 'They were really nice houses … It was so modern and I loved it', while another added, 'It had a bathroom that was another luxury … and what my mother particularly enjoyed was hot water from the boiler, just open the tap and that was it, smashing …'.

At the Ridge an estate was begun in 1944 in anticipation of troops returning from the war. This estate was to be laid out on 'garden city' lines, following the likes of Letchworth and Welwyn in Hertfordshire, which meant wide roads, plenty of trees

40   Scale Hall developments, 1930s. Between the wars there was much more demand for owner-occupation. By now the typical unit was the 'semi' or semi-detached house, with garden front and back and (usually) bay windows. This aerial view shows housing under construction at the junction of Morecambe Road and Scale Hall Lane, halfway between Lancaster and Morecambe.

and grass, and a generous amount of open space. A number of mature trees were included in the new planting, which gave the estate a sense of stability. Extensions to the Ridge estate were approved in 1954 and 1957, the latter group of houses being built by national company Wimpey. The estate can be distinguished by its Lake District names, carrying on the tradition of Freehold. Keswick, Patterdale, Thirlmere and Honister Roads all lie in the area between the canal and Ridge Lane.

Hand in hand with the new developments was a process of slum clearance, especially between 1927 and 1935. It was not without opposition from landlords. It involved areas of sub-standard housing built in the period 1820-50, such as Factory Hill off St Leonardgate, Plumb Street and Monmouth Street on the canal bank, and also older yards and courts in the town centre. Many of these were highly insanitary but picturesque, and many were recorded by local photographer Sam Thompson before demolition. Government subsidy was used to buy out rents and individual cottages were demolished in yards, to reduce density and remove the worst examples. In time all such properties were demolished. Again, this tended to displace poor town centre dwellers to the outskirts, leading to more demand for public transport and roads.

Meanwhile private developers had not been idle. The town's housing stock grew by some 40 per cent between the wars, some of it through the building of council houses, but much through the building of standardised semi-detached houses for private owners. These broke the long but not quite exclusive relationship between Lancaster and stone building. Some brick had been used in the 19th century, mostly under a coating of render. Now alien plan forms and materials began to invade on

41 Pre-fabs at Ashton Road. Built as a stop-gap measure after the Second World War to solve a housing crisis, these pre-fabricated houses offered a compact but desirable standard of living and were popular with their occupants. Many survived far beyond their anticipated lives and the sites live on, since the concrete bases and mains drainage could be re-used for more traditional structures.

a large scale. Estates of semi-detached houses and council estates of groups and terraces were united by being built to a national standard, using brick, usually covered in wet-dash, which can be curiously unattractive and drab in a damp climate such as this. The lack of post-war houses was also supplemented by the building of 'pre-fabs', compact prefabricated houses built by industrial rather than traditional processes, especially off Ashton Road. Many of these saw use far beyond their intended life and the fact that roads, drains, etc. had been laid to them meant that they were replaced on the same sites by more conventional buildings in due course.

In Skerton work was undertaken in the late 1950s and early 1960s which most of Lancaster had been able to avoid: large-scale replanning. Captains' Row, Main Street and the Ramparts were largely demolished and replaced by medium-rise blocks of flats and other contemporary structures. The scale was not extreme compared with other towns, but cost many old topographical features. Elsewhere the prosperity of the 1960s and '70s and '80s led to speculative building for sale of open-plan houses and other 'modern' designs at places such as Hala (the roads named after racecourses) and at Abraham Heights (roads named after American presidents). More recently the tendency has been to recolonise 'brownfield' sites – ones where industry or other uses have ceased. Such sites are usually small and opportunistic but in inner areas of the city, thus fulfilling ambitions to limit outward growth and encourage life without the car. Several of the 'brownfield' sites are related to former hospitals, such as the Royal Albert and Moor Hospitals, 'care in the community' having rendered such large institutions redundant. Their fine buildings are at a premium when converted into housing, such

42 1960s high-rise at Skerton. Skerton lay outside the borough for most of the 19th century and thus its housing standards were not as high as those demanded by the bye-laws. Main Street and the Ramparts were picturesque but squalid, as were Captain's Row and other streets near Skerton Bridge. Municipal improvements were more thoroughgoing in Skerton than anywhere else in Lancaster and we can see here a result of the wind of change which blew more violently in some cities than here. A pair of medium-rise tower blocks are under construction. A number of taller, eleven-storey, blocks were built on Mainway, but the experiment was not continued elsewhere in Lancaster, except at the Ridge, the University (Bowland Tower) and at St Martin's College (the William Thompson building).

as Standen Park, which arose out of the latter, although the prices frequently mean that they are bought by incomers who do not rely economically on the area.

In fact, Lancaster has at present the largest and fastest growing population of any of the Lancashire districts, with an increase of some 10,000 people between 1991 and 2001. This is not matched by growing work opportunities, so it seems that Lancaster is a very popular place to live and that people are prepared to commute some distance to work, in places such as Manchester and Central Lancashire. In planning terms this means that the district has to find additional land over the next ten years or so to house this growing population, even if this means building on green fields and extending inexorably outwards into beautiful countryside. Or should the economic pressure be resisted, if there is not work to match? The concomitant factor is vastly increased commuter traffic, unless home-working on a massive scale becomes realistic.

Four

Lancaster on the Map

There is no surviving map of Lancaster before 1610, but from that date to the present there is an almost continuous sequence. This allows us to compare in a detailed way the various topographical features which make up Lancaster over a period of nearly four hundred years.

John Speed produced his atlas of Great Britain on a county-by-county basis, in 1610. County towns were given a small feature in the top corner – sometimes other towns appeared as well. Lancaster, as county town of Lancashire, accordingly appears on the Lancashire map. The town plan shows a remarkable degree of continuity to the present day, in that the main core of streets remains easily identifiable. In addition the key indicates a number of significant buildings and sites, such as **Greene Ayre**, a large crescent of open land lying between the river Lune and the mill dam, or **Weary Wall**, not closely defined on the plan but a surviving segment of the fourth-century Roman fort wall overlooking the bridge. The **Free Schole** lies below the church-yard, the original site of the medieval school which now stands in East Road as Lancaster Royal Grammar School, while **Olde Hall** appears from its position to be the building now known as the Judges Lodging. **Newe Hall** is not closely defined on the plan but is perhaps roughly on the site of the present *Sun Inn*. Before 1785 the building here was called Stoop Hall. The 1684 plan, however, seems to place New Hall behind Old Hall.

The **Mill**, the ancient town mill, lying on the mill-dam at the foot of Calkeld Lane, was finally demolished in 1769. Nearby stood the **Fishe Market**, apparently at the foot of Calkeld Lane. **Stone Well** was then the point of issue of a stream which ran down into the mill-dam. Of the streets shown, **St Leonards Gate** was named after the leper hospital of St Leonard, which lay just outside the borough boundary, while **Butchers Strete**, also known as Pudding Lane, is now known as Cheapside. **Kelne Lane** seems to indicate what is now China Street, but the 1684 plan assigns this name to what we now call Meeting House Lane, so perhaps it is placed in error. At all events China Street [Lane] seems to be of ancient origin.

The market place is shown in **Market Strete**, with its cross and pillory. Also notable is the way in which the town hall/tolbooth juts out between what is now Market Square and New Street Square, indicating encroachment on an originally larger market place, a pointer back to medieval times. **St Nicolas Strete** is the only ancient central street to be lost, under a shopping centre.

On the outskirts of the town are **The Friers**, site of the Dominican or Black Friars, whose friary stood within twelve acres of orchard and garden. Some ruins appear to be survive in 1610. **White Crosse** was at that time an actual cross in the

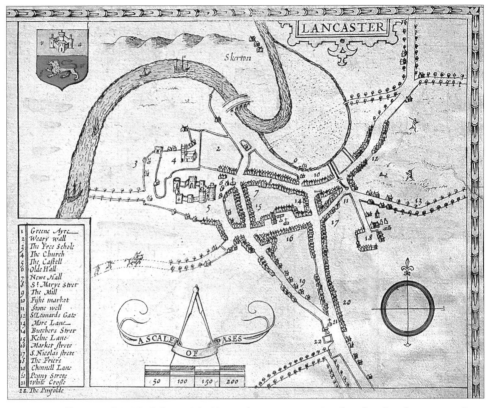

43 Speed's map of 1610. A key with 22 numbers accompanies the plan (modern names in brackets):

1. Greene Ayre [Green Ayre]
2. Weary Wall [Wery Wall]
3. The Free Schole
4. The Church
5. The Castell [Castle]
6. Olde Hall
7. Newe Hall
8. St Marye Strete [Church St]
9. The Mill
10. Fishe Market
11. Stone Well
12. St Leonards Gate [St Leonardgate]
13. More Lane [Moor Lane]
14. Butchers Strete
15. Kelne Lane
16. Market Strete
17. St Nicolas Strete
18. The Friers
19. Chennell Lane
20. Penny Strete
21. White Crosse
22. The Pinfolde

roadway at the southern limit of the town. Later the name transferred to the huge mill complex belonging to Storey Bros., now owned by Lancashire County Council. **The Pinfolde**, now lost, is a reminder of more agricultural days, for it was the enclosure where cattle straying in the common fields were kept until redeemed on payment by their owner. It stood just beyond the White Cross, at the southern limit of the town.

The basic topography of the plan is distorted but the general picture of the town at this date is easily retrieved.

The crumpled survey plans of the map of 1684, and a similar one of Preston, were found in 1952 in the cellar of Towneley Hall, Burnley, and put together by the late Kenneth Docton. The map bears no date and is dated only by internal evidence. It catches Lancaster just as it was developing from a sleepy medieval county town into a centre of the transatlantic trade. The large scale and details of burgage plots allow us to make a number of extrapolations backwards to explain anomalies such as China Lane and Kemps Lane, or what is now New Street Square.

The map contains information on occupiers or owners of property; for the first time we can place individual burgages. The bridge of four arches is shown, with Bridge Lane which, along with China Lane, looks like an afterthought to the town plan; both streets cut through between burgage plots and have none aligned to them. Does this indicate that at some stage before borough status was acquired the old Roman bridge and its access road further to the west were still in use? Green Ayre is still an open space between the river and the mill dam. The mill itself is shown in rather more detail than in 1610. The mill dam has a curious creek arising from it near the mill. Could this indicate that the mill dam only occupied one of several former courses of the river, the creek perhaps pointing to another? Gallows are shown both on the Skerton side of the river and on the Moor at a place called, appropriately enough, 'Tiburn'. The grouping of Free School, St Mary's Church and Castle are as they were in 1610 but the Vicarage House and almshouses (Gardyner's) are shown below the church, together with a large barn, shown by excavations in 1975-6 to be the tithe barn erected by Sion Abbey when the church ceased to be monastic in 1430.

Church Street (St Mary's Street) was clearly the main street, with the most houses, and the most important. New Hall and Old Hall are shown adjacent, occupying the site of the Judges Lodging (itself almost certainly built in the 1630s by Thomas Covell, governor of the Castle). The exact relationship of these buildings has yet to be worked out. Below (east of) Old Hall is the 'Diall', actually the remains of the cross known as Covell Cross, restored in 1902. Further down the street, just beyond the junction with Bridge Lane, is Bonifont Hall, while a little further on, on the right, is Stewp or Stoop Hall (the name refers to the columns which carried a portico out over the street). This property belonged to the Molyneux family, later Earls of Sefton. The presence of these four buildings, the only ones referred to as 'Hall' in such a short space of street, suggests that this was the smart area of the town. None of the buildings except the Judges Lodging complex survives, so we cannot analyse them, but the evidence seems to suggest that these were mainly significant late medieval houses. The medieval building which stood on the site of the Judges Lodging was probably the one built for Sir Robert de Holand in 1322, for which building accounts survive.

Only two inns are shown: the *Mare Maid* at the junction of China Lane and St Mary's Street, and the *Naked Taylor* at the Church Street end of Chancery Lane. A further inn, the *Sun*, is hinted at by the presence of the Sun stables, also in Church Street. This is clearly wrong, as other inns are known to exist at this date, particularly the *George*, at that time the principal inn of the town.

Before the building of North Road, Church Street ran straight on into Stonewell/Rosemary Lane. (That portion beyond Cheapside is now known as Lower Church

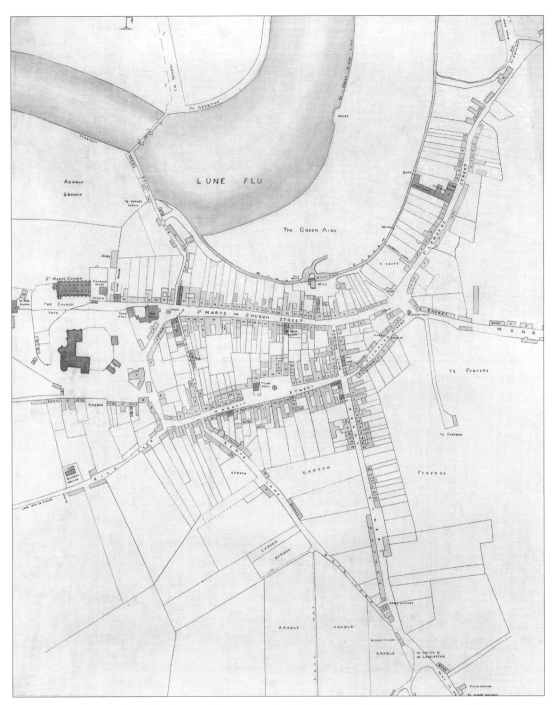

44 Map of 1684. The original survey sheets were found at Towneley Hall and reconstructed by the late Kenneth Docton.

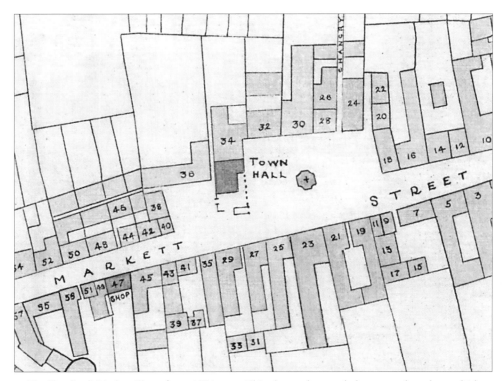

45 Detail of Market Place from 1684 map. This shows the much larger market place which originally included New Street Square and into which successive town halls were an intrusion.

Street.) Further on was St Leonardgate, at this time only partly set out in burgage plots and with a number of empty frontages. It ended at the Jelle Beck, marking the boundary of the borough and the start of Bulk township. The most significant building on St Leonardgate was John Lawson's Sugar House which, with its Still House and Warehouse, occupied a croft between the street and the mill dam. This is the only outward sign on this plan that trade had begun with the West Indies, Lawson being one of the first generation of merchants to seize the opportunities presented.

Running lengthwise through burgage plots in Church Street and Market Street, suggesting that it is later than both, China Lane in 1684 has relatively few buildings along it. Further west lies Castle Hill and Castle Park, not distinguished at that date. Again, buildings are relatively few in number. In front of the Castle gate and at the rear of the Castle are various buildings which must represent encroachments on the moat, presumably later than the Civil War when the castle had last been used militarily. Market Street, another densely packed street, contains the Market Square, the Town Hall (the recently rebuilt structure of 1671) and the cross at which proclamations took place. More interestingly, there appears to be a double or even a triple row of buildings just west of what is now New Street Square. This looks rather like even further encroachment since Speed's time by booths on an even larger original market stance, an encroachment by now fossilised into permanent shops and houses.

Market Street runs into the Pudding Lane [Cheapside]/Penny Street axis, its continuation being St Nicholas Street, now lost, running down to Stonewell. At Stonewell there is a widening leading to St Leonardgate and Moor Lane, a thin straggle of houses and fields leading up onto the unenclosed Moor. An access lane also leads to the Friers, the last remains of the Dominican Friary, whose precinct walls abut the backs of all the burgage plots on the east side of Penny Street, suggesting that the burgage plots in Lancaster were all defined long before 1260, when the Friary was founded. Penny Street has numerous burgage plots, especially on the east side, but seems rather thinly built. It must be remembered that this street had taken the brunt of the Earl of Derby's attack and punitive burning only just over forty years earlier, in 1643. Perhaps it was still recovering, as there is no direct evidence that the compensation offered to the townsfolk was ever paid.

China Lane leads to Kemps Lane and Back Lane, now King Street. King Street is not an ancient name, and not the '*via regia*', meaning 'king's highway', used for any main road in medieval Latin documents. The lack of burgage plots, the few buildings, and the crooked course all point to it being of minor importance up to this date. If this map is any guide, then Penny Street was the more important approach to Lancaster, and may indeed mark the Roman southern approach. At the junction of Penny Street and Back Lane is marked 'almshouses', known from other sources to be Toulnson's Almshouses, long since gone and themselves marking the site of the medieval Herber House.

The 1778 map, by Stephen Mackreth, comes nearly a century after the Towneley Hall plan. There is nothing in between to chart the growth of the town at a time when prosperity and change went hand in hand. Mackreth was a local man of whom little is known and this appears to be his only map. The engraver, B. Grey, also seems to have been a local man. Unlike all the other town plans of Lancaster, this one has south at the top, making it somewhat inconvenient to compare.

The town is still contained within its ancient bounds, from which it was shortly to burst, but with two or three important exceptions. On the south side development has begun in the fields bordering Back Lane, giving rise to the first houses of Queen Street and Queen Square, while High Street and Mount Street occupy the former Head Haugh field. To the north the Green Ayre is beginning to fill up with buildings along the line of Chapel Street and Cable Street, which forms a chord to the curve of the old mill dam, represented by Damside Street. Lesser streets fill in some of the spaces nowadays occupied by the Bus Station. Further to the north-west a wholly new development has taken place on the former Summer Pasture between Vicarage Fields and the river: St George's Quay, as yet only partially developed, is a regular series of warehouses backed by an alley and divided into blocks by lateral streets. Beginning in 1751 under the new Port Commission, this will be virtually complete by the 1780s and thereafter little changed except by the coming of the railways.

Because of the scale of the plan, it is possible to see changes in the 'footprint' of buildings as they are rebuilt. More noticeable is the greater density of building, the filling in of gaps, and the building of new internal streets such as 'Charles or New Street' (1747), New Road (1752), Common Garden Street (once Mackerell Street) and Spring Garden Street, joining older streets and allowing the development of backland. In addition the internal development of burgage plots for cheaper housing

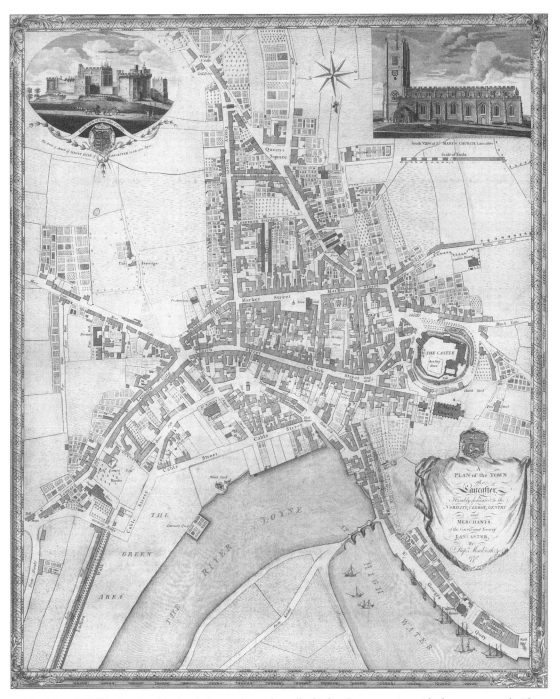

46 Map of 1778 by Stephen Mackreth. Somewhat awkwardly this handsome map is upside down compared with all the other maps of Lancaster. Little is known of the surveyor.

had already begun. Land between Church and Market Streets and between Market and Common Garden Streets had been largely infilled by now with workshops and stables as well as cottages, with a few exceptions such as the bowling green behind the *Sun Inn* and the adjacent pleasure garden belonging to Dr Marton.

A number of individual buildings and features deserve attention. There are the new churches and chapels, such as St John's on the Green Ayre, the Presbyterian chapel off St Nicholas Street, the Quakers Meeting in Meeting House Lane and the Dissenters Meeting in Mount Street. A 'poor house' stands at the southern extremity of the town, shortly to be replaced by a new workhouse to the east. Among industrial buildings and features are the rope walks now appearing in the fields to the east and south, the enlarged Sugar House on St Leonardgate, St George's Quay, and the butchers' Shambles of 1776 running between Market and Common Garden Streets. Also new are Penny's Hospital (almshouses) and the associated Assembly Rooms, which raised money for it, in Back Lane. Over to the east stands the Fryerage and its associated land, blocking development in this direction until some ten years later. The Castle, too, is still in its medieval form, but on the eve of major works to create a modern prison and courts.

The 1821 map was made by local land-surveyor Jonathan Binns just over forty years after Mackreth's map but the changes are profound. Those forty years had been ones of prosperity, leading both to new streets and to rebuilding of city centre property. The year 1821 was a moment of some significance. Both local private banks closed in the early 1820s, with massive loss of local credit, leading to a period of stagnation which lasted over thirty years. The port, too, was declining, unable to offer the infrastructure and facilities of its old rival, Liverpool.

In the south Queen Street was nearly complete, with some gaps on its western side. Fenton Street and Cawthorne Street had been cut to link Castle Hill with High Street, although the development came too late, after demand for building plots had slackened. In the east the most significant change was the growth outwards into what had been the precinct of the Dominican Friars. The property was owned from soon after the Dissolution by the Catholic Dalton family of Thurnham Hall. In 1783 John Dalton got a private Act of Parliament to break the entail upon the estate and started letting out lots in a prestigious new development of the Fryerage lands, which became Dalton Square and its surrounding streets. The Square was to have large houses facing onto it, but the plan allowed for some fifteen other streets to surround it. The map, drawn some 35 years after work began, still shows a number of significant gaps and inconsistencies. There was simply not sufficient local demand by the end of the 18th century for plots as large or schemes as prestigious as this. Many plots ended up empty or subdivided, and away from the Square the size and quality of houses quickly reduces.

To the north a new bridge, Skerton Bridge, had been built in 1788 to create a better entrance to the town than the old approach via Bridge Lane and China Lane. Leading to this new bridge was the wide Parliament Street running into Cable Street. Here again development had been disappointing. The Corporation had intended this to be a distinguished boulevard lined with gentlemen's houses, but had reckoned without a legal dispute with Mr Bradshaw of Halton, which effectively put paid to the scheme.

St George's Quay is now virtually complete, ending in the Pothouse, for a short while in the mid- to late 18th century a manufactory of delftware. Two shipyards are

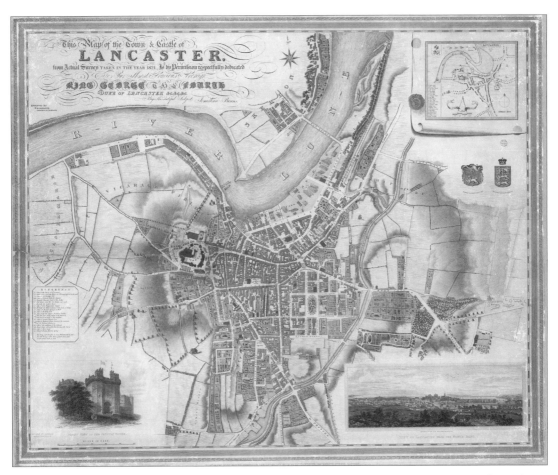

47 Binns' map of 1821. This attractive and detailed map was surveyed by Jonathan Binns, failed farmer but writer on agricultural good practice. Although he describes how it was made and printed in 1821, and although there does not seem to have been a second printing, there are two 1824 references on the sheet which remain unexplained.

shown, Smiths on the north bank of the river and Brockbanks on the south bank, near Cable Street. Numerous woodyards and ropewalks testify to the importance of the maritime trades. The Lancaster Canal of 1797 winds around the south and east of the town and at least two textile mills have appeared on its banks, the shape of things to come. New churches have appeared, such as St Anne's on Moor Lane or the Catholic Chapel on Dalton Square, while other amenities are marked by the Theatre on St Leonardgate and the Bath House out in the fields to the east. The Workhouse overlooks the town from the edge of the Moor. Further up, and off the map, the new County Lunatic Asylum, built in 1816, indicates Lancaster's county town status and its bid to retain its old position over the upstart industrial towns springing up further south and east. The remodelled Castle, too, with its courts and prison facilities, represents the

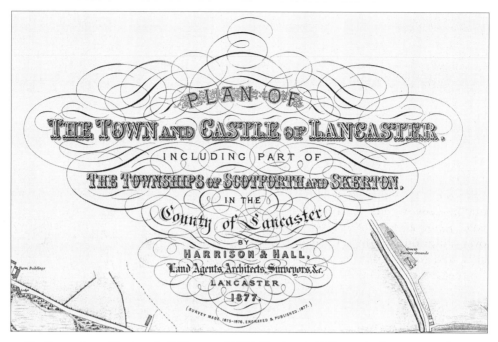

48 Cartouche to Harrison & Hall's map of 1877. Harrison & Hall were land surveyors and must have been acutely aware of the lack of current large-scale maps of the town as it grew. The Ordnance Survey produced nothing here between 1849 and 1891. The firm also produced a much rarer map of Morecambe. (See endpapers for whole map)

importance of the Assizes to Lancaster's economy. This was Lancashire, not Lancaster, money being invested.

The map, being generous around its margins, shows more of the fields than previous maps, and by the time of the next one many of these fields would be built upon.

Harrison & Hall's map of 1877 (they were architects, surveyors and land-agents) shows the mid-Victorian town half-way between the large-scale Ordnance Survey editions of 1849 and 1891. This is a crucial time before most of the larger developments such as Moorlands or Primrose were built. The inner core has filled out and was already becoming unpleasant, leading to the first flush of ribbon development along the main roads, and a number of suburban villas had been built. The only large-scale development is the Freehold. This map is rather awkward. It is large, printed on four sheets, to cover the increasing spread of the built-up area. West, rather than north, is at the top so, like Mackreth's map, it has to be re-aligned for comparisons to be made.

To the south Lancaster has finally broken out of its confines. Several villas, such as Greaves House, The Greaves, Parkfield and Belle Vue, lie strung out along the Greaves ridge, while a series of terraces stretch south from Penny Street bridge and include Springfield Terrace, Spring Bank, West Greaves, Vineyard, Parkfield and Halcyon Terraces, Alfred Street, Alma and Ripley Roads. This suburban ribbon-development, with its attractive names, was intended to draw middle-class tenants away from the increasingly crowded town centre, which as a result became even less attractive, leading to lock-up shops and slums.

Other middle-class development was taking place to the south-west in Portland Street and Regent Street, to the west at Westbourne Terrace and West Place, and to the east at the Albert Terrace, East Road. The larger eastern development of Freehold Park was also supposed to attract middle-class buyers (and Liberal voters), but, again, plot size proved over-ambitious, leading to many gaps, and rows of smaller cottages for rent rather than purchase.

Working-class housing is represented by terraces off Lune Road on the edge of the Marsh and by the complex of streets covering the former Playhouse Fields, such as Edward, Alfred and Lodge Streets of the 1850s and 1860s, or the somewhat later Denis and De Vitre Streets. Smaller back-to-back accommodation of the 1840s could be found in the area south of Dalton Square, such as Marton Street, George Street and Robert Street. Later working-class housing in Lancaster was built to a much better standard. However, at the bottom end of the market there were the cheapest rents of all in some of the two hundred or so yards and

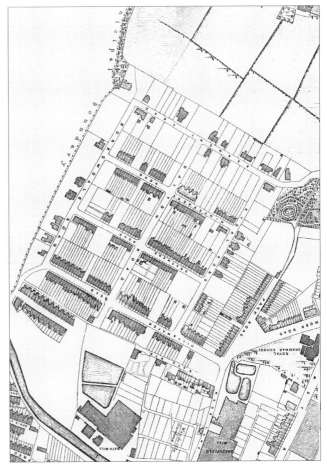

49 Detail of Freehold Estate from Harrison & Hall's plan of 1877. The Freehold Estate was a development intended to swell the Liberal vote by providing housing which met the required level of land ownership. As such it was a failure, but it has left evidence of an interesting social experiment. The shape of the estate was determined by the fields on which it was built.

courts, which became increasingly insanitary and decrepit until a wave of demolition between 1927 and 1935. In addition, many older houses, including Georgian survivals, ceased to appeal to the better-off and so were subdivided for rent. Areas such as Bridge Lane and China Lane became notorious for their lodging-houses, seen by the establishment as the base for much of the vagrant and criminal behaviour in the town, and houses in multiple occupation.

The town was by now ringed with public institutions such as the Royal Albert Asylum, Ripley Hospital (orphanage), enlarged County Asylum and enlarged Workhouse. A Militia Barracks stood at White Cross, while a new Barracks for the recently arrived King's Own Royal Regiment, given a territorial base by the recent Cardwell Army

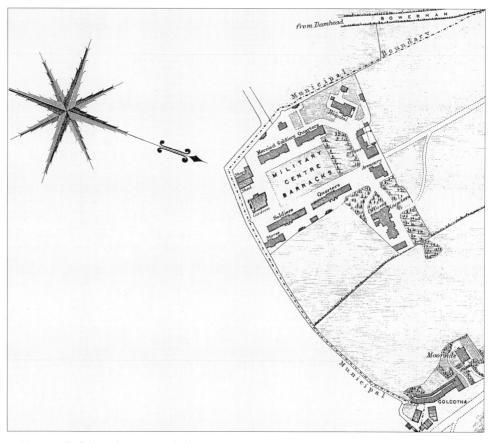

50 Detail of the Military Barracks from Harrison & Hall's plan of 1877. Following the Cardwell reforms of the army in the early 1870s, regiments were given a territory in which to recruit, reflected by their Barracks. The King's Own Regiment (4th Foot) came to Lancaster, and its barracks, after some negotiation for other sites, was built upon charity land at Bowerham between 1873 and 1880. Once the Barracks was built other housing started to move in and soon Bowerham was a busy suburb. The Barracks now forms the core of St Martin's College, opened in 1964 for teacher training. (This map is printed with north to the right, to make it easier to read.)

Reforms, was taking shape at Bowerham. Two railway stations now served the town, Green Ayre to the north for Yorkshire and the growing resort of Morecambe, and Castle Station to the west for the main west-coast line. The older Penny Street Station was by now a private house but a branch line here still served sidings and coalyards.

New churches are represented by St Peter's, now the Catholic Cathedral, and Christ Church on Wyresdale Road or St Thomas' on Penny Street. There has also been great growth in nonconformist building. Industry is all-pervasive, with eight textile mills along the canal corridor, the Paintworks on St George's Quay and the Lancaster Wagon Company on Caton Road. Just off the map to the west, and hinted at by 'to the Varnish Works', Lune Mills, the new home of the Williamson linoleum empire, is beginning to take shape.

Five

Working for a Living

For the last four centuries or so it is possible to reconstruct the working lives of many Lancaster men and women from a great variety of sources. Some we can follow through their entire career, while others come into a focus for a particular moment, before disappearing once more into obscurity. In this chapter I have taken the lives of 15 people or, in one case, a group of people, spread over these last four centuries. Each is chosen because of the nature of their work, which in some way illustrates the opportunities and social customs of their age. More modern citizens I have left alone, because of the need for discretion. Other researchers have investigated these, especially by means of oral history recording, with impressive results, by offering a degree of anonymity to the correspondent, but I prefer to compare like with like and show as much personal detail as can be found out.

John Lawson, merchant and sugar-baker, 1616-89
The founder of a short merchant dynasty, John Lawson was one of the earliest Quakers in Lancaster and actually provided refuge in his house on St Leonardgate for George Fox, founder of the movement, when he was beset by the Lancaster mob in 1652. According to Fox's journal:

> In the afternoon I went to the steeplehouse at Lancaster, and declared the truth both to the priest and people, laying open before them the deceits they live in, and directing them to the power and spirit of God, which they wanted. But they haled me out, and stoned me along the street, till I came to John Lawson's house.

In the early days Quakers were persecuted. Lawson was fined on one occasion £200, which he refused to pay as a matter of conscience, and went to prison for 12 months instead. He was buried in the original Friends' burial ground near Golgotha, but his tombstone was brought back to the Friends' Meeting House in 1951 and now stands in the porch.

He was one of a small group of early entrepreneurs who, with small ships and a primitive financial structure, made a fortune from the West Indies trade and established its importance for Lancaster. He also acquired, it would seem, the Sugar House on St Leonardgate from John Hodgson, his co-religionist and fellow entrepreneur, and was certainly running it at the time the Towneley Hall map was made in 1684. Perhaps in order to bring the raw sugar to it more easily, he also obtained permission from the Corporation in 1680 to build a wharf and crane on the Green Ayre near his house. He had already built a bridge over the mill dam in order to gain access to the Green Ayre. 'Lawson's Quay', as it was called, was the first of a series of wharves built upstream of the Old Bridge by merchants, in the period before the Port Commission had acquired

51 John Lawson's farthing token. During the Commonwealth and the beginning of the reign of Charles II there was a great shortage of small change due to the lack of official coinage. The situation was remedied by tradesmen and merchants who had their own farthings and halfpennies struck. John Lawson was one of about half-a-dozen Lancaster tradesmen who produced such a token, which could be redeemed for silver at his business when anyone had collected sufficient. The significance of the 'agnus dei' symbol on his token remains to be explained.

and built St George's Quay, further downstream. Lawson himself was one of a handful of local tradesmen who issued a farthing token of his own to try to overcome the problems caused by a lack of small change at the time.

The Sugar House seems to have carried on for nearly a hundred and fifty years. The process involved bringing in casks of crude boiled sugar ('muscovado') from the plantations and giving it a secondary refining. This meant boiling the muscovado with lime, egg white or bull's blood to clarify the syrup. This was then mixed with white clay and run into tall conical moulds set over collecting jars. The mixture slowly set, the excess moisture escaping through small holes in the bottom of each mould. The distinctively shaped sugar-loaves which resulted were dried in a domed room heated by charcoal and were then ready for sale. These loaves were often bought complete, but could be broken into lumps using a pair of bladed pincers. Fragments of earthenware sugar-moulds have been found on the north side of St Leonardgate, where the Sugar House stood, and elsewhere in Lancaster. Perhaps they had some second-hand value after they had ceased to be used for sugar? The idea of sugar-refining came to England from Europe and brought with it a number of foreign workers. We know of two Germans who worked at the Lancaster Sugar House in the 18th and 19th centuries; there may have been others. Equally, Lawson may have brought his specialists in from Liverpool, which was ahead of Lancaster in many respects.

William Stout, ironmonger and merchant, 1665-1752
Stout has become well-known to us from his published autobiography, which was written as a sort of retrospective diary, year by year. His life spanned the growth of Lancaster from a sleepy market town to an international trading port and he, along

52 Portrait of William Stout. Stout was apprenticed to a Lancaster ironmonger and became a Quaker. Later he was one of a small group who traded with the West Indies. His autobiography, kept as an annual record of the main occurrences in trade and politics, and things personal to him, gives an immensely valuable insight into the character of Lancaster in the late 17th and early 18th centuries. In particular he painted some very vivid and incisive word-portraits of his contemporaries.

with a handful of others, was one of the prime movers in its development. He became a Quaker under the influence of his master, the ironmonger Henry Coward, to whom he was apprenticed in 1680 at the age of 16. Unlike some of his contemporaries, Stout was not a risk-taker. Indeed he was extremely cautious and held back from a number of enterprises. He was extremely scornful of those who wasted money or time, or failed financially. In part this was his own natural instinct, in part a more general Quaker view which regarded debt as a crime. His autobiography is full of sharp and waspish comments, and indeed, while he was undoubtedly a most reliable and useful man to his community, he can hardly have made himself popular.

Initially Stout worked in his master's shop and slept there, as was the tradition with apprentices who had to serve customers at all hours. From his descriptions, the shop was one of those where the window and shutter hinged away in the medieval manner so that the front was open to the elements. One of his jobs was to make up goods for market day, and, although it was essentially an ironmonger's shop, tobacco, brandy, sugar and prunes were also sold. In 1687, when he came out of his apprenticeship, he took a shop of his own and stocked it partly from suppliers in London. He travelled there with a group of other Lancaster men, and sent his goods back by sea on a Lancaster ship while he went on to Sheffield and bought more goods there, setting up arrangements which would continue for some time after. He later combined these business trips with the Quaker Yearly Meeting in London, where he could be sure of travelling companions, important because of the cash he had to carry. He also brought nails, etc. which were made locally, perhaps in Furness or the Lake District.

Later Stout took on his own apprentices, most of whom were a disappointment to him. Even after he had officially retired from business he kept on being called back to run or sell off failing businesses as an executor for one of his many business acquaintances. He also took responsibility for the rebuilding of the Meeting House in 1708 so that it would accommodate a meeting of the four northern counties. His more adventurous involvement was with sending and bringing in cargoes to and from Virginia and the West Indies. On the whole the risks were high and Stout thought that the profit of less than ten percent on money tied up for a year was not good business. However, the overseas trade opened the eyes of Lancaster shopkeepers to a wider world, in which Stout's small ventures quickly became commonplace and then insignificant. Shopkeepers became merchants, and the scale and value of trade increased immeasurably in a couple of generations.

John Holland (senior), pipe-maker, c.1705-54

John Holland, senior, is the earliest known clay tobacco pipe-maker in Lancaster. He must have started work in about 1705 and by his death in 1754 had built up a considerable business. He married three times and his son John by his first marriage assisted him in business. He marked his pipes 'IOHN HOLAND' with a roller stamp on the stem, in a style similar to that of the pipemakers of Rainford and South Lancashire. Some family event in 1748 led to a dated and fancier version of the mark, including a spread eagle. Several examples of both the marks have been found locally, and, more interestingly, a single example is recorded from the sunken pirate harbour of Port Royal, Jamaica. This must indicate an export business to the West Indies, alongside other goods. We do not know where in Lancaster Holland worked; later pipemakers all worked at Pipehouse Yard, on the eastern side of Penny Street, but so far there is no particular evidence to connect the Hollands with this site.

Holland would have practised the standard method of pipe-making. White-firing pipeclay was rolled out into pipe-sized pieces on a board. Each piece was then roughly shaped and fed into a two-part metal mould which imparted any decoration on the bowl and shaped heel and stem. A plug was forced down into the bowl to create the inner side and a thin wire was passed up the stem to create the bore (this can be a dating tool as the bore became progressively narrower with time). The pipe was then laid out to dry, and the name roller-stamped or impressed into the stem of a certain number. When dried the pipes were placed in clay 'saggars' to protect them and fired in a kiln. After cooling the pipes were packed in boxes in straw, usually by the gross (144), with 16 to the dozen to allow for breakages. Such a fragile item – some 'long clays' could be half a metre long – could easily suffer in transport, especially on a long sea voyage. Clay pipes were very cheap and were often given away by inns; tobacco was by contrast very expensive. The only way a pipe-maker could make a profit was with high productivity and an established market. The former generally meant that the whole family worked at the manufacture.

As a minor trader who had not been apprenticed in Lancaster, Holland, and later his widow, paid the annual Stallenge Roll, a small tax on non-Freemen, from 1737-55, so we can follow their progress, and those of some of their successors, from this source.

Robert Gillow, cabinet-maker, 1704-72

Robert Gillow, the founder of the famous Lancaster firm of cabinet-makers, was born in 1704, the son of Richard and Alice Gillow, both Catholics, at Singleton in the Fylde (near modern Blackpool). His father died in 1717 when he was only 13 (he was aged 77 and so there must have been a considerable age difference between his mother and father). It was a great disadvantage at that time to be a Catholic and another disadvantage to be an orphan, so he was not well placed to succeed. Catholics were fined for recusancy

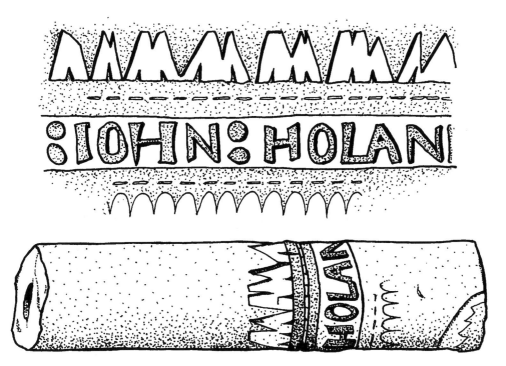

53 Clay tobacco pipe with John Holland's mark. Clay tobacco pipes of the early 18th century were frequently marked with a roller-stamp in the north west. The name was applied as advertising, perhaps to encourage re-order. John Holland had a wide trade in the district as far as Furness and also with the West Indies on the evidence of a marked pipe from Port Royal, Jamaica. Drawn by Wendy Moore.

and were under suspicion of disloyalty to the Crown, especially in 1715 and 1745, when Jacobite armies passed through Lancashire expecting support from local Catholics.

Robert was apprenticed in 1721 to John Robinson of Lancaster, a joiner. It was quite normal for enterprising lads to move to the nearest big town to 'better themselves'. Lancaster attracted many apprentices from the surrounding villages, especially in the Fylde and in the Furness area; it offered a wide range of jobs and excellent prospects. Robinson was a fellow Catholic and likely to be sympathetic to Robert. Alice, Robert's mother, must have sacrificed a good deal to set him up with the £40 or so needed for an apprenticeship, as well as losing his company and any income he could have had while staying at home. At the end of seven years Robert had completed his apprenticeship and went with his master to point out to the town Bailiffs his name in the enrolments of apprentices. He could now become a Free Burgess or Freeman on payment of a fine (£1 6s. 8d.) and so practise a trade in Lancaster.

He joined forces with another ex-apprentice, George Haresnape, and they set up in business together for five years. Almost from the start Robert kept detailed accounts; his first recorded commission was in 1729 for a gun barrel (stock?). In 1730 he was

54 Robert Gillow in the Freemen's Rolls. At the end of his seven-year apprenticeship to John Robinson, joiner, Gillow was able to prove his enrolment in the Apprentice Rolls and become a Freeman of Lancaster, paying £1 6s. 8d. for the privilege. He could now practise his trade in the town and take on his own apprentices, both of which he did. He specialised rather more than his master and became a cabinet-maker, taking advantage of the new taste and money for fine furniture.

secure enough to marry Agnes Fell. Several of their children died in infancy but two sons, Richard and Robert, followed their father into the trade. Initially Robert had supplemented his joinery income with various trading adventures overseas but as time went on the firm began to specialise in fine cabinet-making, using the mahogany and other fine woods now available from the Caribbean. More personal details are recorded in the Return of Papists (Catholics) in the Diocese of Chester made in 1767. From the Window Tax returns of 1766 we know that Robert had a house in Church Street with 21 windows.

Gillows had workshops on the Green Ayre, between what is now Parliament Street and St Leonardgate, and offices on Castle Hill. An 'adventure to London' led to the founding of a branch shop in Oxford Street in 1769, and soon the firm was supplying furniture to the fashionable world. Robert retired from business in 1769 and died in 1772.

As leading Catholics the Gillows took on many Catholic apprentices themselves. They also helped set up the first Catholic chapel in an old barn in Mason Street, among their workshops. Later generations of the family were leading lights in the building of the Catholic chapel of 1798 in Dalton Square.

Dodshon Foster, slaver, 1730-93
Foster was not a native of Lancaster. The son of a Quaker merchant of Durham, he came here and entered the slave trade in 1752 at the early age of 21. Slaving from Lancaster had begun with the voyage of *Prince Frederick* in 1736. Quakers in general found it difficult to square slaving with their consciences and in particular their belief in freedom and equality before God, but so much 18th-century trade was mixed up with a slave economy that the issue vexed the Lancaster Quaker community for many years, and particularly in 1757, which may have affected Foster. Indeed, Quakers were

55 Portrait of Dodshon Foster by William Tate. Foster (1730-93) was one of the most prominent merchants of his generation, profiting from the slave trade and from his connections by marriage with the Rawlinson and Birket dynasties. He held a house and warehouse on St George's Quay, upriver from the Custom House.

in the forefront nationally of the abolition movement. Slaving ships sailed for West Africa with trade goods and exchanged them there for slaves, who were carried to the West Indies to work on the sugar-cane plantations. They were sold or exchanged there for goods such as rum, tobacco or sugar which formed the return cargo to England. This was the so-called 'Triangular Trade'.

Foster married Elizabeth, daughter of prominent citizen Myles Birket. His ship, a snow of only 40 tons, *Barlborough*, made several slaving voyages between 1752 and 1758 when he sold it. Slaving had dropped off with the onset of the Seven Years War, but other opportunities opened out to northern shipping, away from the dangers of the Channel. Soon he was involved in more legitimate West Indies trade with his father-in-law. Between 1755 and 1758 he served as one of Lancaster's Port Commissioners. It may be that slaving was no more than the device of an ambitious young man to make his way in a crowded market.

Lancaster's involvement in the slave trade was fairly brief, although its reliance on the slave economy of the West Indies for a much longer period should be noted. For some years in the middle of the 18th century it was the fourth most important slaving port, with some 180 slaving voyages, although it came a long way behind Liverpool, London and Bristol. Foster was directly or indirectly involved in the shipping of over 700 slaves in his short career.

Richard Fisher, stone-mason, c.1733-85
Richard Fisher was born at Newton-in-Furness, the son of a yeoman. He was apprenticed as a stone-mason to Thomas Thompson of Lancaster in 1746 and gained his Freedom in 1753-4. By 1756 he is listed as 'Richard Fisher & Co', holding a lease to one of the 22 quarries on Windmill Hill (Lancaster Moor). Thus he secured his own supply of building stone, as well as being a contractor on new building work. A later entry in the Borough Court records shows some of the tools of a quarryman on the Moor in 1813:

> In the Quarry, large gavelac, blocks, 3 legs, crane and rope, 4 gavelacs, 3 picks, 4 great hammers, 9 picks, 6 iron wedges, 1 spade, 6 iron wedges, 3 picks, 14 small iron wedges, 2 gavelocs, 3 iron rods, 1 hammer, 1 wood rule staff, 1 water lader, 2 planks, 1 water spout, 1 wheel barrow, 3 scabling hammers, 8 iron wedges, 6 ditto, 1 plank, 6 iron wedges, 8 throughs, 6 large freestones, a quantity of through and parpins, 2 planks, large stone lintel, 2 gate stoops, 1 wood ruler, 9 stone startups, 1 plank, 2 pickaxes, quantity of sough covers and walling stones.

Fisher was the successful tenderer for the Custom House in 1762. With Robert Clarkson, slater and plasterer, and William Sharp, plumber, he was left to interpret the plan and very brief details given by Richard Gillow and turn them into the building we see today. Some of this team had already worked together on St George's Quay and on the Assembly Room a few years earlier in 1759. At that building Bryan Clarke, William Kirkby and Richard Fisher had been the masons. Fisher seems to have been the junior at that time but between 1759 and 1762 his stock had risen. His older partners had been made Freemen in 1739-40 and 1738-9 respectively. Fisher was responsible for taking down the medieval Market Cross in Market Square in 1782, and presumably also for putting up the fish stones and obelisk in its place. At the auction of building lots in the Fryerage (Dalton Square) in 1783 Fisher bought lots 13 and 14, although he did not have enough time to do anything with them before he died in 1785. At the time of his death he was working for the Port Commission on the east side of the Dock at Glasson, where he seemed to be in trouble with his employers for not making as much progress as they hoped. In 1796 his heirs held four houses (built by him?) in St Leonardgate and one in Penny Street.

Richard Dilworth, tallow-chandler, fl. 1792-6
Richard Dilworth first comes into view in 1792 as a well-established tallow-chandler who had just dissolved his partnership with Mr Thomas Noon. The handbill which announces this is probably intended to offset rumours that he was about to close his business. Partnerships of merchants and manufacturers were often short-lived and were often to do with financial backing for enterprises. The difficulty arose over goodwill: who was to take over which regular customers when partnerships dissolved?

It appears from a gravestone at the Priory church that his wife, Jane, had died in 1790 at the early age of 29 (perhaps in childbirth?). Dilworth may have been the individual of that name apprenticed to Elizabeth Walshman and Benjamin Satterthwaite as a merchant in 1776. Walshman was herself described as a tallow-chandler elsewhere. An apprenticeship was usually for seven years, leading to becoming a Freeman. However, the Stallenge Rolls show Richard Dilworth paying this tax from 1787-90 and again from 1792-5. Presumably the gap represents the period in which he was in partnership. He became a Freeman only in 1797-8, which suggests he bought his Freedom. In this case he was either not apprenticed, or his apprenticeship was not in the right trade.

He then appears in the 1794 *Universal British Directory* as a tallow-chandler working in Back Lane and, later on, in 1796, he seems to be living in the Fryerage. His 'Candle-house', however, may have remained in Back Lane. There is some evidence to suggest that Dilworth moved to Liverpool in the early 19th century. The sheer number of tallow-chandlers in Lancaster at any one time is impressive. They must have been the sort of specialised supplier to be found mainly in towns who helped provision the countryside and shipping as well as exporting their wares.

Tallow-chandlers and their near relatives, soap-boilers, boiled down animal tallow and refined it for use, on the one hand, in candles and, on the other, in soap. Tallow candles were much cheaper than wax ones because they smelled, and smelled even worse in the manufacture. In the candle-house the tallow from the slaughter-houses

RICHARD DILWORTH,

TALLOW CHANDLER,

RETURNS HIS SINCERE THANKS TO HIS FRIENDS AND THE PUBLIC,
FOR THEIR PAST FAVOURS,

AND RESPECTFULLY INFORMS THEM

That he continues the BUSINESS as USUAL in the
BACK-LANE, LANCASTER,

WHERE THE FAVOURS OF THE PUBLIC WILL BE GRATEFULLY RECEIVED.

☞ On Account of a report which has been propogated, fince he diffolved
Copartnerfhip with Mr. NOON, that it was his intention to decline the
Bufinefs; he thinks it a duty incumbent upon him to give this Information,
left his Cuftomers may be mifled by fuch Infinuations,

May 21ft, 1792.

56 Handbill for Richard Dilworth, tallow-chandler. This handbill of 1792 records the dissolution of a partnership with Thomas Noon. In the days before there was a regular local newspaper this must have been the best way of putting business news about and avoiding the effects of rumour. The handbill suggests that other tallow-chandlers might have taken over his customers if they thought he had gone out of business.

would be refined to remove impurities. In due course, reheated to a liquid consistency, it would be poured into troughs. Into these 'dipping-frames' containing rows of wicks would be lowered, then dipped and withdrawn repeatedly so as to add layer upon layer to the candles. The candle had to be allowed to cool slightly between dips, otherwise the tallow would not adhere. The whole process had only become mechanised in the late 18th century. Prior to that the dipping had been done by hand, using a 'broach', a rod about three feet long, to which the wicks were fastened. The whole frame was counterweighted so that once the candles reached a certain weight (e.g. twelve or eight to the pound) it ceased to dip, and the candles, when cool, could be unstrung. Larger or special candles might also be mould-made, in metal moulds of a dozen or so at a time.

Georgiana Trusler, schoolmistress, 1795
One of relatively few 'respectable' occupations available to a single woman of good family and with some education was opening a boarding school for girls.

Georgiana Trusler's school has the distinction of being listed in detail in the Borough Court Rule Book as she seems to have got into financial difficulties in 1795. Myles Pennington and two others took her to court. As security for her appearance in

57 Centre of Moor Hospital. This splendid block, finished in 1816, looks more like a country house than the centre of a County Lunatic Asylum. The whole project was expensive and prestigious and so it is no wonder that the instigators wanted it to look dignified. It is mysterious that such a relative unknown as Thomas Standen should gain the contract to design and build it. Ironically, after carrying out its designed function for nearly two centuries, this block and others around it have become prestigious apartments, so its country house image has nearly become reality.

court, officials carried out an inventory of her possessions, in order to distrain upon them if necessary. Her house was in Back Lane. The contents of 11 rooms are listed, including the School Room. The inventory of goods shows 18 delft plates, four bells with pulleys, a quantity of black lead pencils, one hand bell, the contents of school room, three school forms (in garrets) and her personal possessions. We do not know what happened in this particular case, but there was a happy outcome for Georgiana. She married a London attorney, John Price, at St Paul's Church, Covent Garden, in 1802, and went on to have at least four children.

Thomas Standen, slater and plasterer, fl.1798-1830
Standen was a Roman Catholic at a crucial period, when people of his faith were able for the first time since Mary's reign to worship openly. In fact, his first recorded work was on the new Catholic chapel in Dalton Square in 1798-9. He earned £196 for his work here and at about the same time married Susan(na) Rogerson. An 1806 advertisement shows him as a stucco plasterer, moving from 2 Sun Street to Queen Street. By

1811 he had made the transformation to 'architect' of the new County Asylum on Lancaster Moor, a very significant contract (it cost some £42,000 between 1812 and 1820) and an amazing turn of fortune for a man with apparently little previous work to show. Did he have friends in high places? He not only drew the plans but also contracted for the work as builder, beginning by digging out all the foundations with his own labourers. The following year he was advertising in the local press for masons to work on the new asylum, the centre block of which, looking like a country house, still survives. By 1817, according to the transcript of evidence in the Tatham vs Wright trial, he was surveying Hornby church with a view to rebuilding it, but here he did not win the contract. He seems to have taken a share in the quarry at Ellel Cragg in 1818. In June 1822, by now described as 'slater, plaisterer and builder, dealer and chapman', he was declared bankrupt, and seems to have moved to Liverpool. The lack of detail about what other jobs he may have undertaken is quite typical of building craftsmen at this period. He was a lucky man to gain such a lucrative and high profile job as architect of the County Asylum, but this seems to have been the high-water mark of his career.

Mrs. Dorothy Bentham, landlady, fl.1802-26

In July 1803 Mrs Bentham advertised in the local newspaper, 'Genteel Lodgings to Let in an airy and pleasant situation, with Boarding, for Single Gentlemen'. Her house, now 6 Castle Park, is probably the one 'owned by Christopher Bentham's heirs' in a list of 1796. One of her lodgers was the unfortunate Gideon Yates (see below), who was there in 1802 and returned after his release from prison to stay until at least 1807. Another lodger was the famous actor Henry Betterton, who stayed here while performing at the Theatre in the autumn of 1803. Dorothy was the widow of Christopher Bentham, mariner, who had built nos 4, 6 and 8 Castle Park between 1785 and 1792. He died in May 1793. Presumably left with a large house and no source of income, letting lodgings was one of the few respectable openings for Dorothy. She died in 1826 leaving two sons, both stationers, Christopher of Dublin and George of Manchester.

Jane Noon, licensee of the Royal Oak, fl.1803-34

Women have long been associated with public houses but the relationship has been an uneasy one. Yet pubs could not function without them. Wives traditionally ran the household, dealt with the staff, and kept the hotel going (clean beds, prompt food, good service). The role of wives might also extend to daughters, who were sometimes in a position to take over the running of the pub from their fathers. Widows also ran pubs, but in general it seems that women were expected to pass on the pub to be run by a man once things like probate and valuation was sorted out. Just occasionally there were women who ran an inn not just for a couple of years but as a career. Among these were Agnes Starkie, who ran the *Black Horse* in Common Garden Street from 1822 until at least 1856 (an A. Starkie was there in 1818 but it may have been her husband), and Jane Noon, who ran the *Royal Oak* in the Market Place, a coaching inn, from 1803 to at least 1834, taking over from Jennet Warbrick, her grandmother, and her mother, Elizabeth. Three women successively also ran the *Queen's Head* between 1851 and 1864: Mary Wilson, Mary Maychell and Hannah Murphy. More often than not, however, women appear as licensees after the death of their husbands, typically for a

---

ROYAL-OAK INN,

MARKET-PLACE, LANCASTER.

—∞∞∞—

JANE NOON,

GRATEFUL to her Friends, for the Encouragement she has met with in Business, respectfully informs the Ladies, Gentlemen, Travellers, and others, that a large and convenient ADDITION has recently been made to the above old-established INN, which, with its advantageous Situation, renders it particularly well calculated for the accommodation of Travellers, having a great Number of SINGLE BED-ROOMS, SITTING-ROOMS, &c. now finished and neatly fitted up for the Reception of her Friends; and by always keeping a Stock of the best WINES and LIQUORS, with assiduous Attention of herself and Servants, she hopes to merit that Approbation and Patronage, which it will ever be her utmost Study to deserve.

*** NEW and EXCELLENT STABLING, with a CAREFUL OSTLER.

January 15th, 1803.

58 Handbill for Jane Noon. Jane took over the running of the *Royal Oak Inn* in Market Square in or before 1803 (the handbill does not suggest she was wholly new to it) probably from her mother, thus becoming the third generation of women to run it. The phraseology is entirely conventional, like that of a modern estate agent.

year or two. Many probably escape detection because they changed between Trade Directories, one of our best sources, being issued.

The *Royal Oak* existed from at least the 1750s. Jennet Warbrick was the licensee in 1794, according to the *Universal British Directory*. Jane Noon(e) makes her appearance in 1803 with a handbill and last occurs in a Trade Directory of 1834; she died in 1851 aged 89. The inn closed sometime after 1856 and certainly within the lifetime of Richard Bond, who mentions it as one which closed before 1891. Jennet Warbrick, licensee in 1794, died in 1798 aged 89. Her daughter was Elizabeth Noon, who probably took over the inn until her own death in 1802 aged 67. Her daughter was Jane Noon. Jane's younger sister Elizabeth ran a millinery and straw hat business in Market Street from 1804 and also seems later to have run the post office in Market Square. Here we have an example of three successive generations of self-employed women.

Inns were not used just for accommodation or drinking. Farmers left their horses there on market days, relying on the stabling provided, and ate lunch at the 'ordinary', a long table with a set menu. Auctions and sales also traditionally took place at inns.

Gideon Yates, artist, c.1770-1838

Gideon Yates was born probably round about 1770. He pursued the career, first in Liverpool and then in Lancaster, of merchant and insurance broker. In the latter role

59 Watercolour of 'Lancaster from the East' by Gideon Yates, 1811. The view is from Ridge Lane looking down towards St George's Quay and Brockbank's shipyard. Yates specialised in painting numerous copies of particular views in three standard sizes, perhaps using some device to copy the main outline of the picture.

he arranged insurance for ships and their cargoes in the burgeoning seaborne trade of the two ports. We know little about him until November 1802, when his landlady, Mrs Dorothy Bentham, took him to court over some issue. As bail against his appearance, sale was to be made of various personal possessions including 'A box of colouring, a miniature of G. Yates, Drawings etc.' which suggests that he was already an artist of sorts. The fact that he was lodging with Mrs Bentham suggests he was a single man. By March 1803 he was in financial trouble, as a public notice in the *Lancaster Gazette* shows.

The details of his bankruptcy are confused, and Gideon clearly believed charges against him, with his consequent loss of credit, had been trumped up. However, he was committed to gaol on 6 June 1803, principally at the suit of Robert Sinclair, insurance broker of London. His trial at Westminster followed in January 1804 and perhaps both before and afterwards he was imprisoned as a debtor in Lancaster Castle. In a letter to the *Gazette* soon after he endeavoured to explain his good faith, but apparently to no avail.

He spent just over a year in prison. The life of debtors in Lancaster Castle depended very much upon how much money they brought in with them and what support they gained from their friends on the outside. We must assume that poor Gideon could expect little on either count, but help was at hand. In August 1804 a list of debtors 'held at Lancaster Castle not charged in custody on 1st day of January 1804 or since with any debts exceeding £1500' included 'Gideon Yates', formerly of Liverpool, but late of Lancaster, merchant and insurance broker. Under the terms of an Act 44 George III 'for the relief of certain Insolvent Debtors', he and the others on the list stood a chance of being freed. In September it was adjudged that Gideon 'should be discharged and set at Liberty'.

Despite his apparent difficulties with Mrs Bentham he seems to have returned to his lodgings there upon his release; perhaps he had nowhere else to go. In January 1805 he advertised in the *Gazette*:

> Mr. Yates at the recommendation of a number of his friends, begs leave to tender his services to the Nobility, Ladies and Gentlemen of LANCASTER, and the neighbourhood, in TEACHING DRAWING in all its branches, with the PRINCIPLES of CIVIL and MILITARY ARCHITECTURE, LAND-SURVEYING etc - Having made a particular study of Landscape Gardening, he will furnish outlines for beautifying estates. Mr. Y has some New and Original Designs for Villas, Country Houses, Cottages etc. Terms may be known on application at Mrs. BENTHAM'S Castle Hill LANCASTER JAN 2 1805.

Although he was out of prison his troubles were not over. He had still to face two more legal tussles, the outcome of which is not recorded. They were with William Ellithorne in June 1805 and with his landlady, again, in April 1807. The latter is quite revealing, for in the list of goods to be distrained for bail were 'Twenty two Dozin of drawings and sundry Sketches and Drawings in an unfinished state'. Perhaps the new business was not going well and he had fallen behind with the rent?

Gideon Yates had used his time in prison and his irredeemable loss of mercantile credit to change from being an insurance broker to being a professional artist. The change is confirmed not only by the mass of signed and dated water-colour drawings which survive but also by the entry in Holden's *Triennial Directory* for 1811 which records: 'Yeates [*sic*], Gideon. Artist. Penny Street'. His career hereafter has to be reconstructed entirely from his paintings. He seems to have stayed in Lancaster until 1817. Thereafter he set out on a tour which took him to various other picturesque locations in England and Scotland and ultimately to France. Subsequently he settled in London where he painted hundreds of views of buildings, including all the main bridges. He died there in 1838.

Malcolm Wright, Police Superintendent 1836-57
Wright, the last Superintendent Constable of the old Watch (established in 1824) was appointed in January 1835. He went on to become the first Superintendent of the new Borough Police Force, set up in 1836, following the Municipal Corporations Act of 1835. He had to take part in the actual policing, out on the beat with his handful of men, and to lead by example. In 1845 he was shot at with a pistol and this and other injuries shortened his working life. William Hewitson records: 'At its further end [Derwent Road] a house was built, and I think its first occupant was Malcolm Wright,

a big burly Inspector of Police ... [At that time] the Borough 'Force' consisted of himself, one sergeant and eight men. He was afterwards appointed Superintendent in the place of Richard ('Dick') Hogarth on February 21st 1835. He was very roughly handled in one or two local disturbances, and owing to the state of his health he resigned (on pension) in October 1857. He died ... in January 1881.' On his retirement he was presented with an illuminated address by the Watch Committee. A poem by W. Sanderson describing him appeared in the local press:

> How stately and how gallantly
> He moves down Market Street,
> With head so lofty and erect,
> His eyes ne'er see his feet;
> And from him run each boy and dog,
> Such homage is his due,
> Or boy and dog would quickly feel
> The great man's cane in blue.
>
> His coat is buttoned to the chin,
> A nobby air he wears,
> Which is far more imposing than
> A Magistrate's or Mayor's.
> He looks down on the Fish Stones,
> And he looks up at the clock,
> Then stands in thought like Buonaparte
> On St. Helena's Rock.
>
> I wish I were Chief Constable
> Of some small County Town,
> With nothing else the day to do
> But just strut up and down;
> I'd walk up to the station house,
> To visit every train,
> And when come in or when go out
> Why then - walk down again.
>
> As thus in arduous duty would
> Have to be passed each day;
> Is there a man who could assert
> I did not earn my pay?
> I'd suck Seville's sweet oranges,
> Crack Barcelona nuts,
> And fuss about each tradesman
> When at night his shop he shuts.
>
> I after that would send my men
> Upon their different beats,
> And this would save the trouble of
> Parading round the streets.
> Yet in great coat, well muffled up,
> At twelve o'clock at night,
> I'd tap the curb stone with my stick
> And thus make all things - Right.

The reference to tapping the curb stone with a stick is known to mean signalling to the other constables: the sound carried well on a still night.

COUNTER-MARCHING

A LINE OF OUTPOSTS.

60 Houses at Golgotha. Golgotha once stood on its own on the edge of the country and consisted of several terraces of houses, some of them going back to the 17th century. More stood on the opposite corner of Wyresdale Road and were demolished. These houses may have been built to accommodate workers in the stone quarries nearby, but by the 19th century they held a large colony of laundresses, probably attracted by the high and airy position, ideal for drying clothes.

61 A Victorian washerwoman, from *Punch* magazine.

The Washerwomen of Golgotha, 1881

The little hamlet of Golgotha near the gates of Williamson Park has a curious secret. It was probably named after the Quaker Burial Ground established nearby in 1660. The cottages may have been built for quarry-workers at the neighbouring stone quarries, now Williamson Park, but in the 19th century they were home to a concentration of laundresses, judging by the 1881 Census Enumerators' Returns.

The concentration, totalling 20 from only 22 cottages, is quite abnormal. The explanation seems quite simple. This location, high on the edge of the Moor with plentiful exposure to the prevailing south-westerly winds, made a superb drying-ground. There was also space to peg out the washing, or fix it to thorn hedges, and it was quite remote, avoiding the common risk of theft to which drying-grounds were prey. According to the Ordnance Survey map of 1892, all the cottages had outhouses behind, which probably contained both privies and wash-houses. These were operating on a commercial scale, involving the collection and return of laundry from town-centre premises, but it may well have been a cottage industry on the edge of decline, since the first steam laundry (the Princess Steam Laundry) was introduced into the town in 1888 and became the Lancaster and District Steam Laundry Company in 1890. This would have had superior means of collecting (by wagon) and speedier turnaround.

How long had the concentration of laundresses existed at Golgotha? The 1841 Census is of little use, as it does not regularly give occupations of others than the head of household. The 1851 Census, however, indicates possibly twelve laundresses (one is 'formerly' and another is 'laundry maid') but also misses out three houses (nos 3, 8 and 9). The indications are that the occupation may go back a lot further.

1881 Census

1	Golgotha	Jane Swarbrick	61	Laundress, born Heaton
		Mary Heaton	29 (daughter)	Laundress, born Lancaster
2	Golgotha	Esther Wallbank	76	Laundress, born Scotforth
		Eliz "	50 (daughter)	Laundress, " "
3	Golgotha	Agnes Waterwort	26	Laundress, born Lancaster
4	Golgotha	Jane Chorley	55	Laundress, born Lancaster
5	Golgotha	Jane Chorley	16	Laundress, born Lancaster
6	Golgotha	Nancy Garth	68	Laundress, born Skerton
		Margaret Hodgson	27 (daughter)	Laundress, born Lancaster
7	Golgotha	Jane Winder	67	Laundress, born Lancaster
		Martha "	44?(daughter)	Laundress, " "
9	Golgotha	Ann Dawson	59	Laundress, born Lancaster
11	Golgotha	Jane Thirwall	48	Laundress, born Irthington
		Agnes Simpson	35 (visitor)	Laundress, born Lancaster
12	Golgotha	Grace Varey	45	Laundress, born Hornby
		Mary Grime	26 (niece)	Laundress, born Lancaster
14	Golgotha	Alice Salisbury	43	Laundress, born Lancaster
		Ester "	17(daughter)	Laundress, " "
15	Golgotha	Dorothy Martindale	62	Laundress, born Scotforth
18	Golgotha	(occupiers slept at No. 1 Golgotha)		
21	Golgotha	Mary Metcalfe	42	Laundress, born Lancaster

62 Thornfield, Ashton Road. Two rows of houses were built here in the 1890s by a group of men including two involved in the building trade and one, Robert Threlfall, who was a wholesale cheese merchant. Each of the partners retained one of the houses for his family and sold the others as a speculation. The building of these houses is particularly well documented.

Robert Threlfall, wholesale cheese and bacon factor, 1848-1925
Robert Threlfall was born in about 1848. A native of Lancaster, he commenced business in the fast-developing and neighbouring resort of Morecambe as a rather unlikely sounding combination of greengrocer, fish-dealer and cab-proprietor. Morecambe still had few facilities at this time, hence perhaps the multiplicity of jobs. It was in the process of developing from the fishing village of Poulton-le-Sands into the seaside resort of Morecambe, a development which gained much momentum from the arrival of the railway line in 1849. It is not known where he found the money to set up, although perhaps 'Robert Threlfall, Fishmonger, New Market', recorded in the 1851 Trade Directory, was his father. His marriage to Ann, daughter of James Willacy, proprietor of the *Kings Arms Hotel* in Morecambe, may also have helped. Apart from cab business which the hotel may have generated, the marriage allied him to one of the principal fishing families of Morecambe. This could not have harmed his prospects as a fish-dealer. In 1871 he was living in Taylor Street, Morecambe (now Euston Road) with his wife Annie and their five-month-old son Ernest.

He established what was to become the family firm in Lancaster in 1874, with a wholesale warehouse in James Street and, in 1878, with a retail stall on Lancaster Old Market selling 'American provisions'. What these American provisions were we are not told, but Canadian cheeses may well have figured among them, given his later interests. He still maintained a stall here 22 years later. He soon sold on his retail business to I. Hoyle but his firm took a warehouse at 69 Penny Street, Lancaster, and another in Manchester as cheese factors (wholesale cheese merchants). Threlfall himself was a well-known figure at the monthly cheese fairs and often acted as a judge. From the great mass of receipts held by the Lancashire Record Office we know that he bought many of his cheeses from farms on the Fylde area of Lancashire, well-established dairy country, but also from much further afield. He even bought up cheeses in advance of production, or 'speculated on cheese futures' as we would describe it today. [I am grateful to Dr Michael Winstanley for this information.] Billheads of 1896 place him at 14 & 16 James Street as well as the New Market. Between 1896 and 1901 he rebuilt the premises which the firm continued to occupy at 78a Penny Street, known as 'Threlfall's Buildings'. They are still used as a provision warehouse, but are now run by a co-operative.

When the boundaries of Lancaster were extended in 1900 to include the former village of Scotforth, Threlfall joined the Town Council as a member for the new Scotforth ward. His wife Ann died in August 1903 at the age of 56 and he left the Council in 1905, moving to Blackpool and subsequently remarrying. He retired in 1915, handing over the business to his son Ernest. Ernest continued to live in the house, 17 Thornfield, Ashton Road, which Robert had built in 1890. Robert Threlfall died aged 76 in March 1925 and was buried beside his wife in Lancaster Cemetery, Row H, grave 380. There is obviously a mismatch between his age as indicated by the 1871 census, the 1891 census and by the grave record and obituary, which shows how much caution we should use in reconstructing biography.

Apart from Robert's business interests he is marked out by his habit of retaining all his receipts and papers, which are partly in Lancaster City Museums and partly in the Lancashire Record Office. They record not only his business transactions in great detail but allow us to reconstruct the building of his house in Ashton Road from planning to completion.

Six

Entertainment

In the absence of documentary evidence we can only guess at how early citizens of Lancaster entertained themselves. Other evidence in the form of gaming counters and the archaeological traces of eating houses suggests that the Roman inhabitants enjoyed the services of *cauponae* in the settlement outside the gates of the fort, the nearest thing to an inn, in which off-duty soldiers took food and drink, played games and perhaps enjoyed the attentions of prostitutes. All this was standard across the Roman empire.

In the Middle Ages life in Lancaster would have been hard for many, without too much in the way of leisure. However, even the very poor could take enjoyment in changes from routine such as were offered by religious processions, saints' days, the fairs and markets, and the public punishments and executions which followed the Assizes. The church occupied a hugely important part in daily life. Monks and friars would have been a frequent sight in the streets, along with chantry priests, pardoners, pilgrims setting off or returning, and all the business of the monasteries, several of which retained houses in the town for their servants and officers. Not only did the church use the streets for religious processions on particular days, in order to show the magnificence of its ornaments, but friars would regularly preach at the Market Cross and in other public places.

Many of the social organisations were also based on the church; we know of one in Lancaster called the Gild of St Leonard and Holy Trinity, founded in 1377. This was principally a burial club, guaranteeing its members a decent funeral, but evidence from elsewhere shows that clubs existed in the church for all sorts of age groups, such as the young men and young women, who often contributed to building work or new ornaments. Curiously there is no evidence at all for trade guilds in Lancaster in the Middle Ages. There was a brief and short-lived movement to form them in the late 17th century, but we are unclear about how the various trades organised themselves before that. The apprentice-master system tied to the freemanship seems to require the passing of a standard, but if this was run by individual trades it has left no trace.

From the 17th century several nonconformist sects, such as Quakers and Presbyterians, performed important social functions, providing a building, a close-knit social group bonded by links of marriage and affinity, and a wider network throughout the country.

Fairs offered another opportunity for local people to see strange new things. Lancaster enjoyed the privilege of a fair, and a market, as part of its early charter. The charters did not express either very clearly: the rights were based on those of Northampton and Bristol, which the charters of 1193 and 1199 refer to. At all events the people of Lancaster, when challenged on their rights in 1292, claimed a market every week of the year on a Saturday, and a fair every year beginning on the eve of St Michael (28 September) and continuing for 15 days. Over time the fair seems to have broken up into separate components for cheese, horses and cattle.

Fairs served a number of purposes in the Middle Ages and the early modern period. Firstly they allowed overseas trade to flourish. Some, such as Boston or Stourbridge fairs, were mainly about foreign trade and involved commodities like wine, which brought representatives of great families, monasteries and colleges to buy their year's supply. They also encouraged inter-regional commerce, so that specialist suppliers would travel from distant towns with their distinctive wares. This was a period when Sheffield was famous for knives, Ripon for spurs, Ludlow for gloves, and so on. There was an opportunity for shopkeepers to make contact with suppliers of their raw materials. Finally there was the sideshow element, ranging from drinking booths to raree shows, and all manner of exotic things to catch the credulity of local peasants, for the country would come to town on such occasions.

The fairs also brought criminals who hid in the crowds and cut purses, stole horses, or engaged in sharp practice. Summary justice would be enacted on those caught, as most towns operated pie powder (*pied poudre* – literally 'dusty foot') courts to deal with those found out before they could leave the town. Probably the stocks or pillory were most common punishments, involving humiliation and perhaps injury at the hands of the mob. Sometimes it may have gone further. It must have been some such occasion on which the townsfolk hanged Hulle de Ellel, in about 1247, and exceeded their lawful powers. The right of gallows was not exclusively a state prerogative. Some landlords and even abbots had this power.

Boundary ridings
The septennial riding of the boundaries was both entertainment and serious. The entertainment came from the holiday atmosphere and the unusual nature of what went on, while the serious part was originally to inculcate in a largely illiterate citizenry a sense of what belonged to them. Details of boundary ridings are recorded from the 17th century onwards, but there is no reason to doubt that it is a very ancient custom going right back to the origins of the borough. Most parishes undertook an annual tour of their boundaries upon Rogation Sunday, processing in full regalia, singing hymns, and either beating boys against significant boundary markers or giving them presents of food or pins or some such trifle. This 'stick and carrot' approach was designed to remind them into old age exactly where the parish boundaries ran, so that they could testify in court, if necessary, to the parish's extent. The borough had much the same aim and methodology.

By the 17th century this involved a body of citizens, including Mayor and Bailiffs and a trumpeter, on horse and foot, following the boundaries, which by then probably incorporated Quernmore, from west to east. Later on the party included 'colour carriers', who carried banners around the route. By 1837 policemen had joined the party, along with the Bellman and the Pioneer, the second of whom survived into the 20th century. By 1886 the boundaries ridden were much as they had been in 1193, due to the enclosure of Lancaster and Quernmore Moors.

By the 20th century the riding turned into rather a travesty, perhaps as a result of the taking in of Skerton and Scotforth. Groups of councillors were driven by car to several successive points on the boundary and there met up with the Pioneer, who performed the whole journey regardless of obstacles, with axe, ladder or boat – the boat was for the long stretch of river which formed a northern boundary. Afterwards the whole party returned to the Town Hall for a junket. In 1974 the boundaries were again enlarged to take in the whole of the old Hundred of Lonsdale South of the Sands, and the circumference ceased to be a practicable walk. On that occasion the John O'Gaunt Morris performed at a number of key points along the boundary.

The only time the riding has been revived since then was in 1993, when a party of about thirty, led by Museum staff and seen off by the Mayor and Town Clerk, walked as closely as possible the ancient boundary of the borough as it was in 1193, to mark the 800th anniversary of the first charter. It was

63 The 1993 boundary walk. Walkers and flagbearers passing through Freeman's Wood on the Marsh.

surprising how easily identified this boundary still is in many places, despite the passage of time, and despite the various 'no-go' areas now lying along its length, such as the Prison Farm and the delightfully named but deeply unpleasant Nightingale Hall.

Theatre
After the Restoration the theatre became popular again. Because of the curious licensing laws, however, it was not until the late 18th century that most towns had any access to live theatre. Travelling companies offered what little there was and performances would last several hours at a time, including perhaps two plays and an entertainment. For most of the 18th century, outside London, actors were considered to be little better than vagabonds. Initially, travelling players performed in Bulk tithe barn, just outside the borough boundary, where they were beyond the borough's control. By the 1770s they used a strange little building in the yard of the *Horse and*

Farrier Inn in Church Street, but in 1782 a new theatre (now the Grand Theatre) was built by subscription in St Leonardgate. Eight subscribers of £50 each received five per cent from the rent and had a silver ticket giving the bearer free admission. This represented legitimacy at last.

Rev. W. MacRitchie visited the theatre in 1795:

> Put up at the King's Arms …
> Saturday, 4th July … After dinner go to the Play. Mrs. Siddons in the character of Lady Macbeth; her brother Kemble plays Macbeth. The representation very tolerable on the whole, though Mrs. Siddons be poorly supported. Mrs. Siddons Benefit. A brilliant audience; the Lancashire ladies in all their charms …

The new theatre was run by proprietors as one of a circuit. According to Clark, it had been run successively by Messrs Austin & Whitlock, Whitlock & Munden, Stephen Kemble, and Stanton in the 25 years or so of its existence. The players travelled from theatre to theatre within the circuit, performing a large and changing repertoire of plays and roles. It seems originally to have been called 'The Playhouse' but for a brief while in the early 19th century took the name of 'Theatre Royal'. The original name was popular, giving rise to the Playhouse Fields, which were developed for housing in the 1850s and 1860s.

64 Theatre bill, 1772. The theatre was a wooden building in the yard of the *Horse and Farrier Inn* in upper Church Street. It appears that the company had had a number of handbills printed which then had the dates entered in ink. The programme is quite typical.

Raree Shows

The tedium of daily life in a small town was sometimes broken by travelling curiosities, fairs and peepshows. In October 1802 the 'Irish Giant' O'Brien, who was nine feet tall, could be seen for a shilling at the *Bull's Head* in Cheapside. His party piece on evening walks was to frighten the Watch by lighting his pipe from the street lamps.

In 1756 William Hall was prosecuted for 'suffering a Bare to run loose in the publick streets of this borough the same being a public nuisance'. Presumably this was a dancing bear, but we should know nothing of it were it not for Hall's court appearance. Other entertainment of a low nature is hinted at by the visit to the Assembly Room in 1819 of Madame Ingleby, 'the South American fire-proof lady',

65   The Circus comes to town in the 1890s. An essential part of the advertising was the grand entry and parade of the Circus through the streets, caught here by photographer John Walker. It is probably Sanger's Circus, which came each year in the 1890s and performed on Giant Axe Field. Animals which could be trusted, such as the elephants, walked, while the lions were kept in a wheeled cage, pulled by horses. No doubt they were encouraged to roar. Little thought was given to natural habitat or diet.

and to the Theatre in the same year of Mr Usher, the celebrated clown, with his performing tom-cats. In 1828 there was a visit from Madame Tussaud's wax works, which were exhibited in the Assembly Room.

Circus
In 1804 the Circus came to town. The New Circus parked on Green Ayre and put on performances both there and at the Theatre. It featured 'many surprising feats of horsemanship by a capital troop of equestrians', tightrope dancing, and 'antipodean exercises' by Mr Cooke and Master Cimex (aged 8). At a visit by the New Olympic Circus in 1808, Mr Southby, the proprietor, was effusive about the 'liberal patronage already given' and 'overflowing houses'. The Circus, in Cable Street, which gave benefit performances on the New Racecourse to help raise funds for the completion of the course, was prosecuted in the borough court by a number of what seem to be creditors, including the splendidly named Moses Aaron James Gurney, licensee of the *Cross Keys* in Market Street. The Court Rule Book gives a complete description of the Circus, surely a most unusual piece of evidence:

66 Pencil sketch of Mr Green's balloon attempt, 1832. Huge crowds assembled on the Quay to watch the intrepid balloonist and his passenger ascend from the Gasworks. His use of coal-gas was much more dangerous than the customary hot air.

A wood erection, Circus, shed, or building situate on the Green Area in Lancaster with the boards, poles, springers, props, jists, spars, gallery and supporters, consisting of wood thereunto belonging with the iron cramps and nails therein, a quantity of boards round the ring or circle in the inside of the same circus, 5 poles, 2 pair of triangles, 1 spring board, 8 lamps, hoop with tin candlesticks, 6 blocks and ropes, 1 table, 4 wood candlesticks, several old boards, boxes and pieces of wood, 2 step ladders, 12 bass mats, a dressing room consisting of wood, a small wood shade, 7 wood supporters, a wood porch with several other articles of wood … All the boards, planks, supporters and timber with all the materials and fixtures … forming … the Circus on the Green Area … Quantity of green baize, 1 cart and a pair of wheels.

Subsequently it was sold for its materials.

In November 1821 a visiting Circus in the Fryerage, the New Olympic Circus, had its tent blown to pieces by a violent storm. Doubtless there were many others, of which we know nothing because no disaster overtook them. In the 1890s George Sanger's Hippodrome, Circus and Menagerie visited Lancaster twice each summer, performing on Giant Axe Field. It boasted a huge number of performers and animals, and the parade when the Circus came into town was almost as significant as the performances themselves. In the 20th century circuses continued to visit occasionally but by the latter end Lancaster City Council had banned any with animal acts. Ryelands Park is now the usual venue for travelling fairs and circuses.

Balloons

In 1785 Vincenzo Lunardi brought his hydrogen balloon to Lancaster during race week, at the behest of Richard Gillow, for an ascent from the Castle yard. While this does not seem to have taken place as planned (the Gillow archive refers to cancellation notices), it may have gone ahead in the following year.

A balloon attempt of 1832 was captured in a contemporary pencil sketch. Mr Green made two attempts with passengers from the gas works on St George's Quay (his balloon was filled with coal-gas), the first of which had to be aborted near Poulton as he was in danger of being blown out to sea. The second, a month later, was more successful, and he eventually made landfall at Settle.

67 Racecourse on the Marsh, from Yates' map of Lancashire, 1786. The enclosure of the Marsh put paid to this, and it was some years before a new course was opened on the Moor.

Club walks

Many working people joined Friendly Societies, which served as a sort of early union and sickness support club rolled into one. Subscriptions would help less fortunate members in old age or in adversity, and provide for a decent funeral, while a surplus provided a good dinner once a year at one of the inns. There were also walking days, still popular in the south of the county, when the whole club would turn out and walk behind a banner of some sort. One of these was the Marine Society, which provided for the widows and families of masters and first mates of Lancaster ships. Clark, writing in 1807, was aware of no fewer than 13 Friendly Societies in the town for men, and four for women. The total number of men members was 2,027.

Racing

High life and low life sometimes came together. Race meetings were held on the Marsh, initially on Salt Ayre, an island once in the middle of the river but now wholly to the north of its course, from about 1720 until 1797. After a hiatus, racing recommenced on a new course with a grandstand on the Moor from 1809. The races attracted a wide audience ranging from the gentry, who admired horseflesh and enjoyed gambling, down to the touts and pickpockets who infested the crowds. Drink flowed liberally at such gatherings and they were a source of concern to the magistrates involved in maintaining law and order, particularly as half the new racecourse was outside the borough boundary and hence their jurisdiction. This became a real problem when responsibility for policing was divided between the borough and the county police, the latter in charge of the rural area.

Wagers

The local newspapers in the early 19th century are full of accounts of wagers. Walking and running were popular, either competitively or against the clock. In 1813, for instance, a foot-race four times around the racecourse was won by a man named Hinde in just over 23 minutes. The previous year Joseph Blanyer, a cinder-burner of Tewitfield, undertook for a wager to drink 18 gallons of ale in four days and succeeded with time to spare. In 1821 Jeremiah Walmsley, a flour dealer, won a wager to ride his horse from the White Cross to Preston market cross and back in four hours, while in 1823 William M'Mullen failed to walk 40 miles in eight hours on the Green Ayre, but still collected £20 from onlookers for his gallant failure.

68 Handbill for a 'long main' of cocks. The sport of cock-fighting was commonplace but such handbills are rare. This 'long main' (thirteen bouts) took place at Galgate, three miles south of Lancaster, but similar mains regularly took place during race-week in Lancaster itself.

Cock-fights

During race week in summer, cock-fights would also take place at the new cockpit in Back Lane from 1775, but by 1802 this was in use as an extension of the market. Public opinion was moving against such cruel sports by this time, but during race week in 1811 the Gentlemen of Lancashire and of Cumberland fought a main of cocks, the latter winning. Such events went on into the 1830s, at least. Again, both high life and low life combined in these essentially male activities.

The Lure of Speed

Horses had long been an obsession of the squirearchy and the gentry. This manifested itself in races, hunting meets of various sorts, and driving smart equipages. In the Regency period there was a fashion for driving four-in-hand and young bloods sought to imitate the regular drivers of the premier coaches, sometimes even taking over their reins. Speed had an obvious attraction from which even the cavalry were not exempt, for the dragoons quartered in Lancaster in 1802 were accused of riding through the streets at full gallop, which must have been frightening for onlookers. In the same year the driver of the Liverpool coach was presented for 'furious driving' in Penny Street. Some fashionable men went further. In the period 1819-25 there was a fashion for hobby-horses or velocipedes, a French invention and an early bicycle. The rider sat astride a wooden frame with two light wood-spoked wheels and propelled it along with his feet. It was briefly a hit in London, where dandies showed off their mounts in Rotten Row, but there is evidence from Lancaster that a Mr Atkinson (perhaps James Atkinson, gent, of Castle Park) had a velocipede in 1822, which must briefly have been the talk of the town. We should not know of it but for the court records for 2 March 1822 in which a velocipede is listed among his possessions. An example of such a machine also survives in the collections of Lancaster City Museum.

Sport

With a few exceptions sport was not popularly practised in Lancaster until the latter part of the 19th century. Few people had the time, the money or the urge, apart from a fairly small middle class which enjoyed archery, rowing and one or two new sports like tennis. When working people or youths played games on a Sunday, the only chance they had, they were likely to be punished for it. In 1821 three youths were fined by the mayor for playing nine-pins on a Sunday morning, while in 1823 twelve lads from Skerton were fined for playing football on the New Bridge, also on a Sunday. Working-class participation had to wait until shop and work hours reduced, and often depended on employers or churches sponsoring costs of clothing and equipment. Where both classes took part, as in rowing, there was often an uneasy atmosphere.

The John O'Gaunt Bowmen pride themselves on being the most ancient sporting club in the area, dating back to 1788. Archery was definitely a sport for gentlemen in the 18th and early 19th centuries, and by Victorian times was an acceptable sport for ladies. They originally practised in Springfield Park, where the hospital now stands, but for many years from the 1840s the archery ground lay just to the south of Meeting House Lane, where Fairfield was later built. Luneside Bowling Club had its own green to the north of this, complete with clubhouse, from 1831. Bowling must be one of the oldest established sports in Lancaster. There have been bowling greens on Green Ayre from the early 18th century, behind the *Sun Inn* from at least the mid–18th century, behind the *Mitre Inn* in the 19th century, and at Scotforth, at the *Bowling Green Inn*, currently.

Many sports had their local origins in the 1840s. Some were the result of the interest of middle-class patrons in finding diversions for working-class youth, in what spare time it had, while others resulted from a few charismatic people coming into Lancaster with sporting interests. Lancaster Rowing Club was formed in 1843, with the John O'Gaunt Club following in 1867. The Luneside Cricket Club was established in 1841. High subscriptions or entry by nomination only meant limited access, but sometimes outside influences such as the Co-operative movement led to the formation of clubs, and provision of funds, for a wider social mix. The wealthy Lord Ashton's Liberal affiliation meant there was a powerful backer for teams and groups drawn from other

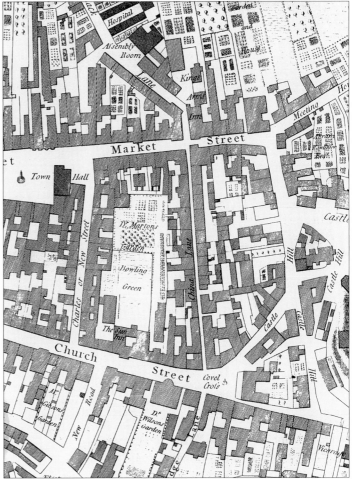

69 Detail of Mackreth's map showing the bowling green at the *Sun Inn*. This was one of the first popular sports available to all classes.

than the professional élite. Lancaster's Football Club originated in 1888, at a time when the game was becoming organised. Rugby was always regarded as the élite game, while football and rugby league were strongly working-class. Water-polo seems an unusual sport for Lancaster, but the town was able to field an excellent team, based on the facilities of the old Gregson Baths in Cable Street, and of the new Kingsway Baths when they opened in 1939.

A handful of people were hugely influential. Edmund Sharpe was one such, coming to Lancaster in the mid-1830s and bringing with him a passion for cricket, rowing, music and a host of new things which arose during his lifetime. An architect and founder of the firm of Paley & Austin, he chose partners (or encouraged them) who had similar interests.

Cycling

Edmund Sharpe owned the first proper cycle in Lancaster, but one of the first people in the locality to take the new sport seriously was Mr S. Dawson. He later became captain of the Lancaster Cycling Club and left memoirs entitled *Incidents in the Course of a Long Cycling Career.* His first experience was in about 1874 with a blacksmith-made tricycle. He graduated in 1878-9 to a Spider Velocipede, which despite its name was a 'high ordinary' with a 50-inch front wheel. He went on to travel great distances by cycle, at home and abroad, at a time when it was suddenly becoming a mass sport. The Vale of Lune Cycling Club was started in 1879, all the members wearing a uniform trimmed with silver braid and badges.

70 Portrait of S. Dawson, cycling pioneer, with his 'high ordinary' bicycle, *c*.1880. At this period the roads were almost deserted and cycling was a voyage into the unknown. However, it was also unpredictable and dangerous, with many a spill resulting from rough roads or farm dogs.

Initially a male sport, cycling rapidly grew to include women, for whom the new 'safety' bicycle with a low crossbar was ideal. It had the incidental effect of simplifying voluminous female clothing and opening new horizons to working-class women who had previously been unable to travel. Clubs such as the Williamson Park Cycling Club and the Lancaster Cycling Club were social gatherings which gave the security of numbers when anyone's cycle failed, and encouraged longer trips. Usually outings were day-long, but some, more adventurous, would spend the weekend away.

Locally, cycles were supplied by Mr J. S. Darque, of Beesley's Yard, Market Street, and Rimmon Clayton of Brock Street, who actually made his own models as well as supplying those of other manufacturers. The 'Lancaster Castle' was one of his products, available in 1894, and he also made a 'Royal Rimmon'. Right at the beginning of the craze, in 1870, the Phoenix Foundry made several rather heavy 'bone-shakers', two of which survive in the City Museum's collection. The multi-millionaire Lord Ashton, safe behind the walls of Ryelands House, had his own cycle-track for exercise, and a specially-made Humber cycle with sprung wheels.

After the First World War cycling was never so popular again, being partially overtaken by cheaper motoring, but it has had several revivals, not least in the health-conscious 1980s and 1990s, with resulting pressures on dedicated cycle-tracks and networks, which led to the opening of the River Lune Millennium Park and Bridge in 2001.

71 Williamson Park Cycling Club, *c.*1895. By now most of the visible cycles are of the 'safety' variety and about half of the cyclists are women. Cycling in company was respectable as well as liberating and exciting for working people who until then had few opportunities for fresh air and travel.

Music Hall

When the theatre waned under Victorian disapproval there was nothing much but the church or improving lectures to take its place. However, the latter part of the 19th century saw the growth of music hall, a popular entertainment with a varied programme of song, dance, monologue and comics. It created its own stars and its own hit songs, which were sung in the streets by ordinary people. At the seaside it spawned pierrot groups and concert parties, which travelled from venue to venue. Places such as the theatre in St Leonardgate ran virtually the whole gamut. Established as a circuit theatre in 1782, as we have seen, its fortunes had sunk by the 1830s and in 1839 it was named the Temperance Hall and was used for meetings and public lectures, including those of the Literary, Scientific and Natural History Society. Edmund Sharpe acquired it in 1843 and converted it into a Music Hall, not of the sort we have just described, but more of a concert hall. It was run by the Atheneum Society, and for a number of years was known as the Atheneum. The true music hall role had to wait until 1884; in the meantime it served a number of purposes, many of them to do with worthy Victorian ideas of self-improvement. The new Gilbert & Sullivan comic operas were produced here and the theatre took part in early flirtations with moving pictures, especially after the fire of 1908. In 1950 it was bought by Lancaster Footlights Club, who have run it successfully ever since for a variety of plays and musicals.

Cinema

Early venues in Lancaster for cinema, invented in 1896, were the Jubilee Hall in Brock Street and the Cromwell Hall in Rosemary Lane. These were merely public halls adapted for the new medium. By 1908-10 the Grand Theatre (burnt out in 1908) and Palatine Hall had been rebuilt as proper cinemas. The latter became the Hippodrome, then the County Cinema. They were joined in 1913 by the Co-op Hall in Church Street and the Picturedrome in Lower Church Street. James Atroy ran both the latter and the Cromwell Hall. A new purpose-built cinema, the Palladium, joined them in Market Street in the following year. Now W.H. Smith, its interiors have been revealed once more by recent building work. Another wave of cinema building occurred in the 1930s, with modern designs reflecting the position of the movies at the height of fashion. The Odeon on King Street opened in 1936. Many more smart and fashionable cinemas served the holidaying crowds at Morecambe. A guidebook of 1936 lists the following cinemas in Lancaster at what was probably the high-tide of the movies: Odeon, Palace, County, Palladium, Picturedrome and Kingsway.

Enthusiasm remained after the war, but a sharp decline set in during the late 1960s and 1970s, taking with it most of the cinemas one by one. Revival in the 1990s was based more on multiplexes, with their range and choice. Morecambe entered this new world first with its Apollo cinemas, but Lancaster has lagged behind, its Warner Bros complex still not complete at the time of writing. In late 2002 the ABC, formerly Cannon, formerly Odeon cinema, closed, leaving Lancaster without a commercial cinema for the first time in a century.

Old Lancaster Exhibition 1908

In order to celebrate the opening of the extension to the Storey Institute an exhibition known as the 'Old Lancaster Exhibition' was organised in 1908. It celebrated the work of local artists old and new, by borrowing from private hands many of the former and having a number of the latter for sale. This accorded with the role of the Institute as art college. In addition a wide range of antiquities, portraits and locally important objects were borrowed for one of the first exhibitions ever to reveal Lancaster's past to itself. While there was a museum collection of sorts at the Institute already, this exhibition must have stirred local desire to see a proper museum of the town's history, which eventually emerged in 1923.

Pageants

Lancaster, in common with many other towns, held a historical pageant in 1913. It also held one in 1930. The 1913 pageant was very typical of its time. The great and the good, or such as were available, were drafted in to chair various committees. A monstrous regiment of women sewed costumes in the Old Town Hall, known for the duration as 'the Pageant House'. The script was written by the novelist Halliwell Sutcliffe, while the Master of the Pageant, and its master-mind, was Rev. Harold Hastings, vicar of Halton.

A series of scenes took the history of Lancaster from the arrival, in a chariot, of the Roman governor Agricola, via the reign of King John (who gave the first charter), through the Pilgrimage of Grace and the battle of Flodden (where Lancashire levies

72 Scene from the Pageant, 1913. King John, Queen Isabel and court jester (foreground, with donkey) at the granting of the borough charter in 1199.

played a critical role in the English victory), via the Lancashire Witches of 1612, to the events of 1715 and 1745. The storyline perfectly imitated the episodic view of history which was taught at that time (and which you may be pleased to see return in some measure in this book). The catalogue is beautifully illustrated with a series of scenes by Fred Kirk Shaw. A cast of hundreds took part in the performance, which took place in Springfield Park.

The 1930 pageant took place at Cross Hill, Torrisholme, since Springfield Park was now occupied by the Royal Lancaster Infirmary. It marked the 500th anniversary of the Priory church becoming parochial, and was more overtly religious than the 1913 pageant, although, oddly, the last scene is a re-enactment of the 1802 election and ends, rather inappropriately, with the reading of the Riot Act! Once again the pageant Master, and now also author of the words, was Rev. Harold Hastings.

In 1937, when Lancaster received its city status on the morning of George VI's coronation, it once more looked to the pageant format for a celebration, but on this occasion, because planning time was very short, did it as a procession. Various groups in the newly promoted city, such as the police and the military, as well as various clubs and organisations, took on particular roles. Since that time, although there have been celebrations for 50 years of city status and 800 years of the borough charter, neither has led to effusions of purple prose or Ancient Britons draped in hearth rugs; the world has become rather more cynical.

Seven

Getting There

Although there are undoubtedly some ancient trackways in North Lancashire which have served human needs since early times, they are not easy to identify on the ground. It is likely that many of our modern routes through areas such as the Lune valley are actually very ancient, since the choices are relatively constrained by the topography.

Roman roads
In fact it is the Roman military roads which are more easily identifiable, since they are axiomatically straight, or at least made up of straight lengths, and are often focused on places which are no longer significant. An example of this is the remarkable high-level route which runs north from Manchester via Ribchester, passing over the fells above Lowgill and ignoring most modern villages. It runs through Overtown, briefly forms part of the A65, and then swings off to form a succession of lanes through Casterton and on towards Carlisle. We can still see its remarkable and ruthless straightness over long distances, generally modified at sighting points on high ground, and its disregard for modern settlements. Even the Lune valley fort of Burrow-in-Lonsdale appears to be an afterthought, attached to this high-level route by a short length of access road.

Other long-distance roads in the area are less obvious in their straightness, being bound more by the local topography, with changes of direction to allow for river and stream crossings or steep hills. The Roman roads north and south of Lancaster must equate roughly to the modern A6, but their routes cannot be plotted in detail. Nor can the probable Roman roads up both sides of the Lune valley. What appears to be a clear series of alignments can be seen leaving Lancaster at Newlands in a north-easterly direction and continuing over the hill into the Quernmore valley past Postern Gates and down into Caton by Forge Mill and so to Caton Green. It seems to be aligned upon the most prominent hill in the district, Ingleborough. Divergences can be plotted where the late 18th-century owners of Quernmore Park built a lake and diverted the road around the fringe of the parkland.

Straight alignments do not necessarily mean a road is Roman, however, since the early 19th-century enclosure period saw many straight roads being incorporated in the new landscape. Some of these can be found in Quernmore. Straight roads are often an indication that they were laid out early, before the modern landscape was created, they were laid out by someone with power to overrule existing property boundaries, or they were laid out by someone with the need to obtain a straight line who was prepared to pay for the privilege.

The local Roman roads are, however, indistinguishable because they show no particular features. Farmsteads and industrial sites must have been linked to the main roads. The Quernmore valley in Roman times was clearly an industrial area, with potteries, tileries and ironworks, but nothing obvious remains today except the line of the road which runs eastwards through the Trough of Bowland, which may have formed the main Roman road from Lancaster to York. Industrial roads probably led off from this but remain unidentifiable.

The quality of the main Roman roads was such that despite centuries of neglect in the post-Roman period they still formed the best way of getting around the country. It is notable that a great many Anglo-Saxon, Viking and medieval battles took place on Roman roads. They were still the only ones capable of carrying armies. The backbone of the medieval road system was made up of Roman road lines, although their surfacing and engineering works such as bridges may have long since decayed. Many routes important to the Romans were still important, such as those linking cities, but the purely military routes linking forts whose purpose had long gone were more likely to disappear, although even these might gain a new lease of life. The fort of Low Borrowbridge in the Lune valley became the site of a cattle fair, and the roads leading to and from it continued as drove roads.

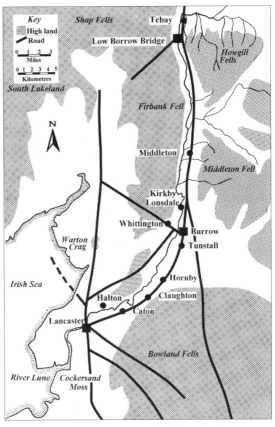

73 Roman roads in Lunesdale. This is the best guess we have at present of the network, but few of the lines are susceptible of proof. However, the topography dictates many of the lines and the choice of routes must have been limited. (P. Thompson/W. Moore)

State of the roads

Our earliest recorded visitor was Sir Guilbert de Launoy, a French knight who passed through on his way to St Patrick's Purgatory in Ireland in 1430:

> Thence to Lancaster, an unwalled town with a large castle, fairly fine, on the Lune; the tide comes up to the wharves, and this is the seat of a duchy. From thence to 'Conequessant' [Cockersand], and abbey of regular canons.

De Launoy's route via Cockersand Abbey, five miles to the south-west, was by coincidence matched by our next visitor, in 1496. Richard Redman, Bishop of Exeter and Abbot of Shap in Westmorland, was one of those rare brilliant administrators that

74 Reconstruction of Cockersand Abbey by David Vale. This view shows the Abbey at its greatest extent and in its last days in 1539. The Receiver's men are already removing lead, bells and other valuables and taking them away by sea. Cockersand was deliberately founded in a remote location on the edge of a marsh and frequently cut off by high tides.

the medieval world threw up. Like others of his kind, he was used on all sorts of important business. On this occasion, acting in the role of a senior Abbot of his Order (the Premonstratensians), he was writing to make arrangements with the Abbot of Cockersand for an official visitation of a junior house. What is of interest is the 'perils of the sea' through which one had to go to travel between Lancaster and Cockersand. His route no doubt lay further west than at present, crossing the river Conder and Pool of Crook at their seaward end.

> Richard, by divine permission, Bishop of Exeter and Abbot of the monastery of the blessed Mary Magdalene at Shap, sends greetings and mutual friendship to his worshipful brother Abbot of Cockersand ... I give you notice by this letter that I intend to make a visitation on your monastery in person on 3rd April next, at dinner-time, or as the tides permit ... Please send a trustworthy man to Lancaster on the 2nd of the month, provided with money for all our necessary expenses, at your cost, so that he can guide me safely amid the perils of the sea to your monastery ... (translated from the Latin)

There is little other evidence as to the state of roads in North Lancashire before the turnpike age. Indeed the absence of mention may signify that the main roads at least were reasonable. It was usually local geology as much as anything which determined

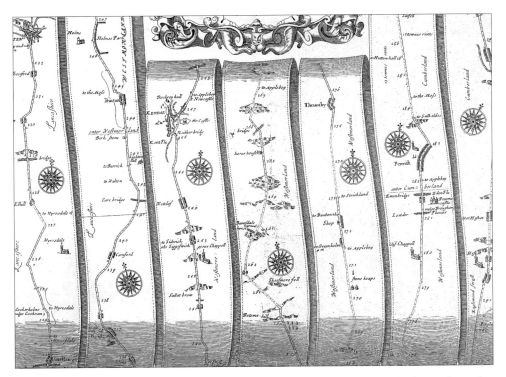

75 Road map by John Ogilby, 1698. This sort of strip map was made popular by Ogilby and carried on by Emmanuel Bowen. It still makes sense for linear features such as roads and canals. This shows the pre-turnpike road from London to Carlisle as it passes through Lancaster, very much on the line of the modern A6 apart from the divergence north of Carnforth. Maps such as this may well have been used by the Jacobites in planning their march south.

conditions, for maintenance of roads was nowhere very good. From the 16th century it depended upon the enforced labour of villagers alongside the route, grudgingly given because they gained no personal benefit. Clay was considered the worst for surfacing, and sand the best. Fast-draining soils, such as those of this area, were most helpful.

The main road we now know as the A6 was the main west-coast road to and from the north. It was by no means as important as the Great North Road (A1) but still carried a good deal of traffic. Indeed, a visit from the Duke of Suffolk and the Chancellor of the Duchy to view Lancaster bridge in the mid-15th century is an indication of its importance, and that of the route it formed part of. Probably the bridge we know as the 'Old Bridge', replaced on another site in 1788 by Skerton Bridge, was a result of this visit.

Celia Fiennes, writing in 1698, described her journey from Garstang thus:

> Thence to Lancaster town 10 mile more which I easily reached in 2 hours and a halfe or 3 hours, I passed through abundance of villages, almost at the end of every mile, mostly all along lanes being an enclosed country; they have one good thing in most parts off this principality (or County Palatine its rather called) that at all cross wayes there are Posts with Hands pointing to each road with the names of the great town or market towns that it leads to, which does

make up for the length of the miles that strangers may not loose their road and have it to goe back againe; you have a great divertion on this road having a pleasing prospect of the countrys a great distance round and see it full of inclosures and some woods; three miles off the town you see it very plaine and the sea even the main ocean in one place an arm of it comes up within 2 mile of the town; the River Lieue [Lune] runs by the town and so into the sea.

The earliest detailed evidence we have for routes is contained in the strip-maps published by John Ogilby in 1675 and the road-book of Emmanuel Bowen in 1720. Both show a road from London to Carlisle which, in this area, is little different in route from that taken by the 1751 turnpike. They also show a road from Lancaster to York which is represented today by the road up the Lune valley through Caton and Hornby. It only diverges from the early turnpike line beyond Hornby, when it dives off through Hornby Park Wood to Tatham, instead of via Wray or Greeta Bridge. The general suggestion is, then, that the turnpike routes were well-established and reasonably satisfactory. Most of the changes made later were to cut out sudden bends and to lower gradients, as the increasing speed of coaching traffic demanded.

Packhorse tracks
Whatever the state of the main roads in the medieval period and beyond, many of the minor roads must have remained narrow and deep in mud during the winter. Goods such as wool or cloth lent themselves to carrying by packhorse. Indeed it is surprising what a range of materials were carried by such means, such as coal, iron ore or salt. The horses would operate in long strings of twenty or more, with a lead horse carrying bells on its collar – the 'bell-horse' – as a warning to others to get out of the way. Each horse would carry a pack-saddle fitted with panniers, long baskets which hung down each side. A man would walk with them to direct them. They could manage in narrow lanes little wider than modern footpaths and they could continue in conditions that would have a cart bogged down.

Much of the cloth trade of Kendal was carried on packhorses up to the mid–18th century, and it is likely that when Lancaster was involved in a small way in woollens in the 16th and 17th centuries they were carried in the same way.

The distinctive feature of tracks used by packhorses is the so-called 'packhorse bridge', narrow stone arches with little or nothing in the way of parapets, which would have got in the way of the panniers. One such can be found on a green lane near Capernwray, perhaps associated with the wool trade of the Bindloss family of nearby Borwick.

'Salt roads' and drove roads
The shoulder of Bowland Forest above Wray in the Lune valley has the farms of Lower, Middle and Upper Salter, the names of which have led to a tradition that coastal salt was carried this way into Yorkshire. Indeed the high level road from Roeburndale to Slaidburn is often known as 'the Salt Road'. Similar names and traditions exist on the moors above Macclesfield, and there is perhaps some truth in the story.

What is clear is that the road up Roeburndale past the Salters is a drove road used amongst others by Yorkshire drovers bringing their cattle to Hornby Fair. Scottish drovers brought their cattle south by various routes, one of which seems closely related to the later Lancaster & Richmond Turnpike, since they came over Cam Fell and traditionally encamped at Gearstones, near Ribblehead, presumably following the natural route on to Ingleton and down the Lune to Lancaster.

Transport of goods

Most local transport from the 18th to the early 20th centuries was by cart. There were professional carriers, who provided a transport service for goods and parcels to and from surrounding villages on set days of the week, usually associating themselves with particular inns where goods could be consigned.

Baines' *Directory* of 1825 gives a good cross-section of carriers from Lancaster. Forty-five carriers provided a service to 30 separate towns and villages around, including quite distant towns such as Leeds, Halifax and Richmond. Locally, Bryan Edmondson and Robert Cornthwaite provided a service to Hornby every Monday, Wednesday and Saturday, setting out from the *White Lion* in Penny Street at 10a.m. and departing from Hornby at 2p.m. Four rival carriers set off for Kirkby Lonsdale from the *Black Bull*, the *Bear & Staff*, the *Golden Fleece* and the *Corporation Arms*, while Wray attracted three rivals, two from the *White Lion* and one from the *Bear & Staff*. Indeed, several of the inns were starting points for several different carriers. The *Black Bull* and *Old Sir Simon's* had six services each, the *White Hart* four, and the two *White Lions*, in Penny Street and St Leonardgate, eight between them. This represents quite a bustle of activity, since some of the carriers ran up to three days per week. In 1881, 33 local towns and villages were served by some fifty Lancaster carriers.

Others provided longer distance transport, such as the wagoners to London or to Liverpool and Manchester, usually with many horses and with wide-wheeled stage-wagons capable of dealing with the difficult roads. In 1794 the *Universal British Directory* noted that a wagon set off from *Old Sir Simon's* every Monday and Thursday at half past ten for the *Castle Inn*, Wood Street, London, returning every Tuesday and Friday, while Scarr's and Atkinson's wagons left on Fridays and Wednesdays from the *Bull Inn* and *Cross Keys* respectively for York. Another firm advertised in the *Lancaster Gazette* in October 1811 that they would set off every day from their warehouse in Manchester, calling at intervening towns on the way, ending up at Glasgow or Edinburgh.

In addition many local tradesmen would have had their own delivery carts as can be seen from these entries in the Borough Rule Book:

> John Ayrey 14/12/1786
> Horse, cart and gear, large quantity of butter
>
> Thomas Sandwick 5/4/1792
> Horse, cart and gear and 3½ loads of coal
>
> William Stockdale 2/2/1804
> Horse, cart etc., butter & eggs
>
> Robert Rumney 10/9/1795
> 2 horses, cart, cover and gear

Some may have stuck to an older pattern. The 'panniers' listed here may well have been for packhorses.

> Thomas Hewertson 20/9/1804
> Cart, horse, 4 panniers and gear

76 Detail of coal cart and horses from a Wray estate map of 1773. The coal available around Lancaster was in thin seams and poor transport alone made it worth winning. When access to the south Lancashire coalfields was guaranteed the local mining of coal practically ceased, except for one or two industries and in time of war. The coal cart here is descending from Smeer Hall colliery.

The local coal mines, which were only viable because bulk delivery from the south of the county was not practicable before the canal and railways arrived, used small coffin-shaped carts pulled by between one and three horses to bring the coal down from the moors. A sketch of one such cart survives on an estate plan of Wray in 1773. It is shown coming down from Smeer Hall colliery. Another, seen on the road near Hornby – perhaps at Farleton - is described by William Wilberforce in 1779.

By Sea
For centuries heavy or bulky goods were sent by sea. Early commercial contact with London must have depended heavily upon shipping. William Stout had all his London ironmongery sent by sea in the *Edward and Jane* ketch in 1687 and he used the same means in 1698 to bring spars and cordage from London for the new ship *Imployment*, which was being built near Warton.

The *Universal British Directory* of 1794 listed no fewer than four coasters trading with London, *Flora, Myrtle, Rose* and *Laurel*, as well as one with Bristol, six with Liverpool, and two with Whitehaven. By 1825 four vessels took it in turn to sail weekly to Liverpool, while a single vessel sailed monthly to Griffin Wharf, London, a measure of Lancaster's commercial decline.

Over the Sands
A very distinctive feature of travel in north Lancashire for many centuries was the route over the sands of Morecambe Bay to Cartmel, Furness and beyond. Although this route was obviated by the railway in 1857, which was able to cut a great deal off the inland distance by road, the route is still followed by walkers for enjoyment today. Until the coming of the Ulverston & Carnforth Turnpike and then the Furness

77 *Waterwitch II.* Seen here in about 1900, moored near the Aldcliffe boathouse, the vessel had had its cabin cut down for use as an engineer's inspection boat. Originally it would have been over one third longer. The cabin originally sheltered up to eighty passengers, the equivalent of some eight to ten road coaches, and the packets could claim to have carried some 16,000 passengers in the first six months alone.

Railway, however, there was little choice for travellers but to cross the sands at low tide. They set off from the shore at Hest Bank, just north of Lancaster, and made landfall again, after a journey which can vary from day to day, according to where the quicksands are, at Kents Bank near Grange. A further crossing could then be made from the far side of the Cartmel peninsula at Flookburgh to a point near Ulverston, while a third crossing, of the Duddon estuary, was also possible.

A schoolboy of 1786 writes to his mother:

> 29 January 1786: Dear Mother, I arrived here [Lancaster] safe yesterday Evening about 7 o'clock after a rather disagreeable passage; it was very thick all the way, and crossing at the low Ford, which was very deep for the Water was near a foot in the Coach, and after that the Sand was so exceeding heavy, that we were obliged to get out, and walk three or four miles …

Millicent Bant described her journey over the Sands in 1804 thus:

> Sept 13th nine o clock Resume our route to Ulverston, over Lancaster sands – I never shall forget it the morning was dark & Gloomy – Sophia in the time of Breakfast entertain'd us with shocking accounts of the peril & Danger of the attempt – from intelligence she had learnt from the wife of the Postman whom she protested she gave up for lost – whenever he left her – her Ladyship was not to be Dismay'd so set forward with Caravan consisting of two stages a cart & Horseman when we reached Hest Bank found the tide too high so alighted at the Ferry House to await it going off – a young person passenger in one of the stages – encounterd in the Garden had she informed me crossed five & twenty times & only was in danger of drowning once but confessed it was not in General conceivd to be safe – this gave us some alarm, but at last we entered on the sands very courageously tho the wind blew the clouds hung as it were in dread suspense over the tremendous mountains …

Mrs Gaskell, the writer, who rented Lindeth Tower at Silverdale, described the scene in 1858:

Looking down on the Bay with its slow moving train of crossers, led over by the treacherous sands by the Guide, a square man sitting stern on his white horse, the better to be seen when daylight ebbs … On foggy nights the guide (who has let people drown before now who could not pay his fee) may be heard blowing an old ram's horn trumpet to guide by the sound.

Despite all the care to protect travellers over the Sands, a great many were drowned over the centuries. Michael de Furness was one of the first casualties to be recorded when, in 1269, he dined too well and stayed too long one evening with the Prior of Cartmel and drowned on his return journey. Cartmel parish registers alone list the burials of 141 victims of the Bay between 1559 and 1880, and most of the parishes around the Bay also show such burials. These were just the bodies that were found. A tombstone in Cartmel Priory church records Robert Harrison, who died on the Sands in 1782, and his mother Margaret, who died in the same place almost exactly a year later. In 1846 nine young people returning from Ulverston fair to Cartmel were drowned when their cart sank into a water-filled hole left by a ship, and in 1857 12 young farm hands met a similar fate on their way to Lancaster hiring fair.

During the Middle Ages the sands were patrolled by guides provided by the monasteries that lay along the route – Cartmel, Conishead and Furness. After the Dissolution these became the responsibility of the Duchy of Lancaster, who paid their salaries. Even Lancaster contributed in a small way to the guides, by paying an annual sum of 2s. 6d. This appears year after year in the Bailiffs' accounts as 'Allowed them paid the Carter of Kent Sands 0.2.6.' The guide, traditionally known as 'the Carter', had the job of checking at every tide where the quicksands lay and where the safest crossing point was of the deep channels. The rivers that flow out into the Bay, Keer, Kent, Leven and Duddon, all create deep channels which shift erratically and can move over a period of time by several miles. These channels vary in depth, and so can be difficult to cross, but older channels often fill with soft silt, a 'lyring', into which the unwary could step and sink. The traditional method of marking the route was with sprigs of laurel, known as 'brobs', which the carter would place upright in the sands at the safest crossings. He would also wait upon the sands during the safe crossing period, from when the tide had ebbed four hours to two hours or so before the next tide, watching for stragglers and blowing a horn if necessary to attract their attention.

78 Oversands travellers. An early 19th-century engraving showing the oversands coach leading a long line of travellers on foot and with pack-horses. The man on the left with the horse is probably the carter. In the background a ship beached close to the route is an indication of likely hazards – it would leave a hollow filled with quicksands at the next tide.

A petition of John Carter, guide, in 1715 is illuminating:

> For managing the said employ the petitioner is obliged to keep two horses summer and winter, and being necessitated to attend the eddy four miles upon the sands twelve hours in every twenty-four hours, his horses thereby and by often passing the waters are starved with cold and so often thrown into distempers that thereby and maintaining them he is put under a very great charge, and that the petitioner undergoes great hardships by his being exposed to the winds and cold upon the plain sands, and being often wet and he by seeking out new fords every variation of the eddy, and upon happening of fogs and mists is often put in danger of his life …

Edward Baines described the guide thus in 1828:

> The Carter seems a cheerful and pleasant fellow. He wore a rough great-coat and a pair of jack-boots, and was mounted on a good horse, which appeared to have been up to the ribs in water. When we came to him he recommended us to wait till the arrival of the coach, which was nearly a mile distant, as the tide would then be gone further out.

There are still guides to the sands. The guide for the first crossing is Cedric Robinson, who has carried out the role for many years. Like most of the previous guides he is a fisherman; the best routes and indications of danger were learnt the hard way by daily experience of catching shrimps and prawns upon the sands in a net attached to the back of a cart.

Turnpikes

The first turnpike trusts in the area were the Lancaster & Richmond and the Garstang & Heron Syke, both of 1751. Like many of the earlier turnpikes, these were routed mainly along existing roads and made only a few changes of course where hills were too steep or awkward. Later turnpikes were built to a much higher specification, with bridges, embankments and tunnels to ease gradients and wide curves to allow speed to be maintained. Many earlier turnpikes were subsequently re-routed.

The Lancaster & Richmond road was designed to link the port with the Great North Road just beyond Richmond itself. It passed through two counties which, to a certain extent, behaved differently. The northern end was managed by Alexander Fothergill, a dynamic individual who kept a diary of his work so it is better known. The first mention of the road at the Lancaster end was when the Bailiffs paid out, in 1749, 'expenses of a journey with Mr Williamson & others to Sedbergh to meet the Gentlemen of Richmond'.

The route up the Lune valley followed the present line of the A683 with several important differences. Firstly, going out of Lancaster it ran along St Leonardgate and what is now Back Caton Road, rather than the lower present route. At Denny Beck there was a toll-house, known as Bulk Gate. Then, at Crook O'Lune, the road took a line much more steeply down to river level than it does now, cutting through what are now the grounds of the *Scarthwaite Hotel*. This part was re-aligned in 1835 to give the present road at Crook O'Lune. At Caton it followed what is now the back road over the Artle Beck up to Brookhouse church and then along Caton Green Road nearly to Claughton. This still remains an alternative to the main road. The diversion appears to date from the 1820s. Between Claughton and Farleton the older road over the hill was abandoned for a much lower and potentially wetter line probably as long ago as

79 Fowler Hill toll-bar. This, the first toll-bar on the Garstang & Heron Syke Turnpike and dating from 1751, stands just north of Garstang. It is unusual in retaining not only the toll-house but also both gate pillars for the gate across the turnpike.

1751 (the present line appears on Yates' Map of Lancashire, 1786). The old road survives here as a pleasant green track. The original toll-house still stands on the right-hand side of the road at Farleton.

Beyond Farleton the road ran on through Hornby and Melling, turning right at Greeta Bridge, where there was another toll-gate, and heading on through Cantsfield to the Yorkshire border. Its subsequent route was via Ingleton and over Cam Fell to Bainbridge in Wensleydale, and then on to Richmond via Askrigg. In 1795 this very steep road was amended to run via Ribblehead and Hawes, instead of over Cam Fell.

The main north-south road was the Garstang & Heron Syke Turnpike, which linked with others to make a longer through route. The rather inconsequential northern end marks the border with Westmorland, near Burton-in-Kendal; the southern end linked to the Preston road, and started at Fowler Hill, where there is a fine surviving toll-house and the posts which carried the toll-gate. It ran north to Lancaster along the route of the present A6, with several small diversions which have since cut off bends. The original turnpike ran through Galgate via the steep Highland Brow and Burrow, a long straight stretch of old road opposite Lancaster University left behind when the line was diverted in 1824 to its present course. The older pre-turnpike course is harder to make out here, though it is likely that the 1751 line incorporated older stretches. At Scotforth was another toll-gate, marked now only by Toll Bar Crescent. North of Lancaster the route followed the present A6 as far as Carnforth. There was another toll-gate at Beaumont. At Carnforth the lines diverge. The old route was via North Road and then by what are now back lanes past Borwick to Longlands, where it crossed the modern A6070 and ran up past Greenlands Farm to the west of Buckstone, re-joining the line of the A6070 just north of the latter, where its former line can be seen on aerial photographs. The modern line was created when a diversion to lower the gradient was made in 1824. From here it ran on to the county boundary at Heron Syke, and thus to Kendal.

These were the main turnpike roads of the district, although the Kendal & Keighley Turnpike to the north-east ran through Cowan Bridge, where Lancaster had long taken a toll on all passing goods, while the 1817 Ulverston & Carnforth Turnpike offered for the first time a reasonable alternative to crossing the Sands.

Canal

Although first conceived in the early days of canals, in 1772, the Lancaster Canal did not come to fruition until 1797, when rising costs and inflation left it unfinished for over twenty years. The original aim had been quite simple: to link the coalfield around Wigan with the Carboniferous limestone in the north of the county, bringing cheap coal to the north and lime for agriculture to the burgeoning south. There were a number of other aims, among which were carrying gunpowder from the works around Kendal, and linking the towns of Preston, Lancaster and Kendal by water. It would certainly help to distribute the goods brought in from overseas via the port of Lancaster. John Rennie surveyed the route. Passengers do not appear to have figured much in the thoughts of the canal projectors. This was a significant oversight, as we shall see.

By 1797, when the main part opened, the canal consisted of one length in South Lancashire, beginning adjacent to the coalfield and terminating above the Ribble at Walton-le-Dale, and a second length running from Preston to Tewitfield, just north of Lancaster. Due to costs and engineering difficulties, the proposed aqueduct over the Ribble never materialised, its place being taken by a tramroad and inclined planes, which meant expensive trans-shipping of goods. The aqueduct over the Lune at Lancaster was magnificent, and still is, but it ran away with £48,000 of scarce capital. The Ribble aqueduct would have been much more expensive. All the northern end was very skilfully built as a 'contour canal', following a contour at a constant 70 feet above sea level, in one long pound of over forty miles. Beyond Tewitfield the land rose, and the solution required locks, tunnels or both. It was not until 22 years later, in 1819, that work was completed to take the canal through to Kendal.

The new route raised the canal 70 feet by means of a succession of eight locks at Tewitfield, and navigated the hilly country that followed by means of a tunnel nearly a quarter of a mile long at Hincaster. To feed the canal, which would lose water down the locks from the top pound, a reservoir was built at Killington. Finally, in 1826, a new branch with six locks linked the main line just south of Lancaster with Glasson Dock, providing access to the canal for sea-going vessels, and incidentally giving Kendal a (remote) sea-port.

Coal and lime were duly carried, despite the difficulties created by the Ribble gap. Coke ovens and lime-kilns sprang up along the canal banks to process the raw materials for easier carriage. In 1802, partly a result of the Preston Gild held in that year, a sedate and modest passenger service commenced, using long wooden boats with overall cabins to protect passengers from the elements.

From this unremarkable beginning rose in due course a truly remarkable fast passenger service. The towpath was, unusually, on one side of the canal throughout, apart from two stretches in Lancaster and Kendal where crossover bridges gave access to the other bank for a short distance. In addition, all of the few locks on the canal were concentrated in one place. This enabled an experiment to take place with William Houston's new light packet boat, first run on the Glasgow, Paisley & Ardrossan Canal, in 1833, which proved a success. Soon a new vessel, *Water Witch*, built of sheet iron and weighing less than two tons despite being 70 feet long, came into use. It was followed by three other similar vessels between 1834 and 1839 named *Swallow*, *Swiftsure*, and *Crewdson* (later *Water Witch II*). With a light cabin made of wood and proofed calico, they could carry up to eighty passengers at an average speed of 12 miles per hour, including stops and passage through the locks. Food and drink was served on board. They only ran until 1846, when the new railway line through to Carlisle duplicated the route between Preston and Kendal, but these packets set a standard of comfort, smoothness and speed which was not bettered for many years. In their first six months of operation they carried 16,000 passengers, a far cry from the handsful carried each day by road coaches. The age of mass travel had arrived.

Sir George Head made a visit to the manufacturing areas of the country in 1835, noting particularly the canals, railways and mills. He travelled by packet:

> Having availed myself, on the present occasion, of one-horse vehicle aforesaid from Wigan to Preston, my purpose was to go by the passage-boat as far as Lancaster, and depart from thence across the sands of Morecambe-bay the next morning. This voyage was rendered particularly agreeable by the companionship of a young and highly-educated Quaker couple, with whom I really regretted it was not then my lot to proceed as far as Kendal; however, when we arrived at Lancaster, although the halt is longer here than during any part of the passage, I had scarcely time to look around, and deplore the change of scene and destiny, whereby I was left behind, bag and baggage, pacing on the Quay, than the whistle was blown, the horses cantered away, and the boat quickly glided out of sight.

The canal continued to be used commercially well into the 20th century. It brought coal to the mills in Lancaster until the hard winter of 1940, when it froze and was not used again for this purpose again after the thaw came. At about the same time the northern end at Kendal sprang a serious leak – it had often caused trouble – and once drained became disused. In the 1960s the M6 motorway and feeders for the Kendal bypass were built over parts of the northern end, which was abandoned from north of Tewitfield. The southern end was also subject to similar development, leading to abandonment of the wharves at Walton Summit (the tramroad went out of use as early as 1859) and the first mile or two in Preston. Fortunes change, however, and a new link is now being built at the southern end, on the line of the Savick Brook, to join the canal to the river Ribble. Equally ambitious plans exist to revitalise the northern reaches, in both cases mainly for leisure use.

A canal was projected to run up through Hornby and Wray in the Lune and Wenning valleys, initial surveys for which survive in Hornby Castle muniments, but it is not clear what its economic objectives were.

Coaching

Coach travel had a relatively brief flowering, from the 1770s to about 1810, when it was acceptably reliable, and from 1810 until the late 1830s, when the state of the roads allowed fast and smooth travel, reaching an apogee just before it was altogether eclipsed by the railways on most routes. Coaches represented an expensive means of travel, and carried a limited number of passengers, usually four to six 'insides' and a slightly larger number of cheaper 'outsides'. Early designs often needed six horses but the number stabilised at four in the 18th century, along with the system of 'stages' at which the horses were changed. The coaches prided themselves on smart turnout and speed, often having names which conveyed a spirit of dignity or reliability. The pinnacle of smartness and speed was achieved by the Royal Mail, which from 1785 dispatched mail-coaches to all parts of the country from London. Local coaching was operated by people like Thomas Cooper, whose son Thomas jnr carried on his business from 1805, or Jonathan Dunn, coach-builder of St Leonardgate, who was able to build himself Ryelands House in Skerton in 1836 from the profits.

It is almost impossible to follow all the nuances of the coaching trade. Names of coaches appear and disappear, times regularly change, and variations elsewhere in the country affect the running of long-distance coaches. The earliest local handbill is for the 'Liverpool and Lancaster Flying Machine' of 1777. Interestingly it was designed to link Lancaster with Burscough on the newly-opened Leeds and Liverpool Canal, where it met and exchanged passengers with the Union Packet boat from Liverpool. In January 1803 the *Lancaster Gazette* advertised the 'only regular coach to London' from the *King's Arms* and *Commercial Inn*. Fares were £2 2s. (inside) and £1 6s. (outside), the service being run by Smith, Bretherton & Co. In August 1807 the *Gazette* advertised the 'Telegraph Coach', run by Dunn from the *King's Arms* and *Royal Oak*, and the 'Royal Sailor', run by Neweby, Varty, Duckworth, Peacock, Gurney and Bell (all innkeepers on the route) from the *Cross Keys* to Preston and Liverpool. The advert refers to a 'Coach office in Market street, corner of Sun street; where parcels are booked, and places taken, to all parts of the kingdom, daily'.

A watercolour drawing by Gideon Yates in 1805 shows the 'John Bull' coach coming into Lancaster through Scotforth, and in the same year the *Gazette* published two adverts for the 'Royal Sailor' and 'North Briton' coaches.

Opposition coaches were sometimes set up to steal a competitor's business, either by undercutting prices or by earlier running. This often led to dangerous driving by the rival coachmen and usually to a price war until one dropped out. In March 1817 Thomas Gregson commenced running the 'Royal Liverpool' coach, in opposition to Messrs J.Dunn & Co's 'Royal Telegraph'. When the former advertised fares of 14s. (inside) and 10s. (outside) to Liverpool or Manchester, the latter immediately came back with fares of 7s. and 5s. However, within three years the two had combined.

A new coach from Lancaster to York started running in May 1815. In 1820 the *Lonsdale Magazine* listed the following coaches through Lancaster: the 'North Briton', the 'Telegraph & Royal Liverpool', the 'Umpire' or 'Union', the Royal Mail and the 'Two Lord Exmouths' (to Newcastle), as well as the oversands coach. In 1829 a coach called 'The Old Times' ran from Lancaster to the *Bull Hotel* in Poulton (Morecambe) in season, to suit the times of sea bathing. A number of local coaches linked up with

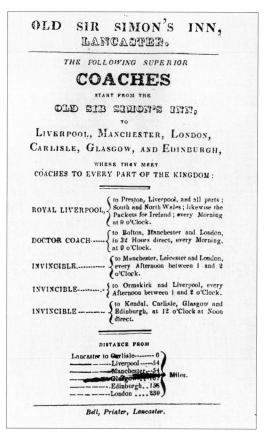

80 Handbill for coaches running from the *Old Sir Simon's Inn* in Market Street. It has no date, but belongs to the last age of local coaching, between 1830 and 1846.

the main roads and served the small band of fashionable people who wished to travel in this way. Post-chaises, light open vehicles, were often hired from inns to get to places off the main routes.

At the peak of the coaching age in 1836 Lancaster was served by such through coaches as the London-Manchester-Port Patrick Royal Mail, and the Manchester and Carlisle coach, while direct coaches connected Lancaster with Clapham, Barnard Castle, Kendal, Preston, Ulverston (two services), Liverpool and Manchester (four services). An undated handbill for services from *Old Sir Simon's Inn*, so probably quite late in the coaching age, lists the 'Royal Liverpool', 'Doctor Coach' and three 'Invincible' coaches. The 'Doctor Coach' is noted as taking '32 Hours direct' to London via Bolton and Manchester. By 1837 the direct coach to London was taking just under 26 hours.

The service over the Sands, between the *Sun Inn* in Lancaster and Ulverston, began in 1781 and was described in the *Cumberland Pacquet* as 'a Diligence or Chaise, which will carry three persons conveniently'. Only light coaches could make it over the Sands, although a handbill of 1848 carries a woodcut of a conventional heavily-laden coach. In 1825 a 'Telegraph Coach' was listed as running to Ulverston from the *King's Arms*. In the absence of railway competition coaches ran on the oversands route until 1857.

The network of coaches met and exchanged or deposited their passengers at coaching inns. You would book the coach from an inn, eat at inns on the way, and probably stay at the inn at your destination. You might also change coach there. Such inns had a yard into which the coach could drive, adequate stabling for the many changes of horses, and facilities for feeding many guests at the same time. They tended to be the larger inns in a town.

In Lancaster the earliest principal inn was the *George* in Market Street, described by a number of 17th-century travellers, but already by 1722 it was referred to as 'a tenement formerly the George Inn'. Its place was taken by others such as the *Kings Arms* and the *Sun*, or the *Royal Oak* and the *Commercial Inn* in the Market Place. The

81 The old *King's Arms Inn*, seen just before its demolition and rebuilding in 1879. The premier inn of Lancaster for several centuries, it clearly spread into several adjacent buildings, hence its rather curious 'footprint', faithfully copied in the new building. This is the inn where Charles Dickens stayed. Thereafter Mr Sly, the landlord, regularly sent him hampers of game, no doubt benefiting from his connections with the writer.

Sun was the setting-off point for the oversands coach. It occupied part of a large courtyard building, possibly medieval in date, which belonged to the earls of Sefton but was rebuilt in its present form in 1785.

In the last days of coaching the *Old Sir Simon's Inn* in Lancaster became the main point of departure for coaches. Canon Grenside, arriving in December 1846 to take up a curacy at Melling, remembered seeing the masons finishing work on the Castle Station, and the two big destination boards outside the *Old Sir Simon's* showing where the coaches went. It was a time of great change. Coaches seem romantic now, but they were expensive and served a very small percentage of the population. When the railways came they were driven off the main roads and tended only to survive as feeders to the trains, until even that market disappeared.

The origins of the *King's Arms* are obscure. Perhaps its first landlord was James Hardman, who lost all in the Royalist siege of Lancaster in 1643. John Hunter was the innkeeper in 1664 and he paid duty on 10 hearths. By 1689 Randall Hunter was assessed on 16 hearths. Clearly the inn was growing in size and importance. Its appearance before 1879 suggested that it had expanded into a number of neighbouring 18th-century buildings. In 1766 it was assessed for 80 windows and by 1825, when John Pritt was the innkeeper, it had become the main coaching and posting inn, with seven named coaches calling each day.

Mr Monson, a Lincolnshire gentleman, had this to say of the inn in 1816:

> The Inn at Lancaster is the King's Arms, very good & civil attendance; they have a curious custom in Lancashire beside the dinner ordered they load the table with all the productions of the house, cold meat, fowls, tarts &c &c without charge for it cheaper than one dish costs in town.

Sir George Head was not disposed to enjoy himself in Lancaster on his 1835 visit and, moreover, met with a common problem of travellers—arriving during the Assizes:

> In a humour, the first moment of landing, to be out of conceit with my present quarters – in due course, as I proceeded up the town, I found more reasonable grounds of dissatisfaction, and particularly when on requesting an apartment in the principal inn, I was conducted to the garrets. The assizes were unluckily on that very day at their zenith: a festival, of which the signs and phenomena below stairs, and in the streets, were apparent; - bloated country coachmen, in their best liveries, stood lounging in the stable-yards and gateways; every servant in the house jostled and trod on the heels of his fellow; dinner tables were laid in all the parlours; sand, in preparation for the scuffle, was spread on the floor instead of carpets; the lawyers ran to and fro in their wigs, and a group of hungry farmers in the passage, all panting and eager for the fray, whetted their large teeth, and licked their lips, as they snuffed up the sweet savour, or fragrant odour, from the kitchen.

In the mid-19th century Joseph Sly was landlord. He entertained many important guests such as Prince William of Gloucester, the Prince of Saxe Weimar, Queen Adelaide, the Queen Dowager, Prince Louis Napoleon and, most famously of all, Charles Dickens. The latter set a short story here, published in *Household Words*, after he stayed here with Wilkie Collins in 1857 ('The Lazy Tour of Two Idle Apprentices').

In 1879 the old building was taken down and replaced by a purpose-built structure, which survives today. The new hotel had stables which could accommodate up to 100 horses and its own horse-bus to meet guests from the station.

82 Drawing of the locomotive *John O'Gaunt* by James Atherton, 1849. This was one of the original locomotives bought for the Lancaster & Preston Junction Railway from Bury of Liverpool in 1839-40. Atherton was locomotive superintendent on the 'Little' North Western Railway and, later, a partner in the Phoenix Foundry, so we can be sure that the drawing is extremely accurate. It may have been done for nostalgic reasons, or for the imminent resale of the locomotive.

Railways

Although the first passenger railway in the world was built in Lancashire in 1830, it was not until 1840 that a new railway line opened between Preston and Lancaster. Not only did it link Lancaster with London by rail for the first time but it also pushed the northern frontier of the growing network forward by 21 miles. For a dizzying six years Lancaster was the end of the line in England. A combination of the Liverpool & Manchester Railway, the North Union and the London & Birmingham Railway had by the late 1830s made sure that there was a through route from London to the north-west. From here a number of new and mostly small-scale railway companies saw the opportunity of extending the network.

Lancaster business people were determined that the railway should not bypass the town, as a plan of 1836 had hinted. The necessary Act of Parliament was obtained on 5 May 1837. The original plan was to bring the line to a point near the canal on the southern edge of Lancaster, avoiding the need to cross valuable town-centre property, with branches to Moor Lane and George Street. These were never built.

Enthusiastic support for the new line came from those who thought it would make their fortune, and from those who saw it as a means of transporting raw materials and finished goods. The potential demand for passenger transport had already been shown by the success of the Lancaster Canal Company's packet boats. The line was surveyed by Joseph Locke, a pupil of George Stephenson and one of

83 Local cartoon of *c*.1842. The Lancaster & Preston Junction Railway Co. and the Lancaster Canal Co. are literally yoked together with the same horse, a reference to the unusual take-over by the Canal. The smiling figure on the left is a 'railway policeman' who in the early days of railways would direct traffic and signal departures.

84 Reconstruction of Penny Street station by David Vale. Quite a lot of the original station of 1839-40 still survives. It shows how the idea of a railway station had not yet been formulated; the station tries to look like a gentleman's villa.

the most famous of Victorian railway engineers. Because of the straight line and easy gradients between Lancaster and Preston the railway presented few diffi-culties and was a model of cheapness and simplicity, Locke's hallmarks. The biggest engineering feat was the building of the long skewed viaduct over the main road and river at Galgate, still in regular use by the modern west-coast main line.

There were six intermediate stations on the line, at Galgate, Bay Horse, Scorton, Garstang, Roe Buck and Broughton. Roe Buck disappeared in 1849, being replaced by Brock. These stations were all extremely basic, built of timber with 'sentry-box'-type shelters. They were later rebuilt in stone and nothing remains today of the Lancaster & Preston Railway period. The day set for the grand opening of the line was 25 June 1840. Directors of other lines and civic dignitaries were invited and over two hundred people boarded a special train. Unfortunately, this was well beyond the capacity of the locomotive, until another one came to its assistance!

By the appointed hour for starting, eleven o'clock, every inch of ground within view was crowded with anxious spectators. In the midst fizzed and fumed the three engines which had that morning arrived from Preston, whilst the beautiful carriages of the company … were ranged upon the rails in lengthened array, awaiting the signal for starting. The scene was exceedingly animated and interest-ing; and the effect was immeasurably heightened by the presence of the fairer portion of creation, who graced the spectacle in great numbers and elegant attire. We should mention that in the town the shops were shut, the factories closed, and the merry pealing of the bells gave token of the general holiday.

Owing to the accident of one of the engines having got off the line on its way to Lancaster, there was a little delay, and it wanted about twenty minutes to twelve before the train started. There were nine first-class carriages and three second-class, all filled with visitors. A capital brass band also accompanied the train. On the first motion of the train the band played 'God save the Queen', and after one or two false starts, as we term it, the whole train fairly moved off, drawn by two engines …

Between 1838 and 1840 the Lancaster & Preston Junction Railway bought the following rolling-stock:

- 6 2-2-0 locomotives with 5ft. 6ins. driving-wheels from Edward Bury of Liverpool, named: *Victoria, Albert, Duchess, John O'Gaunt, Lancaster, North Star.*
- 8 1st class carriages and
- 12 2nd class carriages from Richard Dunn of Lancaster
- 3 3rd class carriages
- 6 horse-boxes
- 10 trucks

(The *John O'Gaunt* locomotive survived to be drawn in 1849 (see p.107), perhaps for sale. Its subsequent fate is unknown.)

Lancaster's new railway station was to designs by Edwin Gwyther of Birmingham, the architect for the London & Birmingham railway, and was built just to the south of Springfield Park. It was known as Greaves or Penny Street Station and looked just like an ordinary Georgian suburban house. It had a very short life, from 1840 until 1849. It was replaced by the new Castle Station of the Lancaster & Carlisle Railway as early as 1846 for through traffic, but in practice the two companies could not agree, so the Lancaster & Preston Company continued to use Penny Street Station until the take-over in 1849. The spur on which it stood was now surplus to requirements and the station and other railway buildings were sold off in 1852. The former station became a private house. The railhead had moved north from Lancaster by 1846 and the town found itself bypassed in just the way it had sought to avoid. Occasional trains still used the spur up until the 20th century, mainly as coal-sidings. The station building itself survives as an administrative office for the Health Authority, and a row of arches at the rear and the original bell, which was used when a train was due to leave, are relics of its former use.

Anthony Hewitson recalls the early days on the Lancaster & Preston:

> The first time I remember riding on the Lancaster and Preston Railway was, perhaps, a year after its opening. I started from the station at Lancaster; the carriage in which I rode was of the parliamentary order – something like a present-time cattle truck, with transversely ranged wooden forms, without backs, for seats, the top being covered with common board-like material, immediately below which was an opening, all round, about two feet deep, through which the wind blew strongly when the train was in motion. The only incident of the journey which I recollect was this: shortly after the train left Lancaster, one of the passengers, a man, who was standing in the middle of the carriage, lost his hat – it was blown right off his head into a field; and this odd incident induced some of the passengers to tie pocket handkerchiefs closely round their hats, &c., and under their chins, so as to obviate further wind antics with headgear.

A reader of the *Lancaster Guardian* complained in 1843:

> Having frequently to go to Preston on business and return on the same day, and being very poor, I cannot afford to pay either for the first or the second-class carriages; I am therefore compelled (there being no other way of getting to Preston) to go in a stand-up carriage – carriage did I say? A stand-up box I ought to say – for which I have to pay 2s. 6d. for going twenty miles, and cannot possibly sit down except on the floor, and if I were to do so I

should stand a good chance of being trodden upon. When the carriages have to stop we all go jostling together.

Now Mr Editor, don't you think this is a most shameful way of getting people's money, and not even allowing them for the rate of 2s. 6d. a seat to sit upon?

The reason, of course, was monopoly.

The Lancaster & Preston Junction Railway gained an unenviable reputation for accidents. Even before the official opening one of the bridges collapsed. Later, a young employee, larking around with his friends, showed them how to start a locomotive. It crashed into a rake of carriages at Lancaster Station, causing serious damage. The worst accident in the line's brief independent history, however, occurred in August 1848 at Bay Horse Station. A local train was standing in the station and the flag signal, which was supposed to protect it, was nearly invisible because of the wind direction. An express train rounded the corner and could not stop in time. One passenger was killed and carriages on the local train were so rotten that they simply fell apart under the impact.

The cause of the accident was the hopeless muddle over who owned the line. Two separate companies were at this time running trains over the same line without consulting each other! Unreliable signalling, common to many early railways, and poor time-keeping compounded the problem. The Lancaster & Preston Junction Railway Company and the Lancaster Canal Company were rivals. For much of the distance between the two towns their lines ran parallel. Usually where such rivalry existed the canal was the loser, but here things were different. The Lancaster Canal was well managed and ran a cheap and efficient packet-boat service for passengers. When the railway opened the Canal Company simply halved its passenger fares and undercut the railway, which in practice made little use of its advantage in speed. Despite this the railway company still managed to carry over 150,000 passengers within its first 14 months of operation, if its annual report is to be believed, but within two years of opening the railway was in difficulty. Not only did it have financial problems, but it had also failed to make any satisfactory arrangements for sharing stations at Preston. From 1841 the North Union surcharged through-passengers who used the line be-tween the two companies' stations in Fishergate. If they refused to pay and instead walked through the tunnel under Fishergate it was often to find that the London train had left without them! In desperation the board leased their new line to the Canal Company for a term of 21 years!

In time the benefits of a through-route to Carlisle became obvious and in 1849 the Lancaster & Carlisle Railway bought the line from the Canal Company. In Sep-tember of the same year all the Lancaster and Preston locomotives and rolling-stock were put up for sale, being no longer required.

The eminent engineer George Stephenson favoured a line across Morecambe Bay and along the Cumbrian coast for the northwards extension, but the line proposed by Locke and eventually agreed was a direct route over Shap Fells, with a branch from Oxenholme via Kendal to Windermere. (This was opposed by no less a person than William Wordsworth, who saw the line as little better than sacrilege. It is ironic to think that had he lived a century and a half later he would probably have been leading the resistance to its closure!) Work began in 1844 and the railway opened to Carlisle in December 1846. It followed a difficult and expensive route, taxing the available locomotive power to the limit, and there were many outstanding engineering feats on the route.

The Lancaster & Carlisle railway station at Lancaster quickly became known as Lancaster Castle Station to distinguish it from the earlier one at Penny Street and the slightly later one at Green Ayre. A simple building in the Gothic style, it occupies part of the 'down' or western platform and can still be recognised among later additions by the cartouches with 'L C' within them. Just beyond the station is the massive Carlisle Bridge, which spans the River Lune. In order to build this the railway company had to pay handsome compensation to the Port Commission for permission to construct the massive piers in the river bed. The bridge has twice been rebuilt; in its original form the stone piers carried a laminated timber superstructure.

The 'Little' North Western Railway grew out of a plan in 1845 to link the West Riding of Yorkshire with the sea, through the Port of Lancaster. When the Act of Parliament was obtained in 1846 the Committee decided to extend the line a few miles westwards to the new harbour at Morecambe. The engineer of the line was Charles Vignoles. Up to now all the railway developments around Lancaster were north-south. Now there was a chance to provide an east-west line, connecting a large industrialised area with the main west-coast route.

Parts of the line were opened piecemeal, as they were finished. The first, in 1848, was the Morecambe Branch, with a station on the shore, later moved to the Stone Jetty when that was ready in about 1853, giving direct access to passenger ferries to Scotland and Ireland. Further sections opened in 1849 but the whole route from Lancaster to Clapham Junction was not ready until 1850. A temporary station was built near Wennington to form the terminus of the line, and the track ran down the Lune valley, passing through Hornby and Caton to a new station in Lancaster.

The new Lancaster station, known as Green Ayre, stood on a former island of that name in the River Lune. At first it was very basic, the North Western Railway Company being extremely parsimonious with its station buildings, and the stone buildings on the site were a much later alteration. The whole station was ultimately demolished and its site is now occupied by Sainsbury's store. There were sidings at Ladies' Walk and along Cable Street, while a new curved bridge of laminated timber, known as Greyhound Bridge, carried the railway across the Lune on its way to Morecambe. A further line linking Green Ayre with Castle Station was opened in December 1849, allowing North Western trains to run through onto the main west-coast line. Apart from one or two minor additions and alterations, the pattern of railways around Lancaster was now established and would remain in use for over a century and a half.

Back to the roads

At the turn of the 20th century the local traffic of farmers' carts and carriers was joined by the first cars, owned by the handful of local gentry and the middle-class managers at some of the industrial concerns. In 1904 a 'John O'Gaunt' car was being built by Atkinsons, the engineers and gunsmiths. Soon local blacksmiths started car repairs and sold petrol in cans. In 1913 the 'Autocar' Road Book, lineal descendant of

85 Battery bus in Market Square during the First World War. These were used to carry women workers to the Projectile Factory on Caton Road, but also served other routes. They were not really suitable for the purpose and often ran out of electricity before they got back to the charging point in Market Square, having to be pushed by their passengers.

all those itineraries such as Ogilby's and Cary's, offered detailed instructions on routes, indicating steep hills, sharp bends and gates across roads. The road to the Trough of Bowland is described thus:

> … past the Williamson Park to Golgotha. Here, inclining left, road descends smartly and then rises, followed by another steep descent (dangerous) and rise.

Electric trams ran in Lancaster from 1903 until 1930, but this was unsuitable terrain for trams, with too many steep hills, and the town was too small. Horse-drawn trams linked Lancaster with Morecambe. During the First World War electric battery buses took women munition workers to the Caton Road projectile factory, recharging their batteries in Market Square. Corporation petrol-driven buses also ran from here from 1925. In 1939 a new bus station was opened on Green Ayre and used jointly with Ribble Motors; this has recently been rebuilt on the same site but a great deal has changed in the meantime. The City Council Transport Department 'floated free' in 1985 and subsequently disappeared in the cut-throat competition which followed. The

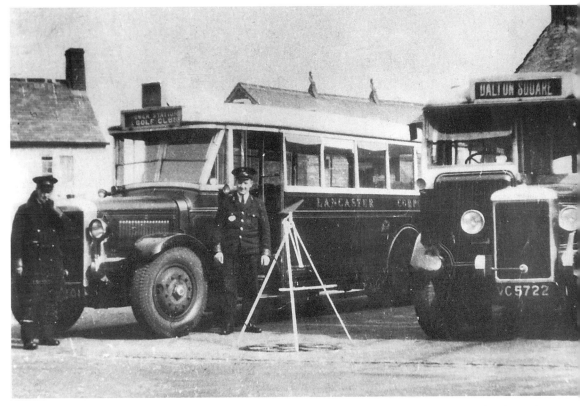

86 Single-deck Lancaster Corporation buses at Scotforth Square in about 1931. These two second-hand Daimler buses are seen with their drivers Harold Jones and Alec Edmondson.

growth of public transport up until the 1950s or so led to the option of living away from the workplace, and helped empty the city centre of housing. The subsequent growth of car ownership and hence the need for more and more parking, and wider, faster roads has continued to cause real problems in a historic city such as Lancaster. The state of the traffic is still one of the biggest concerns voiced by citizens, and is unlikely to improve if the current trend for Lancaster and district to act as a preferred dormitory for people working in central Lancashire and further afield continues.

Motorway
After a long period of neglect and under-investment during the war the county's roads were in a poor state. A Road Plan for Lancashire was published by Lancashire County Council in 1949 at the suggestion of James Drake, County Surveyor and Bridgemaster. This proposed a number of express routes, since the term 'motorway' had not yet been coined. The idea was actually inspired by the pre-War German autobahn, and some plans for a national network had been put forward as early as 1938. Surprisingly, much

of the Lancashire plan actually took shape in the long term.

The very first motorway in the country was the Preston bypass, opened in 1958. The Lancaster bypass, eleven miles long, from the A6 at Forton to the A6 at Carnforth, followed soon after, and was opened in April 1960. By 1965 the intermediate section between the two, with a service area at Forton, was complete. The present interchange at Caton Road (Junction 34) was something of an afterthought, and even then was originally intended only for emergency vehicles. That is why it has such a tight radius, and traffic from both directions carried on the same slip road, surely one of the most sub-standard interchanges in the whole country. Apart from the engineering of the motorway itself, the various bridges over it, many of them for accommodation purposes, were highly thought of at the time. Particularly fine, because of its absolute simplicity, is the bridge carrying the motorway over the Lune at Halton. Unfortunately it is invisible from most points but the river itself.

87 The M6 motorway under construction, *c.*1959. The view is northwards over the present Caton Road interchange (junction 34) and Lune crossing. Initially it was not intended to have an interchange here, but there was concern about the need for access for emergency vehicles to this long stretch of road (Forton – Carnforth) and eventually general access was provided. This explains the substandard nature of the junction, with a very tight radius and single carriageways on and off.

The motorway was very different from what it was later to become. Hard shoulders were originally discontinuous, omitted where there were bridges, and made of no more than a hardened grass verge. There were at first only two carriageways in each direction, and a generous central reservation. Quite soon the lanes were increased, using most of this reservation, and later on crash barriers were installed to stop vehicles crossing over into the face of oncoming traffic. It is remarkable that in spite of these changes, and others, basically the same roads have adapted to carrying numbers of vehicles unimaginable at the time of building.

Eight

Alarums and Excursions

On at least eight occasions in the last thousand years Lancaster has known major panic, mostly as a result of invasion or siege. On six of these occasions, in 1322, perhaps 1388-9, 1648, 1651, 1715 and 1745 the invaders have been Scottish; on the seventh, in 1643, it was fellow-countrymen under the royalist Earl of Derby. On the eighth, in 1698, the visitation was by accidental fire. In fact fire was an agent in several of these events. The effect of all these occurrences has been to destroy most of the evidence for early houses – there are no medieval structures left in Lancaster other than the Castle and Priory church – and an unknown quantity of medieval documents. Lancaster's position on the main west-coast route, only seventy or eighty miles south of the Scottish border, and its possession of an important royal stronghold must have been among the reasons for successive invasions.

The perpetual fear of invasion was most felt by the people of the borderland itself, where an assault by fierce moss-troopers was an ever-present reality, but the road through Carlisle to the south was a magnet to larger and more organised forces. Not all these were hostile in intent. The Jacobites came this way to take control of a kingdom, not to wreck it. Every army had its stragglers, however, and even a defeated or retreating army could be dangerous, having nothing to lose by plunder and rapine. The effect of constant invasion, particularly in the 14th or 17th centuries, must have been to suppress investment in houses or businesses, since they were so vulnerable to theft and destruction.

1322

After the battle of Bannockburn the Scots were able to exploit divisions in the English ranks, especially the rebellion of Thomas, Earl of Lancaster in the spring of 1322, to bloody effect. After a successful invasion of the north in 1316 the power vacuum caused by the Earl's rebellion and then defeat and execution in 1322 led Robert Bruce to march again. Two Scottish armies struck southwards, one probably advancing over Shap Fell and down Lunesdale, via Hornby and Quernmore, while the other, under Bruce himself, crossed the Solway and followed the Cumbrian coast through Copeland, Furness and Cartmel and thus over the sands until they effected a junction at Lancaster. According to the chronicler Holinshed:

> ... they came to Lancaster, which town they also burnt, save onlie the priorie of blacke moonks, and a house of preaching friers; heare came to them the Earle of Murrey and the Lord James Dowglasse with an other armie.

The Scots stayed in Lancaster four days with their plunder and the stocks of cattle and horses they had gathered on the way. Probably the troops were billeted on the town, while the horses and cattle were kept across the river in Skerton, where great damage was done to fields by trampling of crops. On their departure they burnt the town, in which most of the buildings were of timber and thatch. A later petition by the burgesses to the king claimed that the Scots had 'burnt their town and castle so that nothing is left'. Whether the castle was actually taken is not clear, although an inquest of 1323-4 refers to 'herbiage of the ditch around the castle this year 2s; of the issues of the site of the castle he does not answer because it was altogether burnt by the Scots', which is ambiguous. A carpenter was part-paid 48s. from the sum of £5 14s. for 'making the prison and bridge at the entry to the castle of Lancastre burnt by the Scots'. Probably at least the outworks were taken.

What is clear is that there was no organised resistance and the Scots did just what they pleased. Thereafter they went on to burn Preston, and within the month returned to Scotland unscathed. The sparing of the Priory and the Dominican Friary may have been acts of piety on the part of Robert Bruce, but the Scots may have been bribed to leave them alone, as had happened at other monasteries in their path. It is also significant that both had substantial precinct walls. These would not deter an army but they might be enough to deter spontaneous plundering by stragglers. A rental of 1323 shows the reduction in value of local property. One telling comment states:

> ... the said toft (of Agnes de Baldreston) was burnt by the Scots and all the goods and chattels of the said Agnes were despoiled by them through their being there for 4 days and nights within the quindene of the feast of the nativity of St. John the Baptist ... [24th June]

This sort of evidence appears again and again in Lancaster and in all the surrounding villages, which the Scots presumably swept in the search for plunder. Twenty-four parishes in North Lancashire were revalued at one-third of the former value of their benefices as a direct result. Even a couple of years after the event land was lying fallow for lack of tenants, perhaps because of the destruction of houses, or fear of a repeat. This sort of economic damage would have affected a whole generation, many of whom were probably just getting over it when they were struck by the Black Death in 1348-9.

1389

There is only slight evidence for a Scottish raid in this year, and the burning of Lancaster a second time, following the battle of Otterburn on 10 August 1388. Again it was English disunity which allowed the Scots their opportunity. John O'Gaunt was campaigning abroad, leaving the defence of the Borders to others and, during in-fighting between rivals, the Scots slipped through. Evidence comes from a charter of 12 Richard II (1388-9) given 'by the King himself, for the Fine of Forty Shillings and because the Town aforesaid by Misfortune has been often burnt'. If it were referring to the events of 1322 only it would seem irrelevant; surely there must have been a recent catastrophe to give it point.

1643

The Civil War had different impact in different places. Much of the time small armies skirmished around defended country houses and castles with a great deal of noise and relatively few casualties. There were a number of bloody set-piece battles, but the effect on the civilian population was most marked in the siege of towns and cities, and the accompanying plunder and rapine carried out by both sides without discrimination. The civilian population was regarded as a legitimate target, very much as it was in the Europe of the Thirty Years War, where many of the professional soldiers on both sides had gained their training.

Such was the brief Royalist siege of Lancaster in March 1643. The background to this was the Royalist failure early in the war to garrison the Castle, although Lancaster was an important symbolic prize, and controlled the road to the north. In February 1643 a small company of Parliamentary troops under Sergeant-Major Birch marched up from Preston and took the Castle. A Spanish ship, the *Santa Anna*, had been wrecked at Rossall Point. Both Parliamentary and Royalist forces advanced on it, but the Royalists under the Earl of Derby were the stronger. They burned the ship and took some prisoners but failed to rescue its 22 valuable cannons. These were rescued instead by the Parliamentarians, brought to Lancaster and laid up in the Castle yard. Either to lay hands on these or for larger strategic reasons the Earl of Derby, as Royalist commander in the north west,

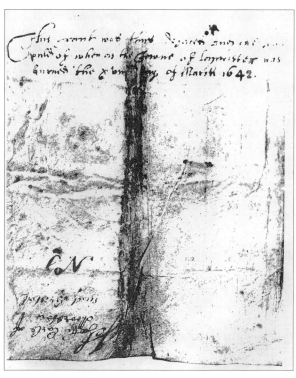

88 Charter of 1193 and wrapper. The wrapper records damage done during the Royalist attack in 1643: 'This Grant was thus defaced and the seale pul'd of when as the Towne of Lancaster was burned the xviiith day of March 1642' (the year did not end until 25 March at that time so this would be 1643 by the modern calendar).

raised an army in South Lancashire consisting of some 600 foot and 400 horse, plus many local levies and sympathisers from the Fylde, and marched on Lancaster. These irregulars were known as 'Clubmen' and were responsible for indisciplined looting both before and after the attack.

The Castle was too strong for such a force to take by anything less than a long siege, but the heavily outnumbered Parliamentary forces attempted to barricade the southern end of the town. The Royalist forces, under the Earl of Derby, Colonel Tyldesley and Sir John Girlington, arrived on the morning of 18 March 1643 and sent a demand to the Mayor and Burgesses of Lancaster offering 'all fair usage' if they submitted and helped and 'the usage of warre' if they did not. Since the townsfolk did not control their own destiny and Captain Shuttleworth stood over them, this request was little more than a pretence. Whichever side won, they were to be the sufferers. Already the occupying forces had commandeered provisions, including all the stock of the principal inn, whose landlord, James Hardman, later petitioned Parliament for redress.

By 10a.m. the Mayor had responded, truthfully, that the town was no longer at their disposal, and that the Castle never had been. This was all that Derby needed. The subsequent attack killed Captain Shuttleworth and drove the occupiers out of their barricades and into the Castle, leaving the town to the mercy of the Royalists. '[They] entered the Towne of Lancaster several waies, there being very few soldiers if any, to resist them save those that kept the Castle …' as one source describes it. Timber and thatched buildings quickly took fire. The principal area to suffer was Penny Street: 'That long street from the Whit croft [White Cross] all was burned Dwelling houses barnes corne hay catell in their stalls.' Other parts suffered as well: 'In the hart of the Towne they burned divers of the most eminent houses.' Even the surviving series of town charters, well-protected as they were, did not escape undamaged. The cover of the 1193 charter bears an inscription declaring that it was damaged and its seal ripped off during the Earl of Derby's attack in 1643. A tract describes the destruction thus:

> The barns, stables, cowhouses, replenished with corn, hay, and cattle that were burned were eighty-six, containing two hundred and forty bayes of building, and one malt kiln of four bayes of building, with three hundred windles of malt therein. By all which it evidently appears that they displayed the banner of the skarlet-coloured beast.

Fearful of being trapped by a relief party from Preston, the Earl called off his men and escaped by taking another road south, perhaps the modern Ashton Road, thus bypassing his enemy, and managed to take Preston for the king. Royalist garrisons at Hornby and Thurland Castles were besieged and driven out a few months later.

Despite the colourful language of several of the contemporary tracts, one is always well-advised to take what they have to say with a large pinch of salt. The savagery and bloodthirstiness of the attack is not borne out by the parish registers. Burials of two soldiers are recorded in July 1643 and two more, possibly three, in 1644. None of these have dates which equate to the siege, nor are the violent deaths of any civilians recorded. Of course, there is the possibility of omission, but the recording of any burials at this period is unusual, and so the presence of at least four must be significant. It may be that some died later of wounds, or were taken elsewhere for burial; possibly the attack was made with noise and bravado but few serious casualties.

In January 1645 Parliament decreed a compensation of £8,000 to the townsfolk for their loss, but it was to be gained by the victims themselves from the estates of such Royalists as were present at the burning. It is unlikely that much redress, if any, was ever obtained.

Twice more in the next few years armies passed through Lancaster, generally in peace. During the second Civil War a huge army of Scots under the Duke of Hamilton, numbering between 18,000 and 24,000, came through in August 1648, soon to be defeated at Preston by Cromwell, while in 1651 Charles Stuart, later Charles II, and a Scots army under General Leslie passed through Lancaster on 11 August, proclaiming Charles as King at the Market Cross, a shape of things to come. This army too was defeated, at the battle of Worcester.

A mound on the southern edge of the town near Aldcliffe Road, destroyed when Cromwell Road was built, was traditionally called 'Cromwell's Mound' and described as the place he set his cannon to besiege the Castle. Cromwell, however, is not known

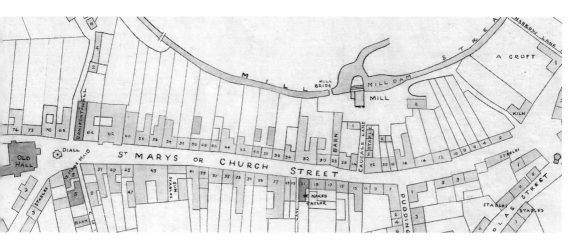

89 Detail of Church Street from 1684 map. This shows the area shortly to be affected by the fire of 1698.

to have had any part in any siege of Lancaster. Perhaps the site was actually a cockpit hill or a post-mill mound. The character of the finds from it suggests a 17th-century origin.

1698

On 21 February a fire destroyed at least twenty houses in Church Street. William Stout describes it thus:

> It begun about 9 in the morning, the 2d day of the week [Monday], in the north-west corner of the house belonging to John Johnson's children where their mother then dwelt, by her daughter Ann Tinkler, aged about 15 years, carrying out ashes to that corner not well quenched. The thatch being not two yards above it, a spark got to it and was not discoverd till it got to the roofe. And there was a strong east wind and a dry season; it spread in an instant, and, in half an hour, to the farthest, where it was stoped by stone and slated buildings. It was so quick and violant that people had not time to get out their most nessesary and valuable goods. All that was burnt was on the north side of the street, exept one house, and the main industry was to keep it on that side. There was two stone and slated houses which were burnt round, yet escaped … The whole loss was computed at about two thousand pounds, and a breif got, and some colectors apoynted … but … not one fourth of the value lost did not come to the sufferers.

A list of those sufferers is to be found in the Lancashire Record Office. Thirty-one names are listed, but some may have shared houses as surnames repeat:

> Ellen Johnson; Isabell Tompson; Sarah Tompson; William Garner; Thomas Parkinson; Charles Jackson; Robert Fletcher; Christopher Simkinson; Henry Simkinson; John Millner; James Clarke; Margret Waller; Margery Batty; William Gunson; James Harrison; Margret Brown; John Robinson; George Hodgson; Robert Bond; Richard Gunson; Edmund Townson; Elizabeth Chapman; John Simpson; John Fell; William Hind; Jennett Troughton; Francis Green; Jeoffrey Braithwaite; Elizabeth Barsley; Thomas Grocock; George Deys.

The effect of the fire was to instill a very healthy respect for the safety factors of stone and slate building and speeded up the conversion of the town from one of timber and thatch to one of stone. The common incidence of fires in other towns in the late 17th and early 18th centuries became well known to ordinary people through the system of briefs read in church, to raise money, as had happened in the case of Lancaster, according to William Stout.

1715

After the Catholic James II was driven out in the so-called 'Glorious Revolution' of 1688 in favour of his son-in-law and daughter, William and Mary of Orange, England settled down to some years of peaceful Protestantism. Mary's sister Anne succeeded them in 1702 but on her death in 1714, by a sleight of hand, the succession went to George, Elector Palatine of Hanover, and heir eventually to a sister of Charles I, whose proximity to the throne was probably a good deal less than James and his heirs. Even some Protestants felt that something was wrong, while Catholics were outraged. There was mob protest in Manchester, and the leaders were subsequently imprisoned at Lancaster. Within the year two separate rebellions had begun, in the north under the Earl of Derwentwater, and in Scotland under the Earl of Mar, in the name of James Edward Stuart. The rebels marched south via Penrith, gaining strength as they went. Many local Catholic gentry came to join the army, particularly in Lancaster, where it arrived, about 1,400 strong, on 7 November 1715. Albert Hodgson from Leighton Hall, John Dalton of Thurnham, and Squire Carus of Halton were among the Catholic gentry who joined here, but there were others, such as Edward Gartside, a barber, and an unnamed joiner, who also threw in their lot with the Jacobites.

Sir Henry Hoghton and Col. Charteris, of Hornby, with about six hundred of the local militia, represented the Hanoverian forces available to resist the Jacobites. After vainly seeking to demolish the bridge over the Lune and to remove the guns from a ship of Robert Lawson lying at Sunderland, they decided to fall back towards Preston. The only positive action was to dump the town's supply of gunpowder in the well in Market Square.

The rebels proclaimed 'James III', James' son (the 'Old Pretender'), at the market cross. They released the Crown prisoners from the Castle, sought money and arms, including the six cannon from Sunderland, and were billeted on the townsfolk. William Stout recorded in his autobiography:

> … it was a time of tryall, and in fear that the Scots and Northern rebells would have plundered us; but they were civil, and to most paid for what they had; but I had five of the Mackintosh officers quartered on me two days, but took nothing of them.

Another source tells how the gentlemen soldiers took tea with the ladies of the town on the second day, all dressed in their best. They left Lancaster on 9 November and within five days had been defeated by government forces at Preston.

William Stout wrote of 1716:

> After the Rebelion at Preston was supressed, about fower hundred of them were brought to Lancaster Castell, and a regiment of dragoons quartred in the town to gard them … [the prisoners] laid in straw in the stables, most of them. And in a month time, about one hundred of them were conveighed to Liverpoole to be tryed, where they were convicted, and near 40 of them hanged at Manchester, Liverpoole, Wiggan, Preston, Garsting, and Lancaster. And

about two hundred of them continued a year, and about 50 of them died, and the rest were transported to America; exept the lords and gentlmen, who were had to London and there convicted and their estates forfeted …

Nine of the Jacobites were executed at Lancaster, four on 18 February 1716 – Hercules Durham, Donald Robertson, John (or Robert) Crow of Aberdeen, one of the Mackintosh clan – and five on 2 October 1716 – Captain John Bruce, [ ] Charnley, George Hodgson, Thomas Shuttleworth, John Winckley. Forty-three who died from other causes are recorded in the parish registers. The sequential death of so many men from the same place and with the same names suggests that comrades-in-arms caught some infection from each other in the unhealthy conditions in which they were held. Of the two hundred prisoners detained beyond the first month, more than one in five died in captivity. A number of deaths of soldiers, who may have been the guard or garrison, and their dependants are also recorded.

The Lancaster Borough Records note merely two items of expenditure (the financial year ran from October to October and payments were authorised at the end of that year):

1716 pay'd to the Militia and for swords and other arms £12.09.07
1717 Expences upon the Soldiers at the Guard house viz in Coals, Turf, Candles & other charges upon yᵉ rebell prisoners £17.12.5 ½.

1745

Thirty years later another army marched south, proclaiming another Pretender, Prince Charles Edward ('Bonnie Prince Charlie'), as regent for his father. This time the army was bigger and more effective (perhaps 6,000 strong), but many things had changed in the intervening years. Few local Catholics joined forces with the Jacobites this time. Recollections as to what had happened to supporters last time, mixed with greater prosperity, fading memories of the Stuarts, and a gradual reduction in tension between religious groups, all led to apathy or caution. But there is no doubt that the Jacobites were a powerful force and modern analysis suggests that had they pursued their goal of London, instead of turning back at Derby, they might well have overturned the crumbling edifice of Hanoverian rule. Even in retreat, when all was against them, they inflicted a number of salutary defeats on the Hanoverian vanguard.

On Sunday 24 November the first of the Jacobite troops arrived in Lancaster: a dozen hussars appeared at 11a.m., some more troops at 12 and a body of 200 Athollmen led by Lord George Murray just after 2p.m. All of these, and later arrivals that day, were billeted on the inns and on the townsfolk. Meanwhile Lord Elcho and about fifty mounted Lifeguards called round by Hornby Castle to check for forage and dined there on the way to Lancaster, just as their predecessors had done thirty years before. Elcho had a particular reason for calling there, since he was David, eldest son of the Earl of Wemyss. Through his mother, Janet Charteris, the family owned Hornby Castle as well as their ancient Scottish estates. He and his men would be very welcome there. He had even become a Freeman of Lancaster by purchase in 1742-3, at a cost of seven guineas. As a result of the failure of the '45, however, Elcho

90 Fred Kirk Shaw's pageant painting of Bonnie Prince Charlie. This appears in the souvenir programme of the 1913 Pageant and shows Prince Charlie arriving outside what is now 76 Church Street, where tradition states he lodged and held a council of his officers. It seems unlikely that the house of recently-deceased prominent lawyer, Oliver Marton, and father of the MP, Edward Marton, would have been put at his disposal, and there were no recriminations afterwards, so this tradition must be resisted.

spent the rest of his life in exile and his younger brother Francis eventually inherited the title of 7th Earl of Wemyss. Elcho's men were described as:

> … all brave men, poorly mounted and in good spirits … They are dressed with two pistols on each side, a musket slung over their shoulder and a broadsword. They have plenty of money, principally French guineas.

A large army, mostly on foot, took a long time to assemble and for much of its march would be strung out along many miles of road. This meant that different elements of it could be billeted on different towns and villages along the way. The rearguard was still in Kendal after most of the vanguard had arrived in Lancaster and a curfew been declared at 9p.m.

One of those who came with the main body of the army on the following morning, John Maclean, described the event in his journal:

> … Monday the 25 all the Calvallry and infantry we had there were turned to a Parade at the Cross, and the Provost and Bailies were Called & the Provost Appeared in his velvet Gown and a Black rod with a Silver head. And upon the Cross they proclaimed the King …

It is often claimed that the Prince stayed at 76 Church Street, until recently the Conservative Club, and that this had also been used as one of the leaders' lodgings during the 1715 rising. It seems an unlikely choice in 1745 since it was the house of Oliver Marton, a successful London lawyer, whose son Edward was MP for Lancaster. Other than a couple of inns, we do not know where the leaders or the soldiers were billeted. The town authorities were mainly hostile to the Jacobites, but some of the citizens were better disposed. However, the army of 1745 was disappointed by the lack of English support as expressed in actual recruitment or in gifts. Most people heard the proclamation of King James in silence, perhaps all too aware of what had happened last time.

On that Monday two doctors became involved with the Jacobites in very different ways. Dr Burton came over from Yorkshire to show his support for the cause, but because of the somewhat farcical circumstances of his arrival he was greeted with suspicion and spent some time trying to find one of the Jacobite leaders who would vouch for his not being a spy. Having achieved this he obtained a pass to return safely to Yorkshire. Dr Henry Bracken of Lancaster really was a spy, inasmuch as he was a Whig supporter and used his previous acquaintance in Paris with Lord Balmerino to find out what the plans and strength of the Jacobites were. Because he had been seen talking with the enemy he had later to prove his innocence of involvement.

On the morning of Tuesday 26 November the main force departed for Preston, the vanguard having already moved on to Garstang. The rearguard under Lord Ogilvy left Burton-in-Kendal and came on through Lancaster. Soon after Dr Bracken revealed his true allegiance and, with an armed posse, was able to pick up a number of stragglers from the army. The Jacobites moved on through Preston and Manchester, where they gathered more recruits, particularly in Manchester, creating a Manchester Regiment. After successfully avoiding the Hanoverian army awaiting them, they arrived in Derby on 4 December. The Prince stated his desire to march on London, but the other leaders overruled him on the basis that there was little evidence of English support, and so the decision was taken to turn back towards Scotland.

The advance guard of returning Jacobites entered Lancaster on Friday 13 December. Dr Bracken made himself scarce, but the army sacked his house and demanded £600 from his wife, who, however, managed to escape through a cellar window. The vicar, Dr Fenton, was also a target of their wrath, and his house was ransacked and threats were made to his wife and servants. The mood was obviously now uglier and more dangerous. The main body entered Lancaster and one of the Manchester Regiment, called Chadwick, defiantly played 'The King shall have his own again' on the organ of the Priory church.

The pursuing Hanoverian cavalry met up with the rearguard at Ellel Moor, a few miles south of Lancaster, but had the worst of the skirmish. However, that night the Jacobite army was on full alert in case the Duke of Cumberland brought his main force up against them. They patrolled the Preston road from a base at a windmill about half a mile from the town, which must have been the one at Scotforth, and also the Hornby road in case General Wade's army in Yorkshire sought them out. The next morning, 14 December, Lord George Murray with O'Sullivan and Donald Cameron of Lochiel investigated several positions south of Lancaster where a stand could be made by the whole army. From the descriptions it seems likely that the slopes of Hala Hill or the ridge of Bailrigg was the place chosen. It might easily, had the Hanoverian troops pushed closer, have become an English Culloden, but it is quite probable the result would have been very different! In the event the leadership decided strategic withdrawal was the best option.

On 14th and 15th the army withdrew from Lancaster in stages, their rear covered by Elcho's Lifeguards, who had to turn and threaten to fight on several occasions as the Hanoverian cavalry began to appear and press them. That, for Lancaster, was the end of the affair, although Dr Bracken was unfairly imprisoned in the Castle until he could prove his innocence of involvement with the Jacobites, and his son Henry, visiting him there, caught the gaol fever then prevailing and died of it in May 1746.

During the retreat to Scotland the Jacobite Manchester Regiment was left behind at Carlisle to garrison the Castle. They surrendered to the Duke of Cumberland in the face of overwhelming odds before the end of December and many of them, it would seem, were sent to Lancaster Castle as prisoners. Once again fever, as well as inadequate food, decimated the prisoners. Some sources indicate 80 prisoners died as a result. The parish registers do not show so many, and it is also more difficult to distinguish the rebel prisoners from others, since all have English names. In addition, many soldiers, including an Irishman, and their dependants are listed, presumably because fever would spread readily to the guards. These burials are shown in the parish registers for 1745-6. There are occasional soldiers or prisoners before 1745, but these 18 soldiers (or their relatives) and 11 prisoners represent an anomaly: *either* they indicate a general gaol fever affecting both garrison and prisoners in the Castle, *or* the prisoners were from the Jacobite army and the soldiers were their guard. Bearing in mind the large number of insurgents who died in Lancaster Castle in 1716, this could be a repetition of events, only among English adherents of Prince Charles.

Again, the Borough Records only refer in passing to the great events which had taken place. The Bailiffs' Accounts give:

> 1746   Allowed them several incidents occasioned by the Rebellion £49.12.09 ½
> Allowed them for the charges of raising and subsisting the militia £17.10.00
>
> 1747   Allowed them paid to John Troughton and Thomas Cartmell for two horses lost in assisting the King's forces at the late Rebellion £4.00.00

So ended the last armed invasion of Lancaster, at least so far!

Nine

Priory and Castle

The reason for Lancaster's existence is the long, whale-backed hill lying immediately to the south of the lowest bridging point of the navigable river Lune. This hill, known rather ambiguously as Castle Hill (the address of Castle Hill now refers to one small part of it), attracted Roman military engineers as the site for a fort. Roman civilian settlement, medieval town and modern city all followed. The site's continued use is probably the result of two factors: firstly its continuing strategic importance, the second being locational inertia. The fact of the Roman fort being built here led the medieval castle-builders to utilise its surviving earthworks and recycle its stonework; the fact of the medieval Castle being here accounts for continued investment in both courts and prison, long after any strategic benefits had been nullified by modern armaments.

The location of the Priory church adjacent to the Castle might be seen as a typically Norman pairing, the lord's castle and lord's church standing side by side. However, it is clear that there was a church or monastery on this site at least as far back as the eighth or ninth century given the large number of fragments of stone crosses found in the vicinity or built into the fabric. Equally, a significant number of small Anglo-Saxon coins has been found close by, including a small hoard. Both are powerful evidence of a well-connected church or monastery, probably the latter. Documentary evidence for that period is altogether lacking for the north west, in contrast to the Northumbrian heartlands; this area was on the borders of the warring kingdoms of Northumbria and Mercia and probably fell to whichever was the stronger at the time. Indeed, Lancaster may owe the foundation of its church to apostolic work in Northumbria in the seventh century, but at present that is beyond proof.

Some have sought to take the connection back to Roman times, but the location and orientation of the church within the plan of the Roman fort is reminiscent of the setting of other monasteries and churches within the ruins of forts in the post-Roman period, as for instance, in the Roman forts of the Saxon Shore around the south and east coasts of Britain. There may well have been a feeling among Anglo-Saxon land-owners that the Christian church was the legitimate descendant of the Roman Empire, and so an appropriate occupant of former Roman sites, but the sites, in the gift of local landowners, were no longer occupied by them. As surplus land, as spaces protected by earthworks, and as ready quarries for stone, they would appeal to both donor and recipient. The origin of Castle and Priory is probably the combination of a local Anglo-Saxon chieftain's hall with a church, both set within the decaying walls of the late-Roman fort. This had been rebuilt in the latest defensive style, probably in the 330s or 340s A.D., incorporating high and thick stone walls and strongly defended corners protected by angle-bastions carrying artillery. The earlier doctrine of Roman

91 Reconstruction of a seventh-century chieftain's house and church in the ruins of the Roman fort, by David Vale. By the seventh century the site of the late Roman fort, ruined but with much of the outer wall still standing, may have served both secular and ecclesiastical purposes. This pattern is reflected today by the presence of both Castle and Priory church.

forts as relatively lightly-built centres for defence-through-attack had been quite abandoned. What resulted was something like the traditional medieval castle, albeit lacking a main tower or keep. Such walls had the potential to survive several centuries. That they did is evidenced by the use of one of the fort walls as a boundary marker as late as 1094 A.D. perhaps. We must therefore envisage a range of early timber-and-thatch domestic buildings sharing the space in the eighth century within the crumbling but still massive walls with a church of either timber or of reused Roman stone. This relationship survived the gradual decay and robbing of the walls, which still form an invisible *cordon sanitaire* around the Priory and Castle. Oddly, though, the Priory church maintains an orientation owing more to the internal roadway of the older Roman fort than that of the fourth century A.D. Perhaps some of the old buildings had been retained and their ruins or, more probably, the roadway that they fronted acted as a geographical constraint.

The Priory Church
We do not know what the pre-Norman church looked like. If it lay on the same site and orientation as later versions, as seems likely, its plan may never be revealed. In 1911 the floor of the present chancel was sealed by a thick layer of bitumen in order to stabilise it and to counteract the effects of centuries of burials in vaults within the building, which had caused the interior to slump into the myriad cavities. The nave and chancel had been deeply concreted in 1860. If any trace of the pre-Norman building survived the grave-cuts, then the consolidation work may well have put them

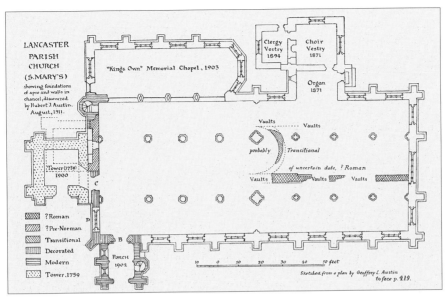

92   Hubert Austin's plan of discoveries in the Priory church, 1911. Of most note are the fragments of the apse, which should be Norman, and the long wall extending east from it, which may represent the extension of the late 13th century.

beyond reach. The earliest evidence which Hubert Austin, architect of the 1911 work, found was fragments of an apse underlying the present choir. He believed this to be Roman, but it is much more likely to belong to the first Norman church, perhaps the first stone church. At the west end is a rough wall containing a disused doorway with a 'Caernarvon arch' lintel. This is often claimed to be 'Saxon' without any supporting evidence other than the crudeness of the wall and arch. It is much more likely to represent the Norman west wall. This would give us a narrow aisleless rectangular church about 90 feet long with an apsidal east end and, perhaps at this stage, no tower. The church may already have been monastic, but what is certain is that in 1094 the new Norman lord, Roger de Poitou, gave the church to the abbey of Seez in Normandy, and thereafter for some three centuries it acted as a so-called 'alien priory'. These alien priories were common in the early days of the Conquest. Norman lords who had come over with William I became concerned as they aged about the health of their souls. Many gave existing English monasteries to the abbeys of their home district in Normandy or wherever they came from. These alien priories were usually too small to maintain proper canonical hours and have much of a common life, and they tended to be regarded as local rent-gathering centres for the Norman abbeys. Lancaster produced a rental of 50 marks for the mother house of Seez. In time this became a thorn in the flesh of English kings, who saw English resources heading off to France to support, as they reasoned, a hostile regime.

In small alien priories it was not uncommon for the conventual buildings, where the monks would sleep, eat, entertain guests and store produce, to be to the north,

93 Reconstruction of the Priory in the 12th century by David Vale. The east end terminates in an apse, and the buildings housing the few Benedictine monks lie to the north, rather than the south, of the church, quite common in alien priories.

rather than the south, of the church, and to be rather less conventionally organised than those in the larger abbeys. It is very likely that at Lancaster the buildings lay to the north, and were not much altered in three hundred years. The north wall of the nave, which survived until the building of the King's Own Memorial Chapel in 1903, seems to have been the original Norman north wall, against which the conventual buildings stood. At all events it was found to contain many pieces of Anglo-Saxon sculpture, which was wholly absent among the newly quarried 15th-century stone-work of the south side. The conventual buildings may have acted as a boundary, so that all subsequent expansion had to be to the south. A further deep wall foundation, discovered by Hubert Austin, running east-west beyond the apse, may represent the eastwards extension of the original church in the late 12th or 13th century. In 1281 Archbishop Wickwayne of York put off for two years the consecration of a 30-foot extension to the east, presumably because it was not finished. The wall foundations could represent this, although Austin thought they ran too far.

By the 14th century a south aisle seems to have existed. The south-west corner of that period, including an earlier but perhaps reset south door, a Decorated doorway now leading into the tower but blocked and covered in plaster until 1899, and a porch replaced only in 1902, appear to have survived the massive building campaign which followed in the 15th century, when the Priory was dissolved and became a parish church. The other significant feature of the mid–14th century is the set of flamboyant choir-stalls which is the glory of the Priory today. These stalls, with flowing Gothic tracery above and a series of carved misericords below, have had a very chequered life, being moved around the church as fashions changed. Despite stories that they were brought from Furness or Cockersand abbeys at the Dissolution, there seems no reason to doubt that they have always been at Lancaster. The only odd feature is the number and quality of stalls, disproportionate to the small number of monks and the relatively low status of the monastery. A list dated 1374 shows that the Prior was responsible for serving churches and chapels at Poulton-le-Fylde, Bispham, Stalmine, Caton and Gressingham, as well as the Priory. All the others apart from the Priory were farmed out to other clerics, who made what living they could from the difference between what they paid and what they received. The Prior himself was accompanied by five monks, two chaplains, two clerks and a domestic servant. There does not seem to have been any larger establishment earlier.

When alien priories were dissolved links with Seez were severed, and in 1414 Henry V gave the revenues of Lancaster to his newly founded Bridgettine nunnery of Syon in Middlesex; later he gave them the Priory itself, after the death of the last Prior. The nuns had to wait until 1428 to gain possession of the buildings, but in 1430 the church became a parish church and so it has continued to the present day. The nuns continued to own estates around Lancaster until the Dissolution, and may be remembered in 'Ladies' Walk', near the river above Skerton Bridge.

Associated with these changes was an ambitious programme of rebuilding, which has resulted in the removal of most traces of the original monastic function, apart from the south doorway of c.1200 and the west wall. The church we see today, with integral aisles and consisting of four bays to the nave and four bays to the chancel, is mostly a creation of the 15th century, beginning in the west and working eastwards. The exterior is mostly constructed of very large blocks of newly quarried sandstone, contrasting with the rubble walling of the older parts and the interior of the nave, which were not intended to be seen and were probably always lime-washed. When it was completed the new interior must have seemed exceptionally tall, light and airy, with its lofty arcades and clerestorey. It took later generations to fill the large windows with stained glass and the interior with pews. The building programme seems to have run from about 1430 until 1479.

In the later Middle Ages fear of Purgatory led many rich people to found chantries, private chapels within churches and friaries where priests prayed for the souls of the founder and his family. The Priory church had several, partitioned off from the body of the church by timber or stone screens. Two were set up in 1472 by John Gardyner of Bailrigg in the south aisle of the chancel at the altar of St Thomas à Becket; there may have been two more dedicated to St Patrick and St Loye in the matching north aisle. John Gardyner's chantry priests also ran the Grammar School in the churchyard and the small almshouse known as Gardyner's Chantry at the foot of the church steps. The inmates of the almshouse would also have been expected to pray for John Gardyner's soul at his tomb.

Medieval parishes in the north of England were often very extensive, with many townships contributing towards one large church. Lancaster Priory served a huge

94 Reconstruction by David Vale of the Priory church in the late 15th century. Work is just coming to an end on the north-eastern corner, probably the last part to be rebuilt. The remains of the conventual buildings to the north will shortly be removed.

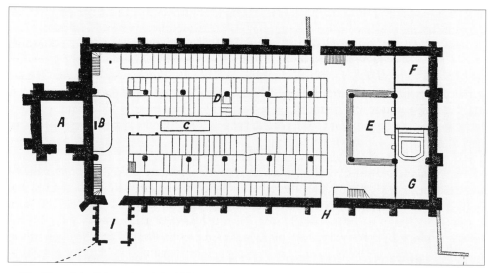

95 Plan of the Priory church in 1819. North is at the top. The interior can be seen filled with box pews, pride of place among which went to 'Noah's Ark', the great pew marked 'C' occupying the centre of the nave just below the pulpit (D). The focus of the whole church at this time was upon preaching, the altar (E) being relatively unimportant. At the east end the medieval choirstalls were used to screen off a vestry and consistory court (F) and (G), where wills were proved.

parish mainly centred on the lower Lune valley but with detached portions as far away as Toxteth Park, some fifty miles from Lancaster. In consequence it had no fewer than 24 churchwardens or vestrymen, known as the 'the 24^{tie}' or 'the Four-and-Twenty'. These comprised five plus the current Mayor for Lancaster itself, two each for Scotforth, Skerton and Wyresdale, and one each for Aldcliffe, Poulton, Stodday, Bare, Middleton, Quernmore, Torrisholme, Ashton, Thurnham, Bulk, Heaton and Overton. The vicar had six curates to assist him.

In 1743 the parish agreed to buy a new peal of bells from Abel Rudhall of Gloucester. In order to make their sound travel further, the churchwardens unwisely decided to have the tower itself raised 'ten yards higher'. Within a very short time the tower started to collapse under the unaccustomed strain. It was necessary to take it down and rebuild it completely to the designs of Henry Sephton of Liverpool, which was done by 1756. The new tower still stands and is a very fine complement to the church. Its predecessor was not attached to the church but stood a few yards apart, with a charnel house in between. There were stored the bones dug up in the church-yard when new graves were made.

Although the exterior of the church has remained relatively undisturbed since the 15th century, the interior has seen many changes. The medieval church probably had few seats in the nave; most of the congregation would stand. The high altar was enclosed by a rood screen and out of sight of much of the congregation, just as much of the mass, being in Latin, would pass them by. After the Reformation, use of the vernacular for services, and later the Authorised Version of the Bible and the new Prayer Book, led to a concentration on 'the Word' instead of upon ritual. Emphasis was placed upon the congregation seeing and hearing, and the church interior began to resemble a theatre, with seating focused upon the pulpit. By the 18th century the interior had filled up with box-pews and with galleries to increase the space.

In 1724 it was resolved to build an additional gallery at the west end and to provide in it a convenient number of seats for the west gallery singers, whose stock in trade would have been the Metrical Psalms and contrapuntal versions of the hymns, perhaps accompanied by fiddles and bassoons. In Lancaster this tradition was stifled more quickly than in the countryside. Within a few years an organ had been installed and charity children replaced the singers. Later both organ and choir, now robed, were moved forward into full view of the congregation, representing the victory of polite values over the cruder, popular traditions of the 18th century.

One of the pews was very large and occupied a prime place in the centre of the church, right in front of the pulpit. It was known as 'Noah's Ark', and after it was moved into the chancel in 1824 the owners sought recompense for their loss of amenity. Seats in pews and galleries were private property and could be bought and sold. The Corporation had its own pews and its members usually attended church in full regalia. A good description of the church by Rev. Benjamin Newton survives from August 1818:

> We were shewn into the Duke of Hamilton's seat by the desire of the landlord of the inn. The prayers were read very well by another gentleman, five banns were published, there is a very good organ with a most delightful flute stop, two voluntaries were played and the psalms sung. The Mayor's Mace was hung at his seat door the opposite side the aisle to which

96 Engraving of the Priory church looking east as it was in the 1840s. The pulpit with its crown, the side galleries and the box pews running right through into the chancel can be seen. The east window is at this date of clear glass. From a lithograph by F.S. and R.K. Thomas.

97 The medieval choirstalls. These flamboyant 14th-century stalls are unexpected in the sober setting of the Priory church. Their history is chequered, having been moved around to numerous different positions. The wonder is that they survive at all. The splendid needlework was carried out by local women to designs by Guy Barton.

we sat and it was a very superb and handsome one, two smaller ones were carried in front of him, then two serjeants, then the Great Mace, then the Mayor and one other Alderman without gowns, which surprised me. The Church is a very light Gothic building and all the pews were occupied promiscuously and the poorer sort seemed to have the seats nearer the reading desk and pulpit, the genteel people were mostly in the galleries and excepting the Duke of Hamilton's where we sat I saw no people of condition near the pulpit.

In 1827 a new vestry and registry was built onto the north side of the church, which enabled the eastern bays of the chancel and its aisles to be thrown into the body of the church. Hitherto the east end had been divided into a series of small spaces, the chantry chapels of the 15th century being replaced after the reign of Edward VI by a vestry and a consistory court, in which church courts were held and wills proved. The splendid medieval choirstalls were now used as a screen across the east end. In the Victorian spirit of recreating something of the ritual and feeling of the medieval

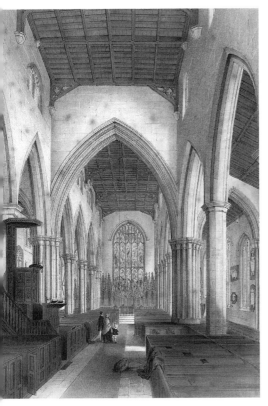

98 Engraving of the Priory church looking east in about 1864. The box pews remain but the galleries have gone and the pulpit has been cut down. The east window is now filled with stained glass. From a lithograph by E.H. Buckler.

99 Engraving of the Priory church after 1864 and the fitting of the new oak pews. Compared with the earlier views the church is very much less cluttered. The moving of the choirstalls back to either side of the chancel was to reduce this open appearance. From a lithograph published by Thomas Edmondson.

church, a large-scale rearrangement took place in 1864: the old box-pews were removed and replaced by oak benches; the pulpit was moved up the nave and the difference between nave and choir once more asserted; the rich medieval choirstalls were once more moved, this time to approximately their original positions; chapels were recreated in the ends of the aisles, again in imitation of the former chantry chapels. More work took place at the end of the century.

In 1886 a new peal of eight bells was installed to replace the somewhat motley collection which then existed. In 1879 John Gardner of the Greaves had left £1,000 to St Peter's Catholic church for a peal of eight bells, which were subsequently cast by Warners of London. The Priory authorities became dissatisfied by the quality of their own bells but the vicar, Dr Allen, refused to put their replacement out to public subscription. Instead, in a letter to his parishioners in 1884 he wrote,

It would be a nobler thing for some wealthy citizen of Lancaster to devote £1000 of his money to providing a really fine peal of bells and clock for the tower of one of our most venerable Parish Churches …

As he must have intended, the multi-millionaire Anglican James Williamson, MP for the town, rose to the bait, and obliged. A magnificent heavy peal of bells to outdo the Catholics was ordered from Taylors of Loughborough in 1885, and still does duty today.

A new porch was added in memory of James and Emily Langshaw in 1903, and the same year saw the building on the north side of the King's Own Memorial Chapel, commemorating those of the local regiment who died in the South African War. In the early 1920s there was considerable pressure to make Lancaster the seat of a new bishopric for Lancashire, and the Priory its cathedral. Eventually the decision went in favour of Blackburn, which gained considerably from the move, and saw its parish church ennobled and extended. It is interesting to conjecture what such a move might have done for Lancaster. In 1992-3 considerable improvements took place, including the lowering of the altar, stripping of plaster from the chancel and replastering of the nave. The whole church was scaffolded, enabling details such as old roof bosses to be seen at first hand. This revealed yet more evidence of the building's history.

Other Churches and Chapels
Although it is the oldest and most important church in Lancaster, the Priory church is not the only one. In the 17th century a number of sects grew up which were at odds with the established church for one reason or another. Not all were in a position to build their own meeting houses or chapels, and a number met in private houses. The Anglican church also provided for the growing population with two new churches in the 18th century and a further series in the new suburbs in the 19th century. The Methodists arose in the 18th century, and at the end of the 18th century the Catholics, who had until then worshipped in degrees of secrecy, were at last permitted to worship publicly, leading first to the building of a chapel, then of a church which became the Cathedral. Two notable late 20th-century additions have reflected the post-war ethnic mix: a mosque in the former Friends' Hall and a Polish Catholic church in the former Nelson Street chapel.

Of these the earliest was the Friends' or Quakers' Meeting House, built in 1677 in what was then open country to the west of the town centre. This was rebuilt in 1708 and again extended in 1779 and 1789-90, mirroring the success and growth of the Friends, who moved from persecuted renegades to respected members of the community in a couple of generations. The Presbyterians had their chapel in St Nicholas Street from the 17th century; it was rebuilt in 1786 but demolished in the 1970s to create a new shopping centre.

New churches in the 18th century included St John's on the Green Ayre in 1755 and then St Anne's in Moor Lane in 1796, now the Duke's Theatre, the latter originally for the 'Enthusiastic' wing of the Anglican Church under Rev. Housman. The Congregationalists, or Independents as they were then known, built their first chapel in High Street in 1774 and later the Centenary Chapel in Stonewell. The Methodists built a simple chapel in Sulyard Street in 1806 and replaced it with a much fancier structure in 1874. The Catholics worshipped first in secrecy in a number of dispersed mass centres such as Dolphinlee, an isolated farmhouse high on the Ridge, but by the 18th century a degree more tolerance and the support of the influential Gillow family allowed them to use an unofficial chapel in Mason Street, where the Gillows had their workshops. In 1797-8 they were able to build a chapel in Dalton Square, now Palatine Hall, and later, in 1857-9, St Peter's Church in East Road, which was to become the Cathedral. The Baptists acquired a large new chapel in Nelson Street in 1894-7.

The Anglicans built several more churches in the town during the 19th century,

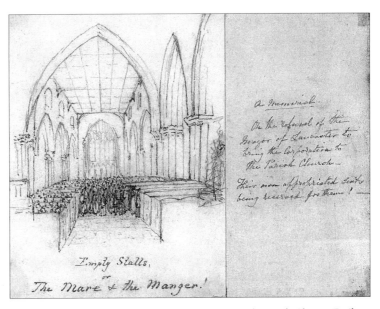

100 'Empty Stalls or The Mare and the Manger' by Emily Sharpe. Emily was the sister of Edmund Sharpe and a number of her sketchbooks survive to show that she had a considerable artistic talent. This sketch, dating from 1836, records the refusal of the Mayor to bring the Corporation to the Priory church and use their allotted pews, while dozens of citizens had to stand.

not only to serve the growing population, but also to cater for the many shades of worship from High to Low. First was St Thomas' in Penny Street, dating from 1839-40 and in a new spiky Gothic style which marked the arrival of Edmund Sharpe. Its tower and spire came a little later. Christ Church, on Wyresdale Road, was the gift of the Liberal MP Samuel Gregson, and intended to serve the new Freehold Estate as well as the Grammar School and Workhouse. Its twin western spires are very distinctive and, from certain angles, aligned with the dome of the Ashton Memorial, create a vision of Agia Sophia in Constantinople! St Luke's Church, Skerton emerged in 1833 while Scotforth had to wait until 1874 for its church (St Paul). Many local churches were either designed or extended by the notable Lancaster architectural practice begun by Edmund Sharpe and continued by E. G. Paley, H. J. Austin and H. A. Paley.

Lacking, with a few exceptions, the funding and the big backers of the Anglicans, other denominations struggled to extend their reach into the new suburbs. The Wesleyans, with the support of Sir Norval Helme, built two beautiful Art Nouveau-inspired churches on the Greaves and in Skerton in 1909 and 1910 respectively. Sad to say the latter has been demolished and replaced by a perhaps more convenient but certainly less attractive building. The Catholic effort focused on the St Peter's site with its ancillary buildings, but the backing of the wealthy Coulston family enabled the building of a new church, St Joseph's, in Skerton in 1900.

During the 20th century the fissile nature of the noncomformist sects has been marked by an excess of chapels built to accommodate breakaway elements, which

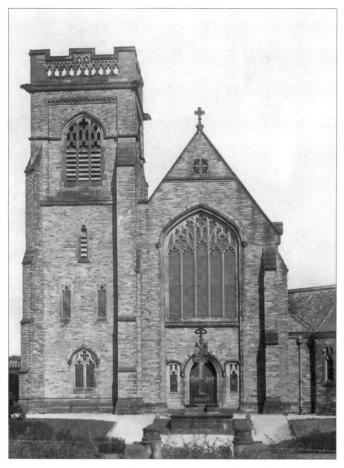

101 St Joseph's Catholic church, Skerton. The church was built to serve the growing Catholic population of Skerton by the wealthy Coulston family. The nearby school stands on the site of their former tannery.

have tended to become surplus to requirements. Many have adapted to secular use, a tendency which the Anglicans have followed. St John's and St Anne's have both become redundant and now have other uses. Luckily the design of both, from the preaching age of the Georgian church, is such that they lend themselves to public functions without too much intervention in the historic fabric.

The Castle
The early form of the Castle, like its neighbour the Priory church, remains an enigma. Its earliest stone phase dates from the mid-12th century, but there must be some seventy years of its history before that to account for. We must use a combination of two things to assess what it may have looked like. One of these is our knowledge of how the Normans dealt with similar defensive issues elsewhere. The other is the possibility of an earthwork phase fossilised in the later stone defences. While examples of demolition and wholly new construction are known, there is a presumption against unnecessary rebuilding or re-alignment, simply on the basis of cost, so early features can exert a powerful influence on later structures.

The Normans would have been presented with an urgent need to defend this site. They were after all an embattled and hated minority within a hostile land. The pre-Norman head of this particular manor was based at Halton, according to Domesday Book. Halton has a small earthwork castle, probably of immediately post-Conquest date, but so have a number of villages in the Lune valley – Hornby, Melling, Arkholme, Whittington and Kirkby Lonsdale. The purpose and significance of these, one of the densest distributions of castles outside the Welsh Border, is still not understood. Lancaster must have been an important military site in late-Saxon England. It seems most unlikely then that it was not provided with an early Norman castle. Roger de Poitou, who founded the Priory, would have found a number of material advantages to hand.

102 Reconstruction by David Vale of the Castle in Norman times. In this reconstruction the assumption has been made that it was a motte-and-bailey castle to start with. It could equally have begun as a ring-work.

There was the naturally defensive Castle Hill, for example, and the ruins of the late-Roman fort, which could afford both a degree of protection within its crumbling walls and a quarry for stone. The stone may have been least important in the early phase, as earthworks and timber revetments could be built more quickly with unskilled labour. The Normans probably used a mixture of elements of the fort walls, temporarily strengthened, and earthworks topped by timber stockades to reduce the defensive circuit to manageable proportions. If any gates or towers survived from the Roman fort – and their massive structures would give them a higher chance of survival – they would either have to be incorporated into the circuit or demolished to deny them to an enemy.

The earliest surviving plan of Lancaster Castle shows a sub-circular layout with anomalies such as the site of the medieval hall, flanked by 13th-century round towers, or the 12th-century Lungess Tower, which was orientated diagonally to the earliest stone curtain wall. The Lungess Tower, or Keep, could be an addition to an earlier circuit or could replace a motte, the earthen mount capped with a timber tower which provided both private rooms and a final retreat if all else failed. In the 1790s, when the Crown Court was being built, labourers levelled a 'high bank of earth' just to the west of the Lungess Tower, perhaps the flattened remains of a motte. On the other hand, a perfectly good model for an early Norman castle would be a ringwork, a more-or-less circular bank and ditch with a timber stockade, any important building being incorporated within the gatehouse, which assumed an enhanced strategic significance.

Whatever the earliest form of the Castle, its growth thereafter appears fairly straightforward. In the mid-12th century the Lungess Tower was built, either by

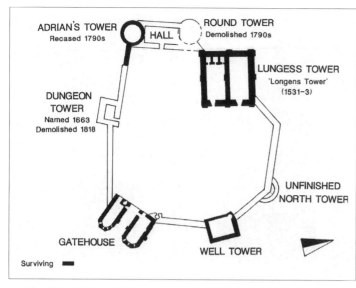

Plan of the Castle prior to 1788, with the names of towers. (P. Lee)

103

Stephen of Blois or Henry, son of King David of Scotland, who was Lord of Lancaster from 1139-53. In the confusion of the Anarchy, parts of north-west England reverted to Scotland. The bailey, containing timber domestic buildings, would have been surrounded by an earthen bank and a stockade broken only by a powerful timber gatehouse.

In 1199 the Castle was besieged by Hubert de Burgh. Some nine years later a writ instructed Ranulf, Earl of Chester, Robert de Gresley and others to cut ditches and repair ramparts, and these ditches, or moat, were to remain a significant feature of the townscape until it was demilitarised in the 17th century. Even then part of the southern moat was retained for a long time as a source of static water. In 1202-3 the Pipe Rolls record expenditure on 'repairs to the King's lodgings in the castle of Lancaster and on repairs to the tower'. Further work under John, first as Earl of Mortain and then as King, cost the enormous sum of £630 between 1193 and 1215. No doubt this was sufficient to build at least some of the stone curtain wall, the great hall and some of the round towers. Of these only Adrian's Tower survives today, and that is greatly altered.

It appears that the Castle was substantially garrisoned at this time of civil strife. Eighty live cows and 130 sheep were brought into the Castle in 1215, perhaps to be slaughtered as required. In the meantime they had to be accommodated in sheds and pens in the bailey. The Pipe Rolls for the same period show the purchase for £40 of 240 quarters of wheat for the provisioning of the Castle:

> et pro cc et xl quarteris frumenti emptis ad warnisturam castri de L xl li.

In 1243-4 £128 was spent on the gate, bridges and stockade (the curtain wall was still incomplete), and in 1254 work on the curtain wall and the gateway cost £257. By now the Castle consisted of the Lungess Tower and a stone curtain wall pierced by a gateway flanked by two round towers (a 13th-century stair turret is still to be seen at the north-west corner of the present 15th-century gatehouse). Further towers, between three and five in number, punctuated the curtain wall. Of these two, Adrian's Tower and another round tower demolished in the 18th century stood on either side of the Hall and lodgings on the west side of the Castle, adjacent to the Keep. Another round tower, described in 1476 as '... a Towre begonne of old tyme on the north part of the castell and ... not passing x fete above grownde ...', stood on the northern curtain on one of its sharp changes of alignment, which were capable of being undermined if not protected by towers. Clearly, this 13th-century phase was left incomplete, so we can only conjecture whether other round towers stood where they would make military sense, on the sites of the later Dungeon Tower and Well Tower.

In the late 13th and 14th centuries little work was recorded by expenditure, although internal buildings may have been constructed from some of the 260 oaks from Quernmore Forest provided in 1377. The building of the square Dungeon and Well Towers in this period seems to have gone unrecorded. While the Dungeon Tower was demolished in the early 19th century, the Well Tower remains. Both seem to have been built as lodging towers, that is, provided with domestic accommodation, perhaps for important visitors and their retinues. Windows are larger and more decorative than before, and fitted with seats. Fireplaces and domestic layout, with plentiful timber in floors and ceilings, mark them out from the older, more spartan tower layout.

The last feature to be added to the medieval Castle was the great gatehouse which still stands today, dominating the approach from the south-east. Although often called 'John O'Gaunt's Gate', this is clearly work of the early 15th century, dating from after the Duke's death

104 Interior of the Well Tower, showing a window seat. The tower was fitted out as lodgings to accommodate an entourage, as was the so-called Dungeon Tower. The standard is domestic, rather than purely military, although from the outside the difference was not apparent.

and carried on by his son and grandson, Henry IV and Henry V. The Duchy's Receiver was instructed to spend £133 annually on the Castle, and over twenty years some £2,500 was spent but it is not clear how. The gatehouse was massive and modern, fulfilling many of the functions formerly expected of the Keep. It was very much in keeping with the seignorial ideas of the time, borrowed from France by great magnates who fought there, that building a massive tower onto an existing castle indicated status and power. By the end of the century such towers were commonplace, famously at Raglan, Caister or at Tattershall, but locally at Hornby and at Greenhalgh Castle near Garstang. It is not surprising that kings of England were early exponents of this trend.

105   The great Gatehouse of the Castle. Like the 'prodigy towers' of many other castles inspired by French examples, this early 15th-century mass of building was intended to express the status and raw power of its owner, in this case the Crown.

After the building work of the 15th century little other than minor repair was done for over three hundred years. In 1562 the Lord Treasurer of the Duchy described the Castle as '… a greate strengeth to the Cuntrey and a succor to the Quene's Justices and officers …'. To assist Duchy deliberations on their far-flung responsibilities, the Chancellor had drawings made of many of the castles and mansions in the north. That of Lancaster Castle is the earliest surviving image of it.

Royal Commissions might look at the state of the Castle during the reign of Elizabeth, such as the survey of 1577-8, but there is no indication that anything followed from these. Steady decay was to be its fate, with a few interventions. Because it was used by the judges of the Northern Circuit and because it was a receiving centre for rents for the Duchy of Lancaster, certain elements of accommodation were probably maintained, but militarily it was left to rot. It may have been fear of Spanish invasion which led to some work on the Lungess Tower, as an inscription dated 1585 survives below the battlements, or it may have been a late response to the Royal Commission, prompted by complaints from the judges, who sat and lodged here.

LANCASTER CASTLE in LANCASHIRE.
*Built by EDWARD the third, is together with Seven other Castles taken from Draughts now remaining among
the Records of the Dutchy of Lancaster (by the Permission of the most Noble JOHN Duke of RUTLAND,
Chancellor of the Dutchy) Copied and Engrav'd at the Expence of the Society of Antiquaries, London, 1734.*

106 Vertue's engraving after the 1562 drawing of Lancaster Castle. The Duchy Council had drawings
made of a number of its far-flung possessions in 1562. These included Lancaster. In 1734 the Society
of Antiquaries had a series of old images engraved by George Vertue to make them more accessible.
The view is quite recognisable, even if the perspective of the Castle is a bit wrong and the Priory
church looks Italianate!

Carlisle Castle was extensively adapted for and against gunnery but Lancaster remained essentially medieval in its defences.

In the Civil War it served as a useful stronghold for both sides, and neither could
muster sufficient troops for long enough to take it by siege. It is likely that rampart and
ditch outworks were added to keep gunnery at a distance, and they seem to be referred
to in an order to 'disgarrison and slight the new works' in 1647. A sequence of orders
followed the refusal of the governor to demolish the Castle fabric, which were intended to render the Castle untenable and demolish all those parts not used as a gaol.
The deputy governor must eventually have seen to the demolition of much of the old
curtain wall by 1651.

By 1664 plans were afoot to remilitarise the Castle, which would have cost nearly
£2,000. This was not done, but some alternative and lower walling was certainly built
between the mural towers before the 18th-century improvements, as can be seen from
S. and N. Buck's engraving of the Castle in 1727 and in their north-east prospect. Only
one short stretch of original curtain wall survives, on the south side, adjacent to
Adrian's Tower.

In the late 1670s responsibility for the gaol and Shire Hall in the Castle passed
from the Duchy of Lancaster to the county authorities. No really significant effort was

107 Watercolour by Thomas Hearne showing the rear of the Castle. Hearne's visit to Lancaster in 1778 caught the Castle on the eve of great changes. Within twenty years it would be converted into modern courts and gaol. This view shows the then-exposed side of the Lungess Tower (Keep) and the back of the second round tower which matched Adrian's Tower. The wet moat on this side of the Castle can also be seen to the right.

made until 1788, despite various proposals put to the county authorities some ten years earlier, by which time the Castle was seriously decayed, with missing roofs on the lodging towers and on half the Keep. Eighty-seven prisoners were held here in 1774 but numbers grew, and, as well as felons of both sexes, lunatics were held here until the building of the County Asylum on the Moor in 1816. More significantly there were a large number of debtors held for as little as £2. There could be several hundred here at any one time. The immediate spur to work on the Castle was a serious outbreak of gaol fever in 1783; work continued until 1823 and cost, it is estimated, about £140,000. In the early days the work was overseen by Thomas Harrison, but gradually relations between him and the county authorities worsened and he moved on to Chester to effect improvements to the castle there. His work had been understudied by Joseph Gandy, who took over and finished off much of the work, acting as architect until at least 1819.

The new work included an integral Governor's House on the east side, near the gatehouse, the Shire Hall, which extended the western side beyond the old defences, and a new Crown Court inside the former Hall area. Both Shire Hall and Crown Court were immediately recognised as being of the very highest standard. The Shire Hall, in particular, being half of a 14-sided figure in plan, with details in the Gothick

108 Watercolour by Robert Freebairn showing the Shire Hall. Freebairn's series of views were painted by around 1801 and presented to George III. They show the first phase of work – Shire Hall, Crown Court, Governor's House and Male Felons' side – more or less complete.

style, became a focus for visitors. Next to the Keep and the Crown Court another circular tower-like structure was built to match Adrian's Tower, containing the Grand Jury Room. This tower also gave access to the temporary scaffold on which executions took place from 1800.

The work also involved the demolition of the whole northern side of the medieval Castle and a new extension to incorporate two sleeping towers for male felons, with associated workshops and integral wedge-shaped yards for exercise, centred on a 'panopticon' or watch-room. Most of the work was carried out in stone, to increase security and avoid the risk of fire. All of this work took until about 1815. Subsequently a new arcade was constructed for debtors around the base of the Lungess Tower. Last of all the old Dungeon Tower was demolished in 1818 and accommodation for female felons, mostly in single cells, provided here by 1823. Towards the end of the work a new statue of John O'Gaunt was set over the main gate, carved by Claude Nimmo, a stonemason.

Millicent Bant came here in 1804 and saw the new arrangements:

> … paid a visit to the Castle – the principal Gateway & two or three towers are the only original parts remaining, it is now dedicated to the purpose of a prison for Debtors & Felons kept in the nicest order – they have restor'd the Delapidated parts to its original spendour

> & made considerable additions in the true Gothick stile, the Courts of justice are very fine
> & make part of the Building, The Felons are admitted through a frightful Trap Door to the
> Bar, a subterranean pasage leads from their Cells to the Court of Justice …

Dr Spiker, librarian to the King of Prussia, who came here in 1816, took a great interest in conditions:

> We ascend by stone stairs to two large sleeping apartments in this tower. From their height we
> may conceive the great elevation of the tower itself. From the thronged state of the prison,
> instead of only sixteen or seventeen persons, which these rooms were originally intended to
> contain, twenty-six persons now slept in them, which is calculated to render the atmosphere
> of the rooms very unwholesome. From the top of the tower we looked down into the court
> of the prison, and were enabled to form a distinct idea of its internal arrangement. Each tower
> has its own peculiar division of the court in front of it, enclosed by a wall, in which the
> prisoners may walk at stated times, without having any communication with the prisoner of
> the other towers. The ground in these divisions is flagged, that it may always be kept clean, and
> a well supplies the prisoners with water during their walk. The two towers next to Adrian's
> tower, contain forty cells each; and a new one, which will contain room for 120 women, was
> building, for the which, alas, the beautiful Gothic tower beside it was to be demolished! The
> number of persons confined in the different receptacles was considerable, even for a county of
> the extent of Lancaster; there at this time 197 male and 53 female criminals, and 150 debtors,
> amounting in all to 400 persons. Of the former, 34 men and 11 women were sentenced to
> transportation, and on 17 no sentence had yet been passed.

Since the 1820s relatively little has been added or subtracted, although uses have changed immeasurably. A new galleried wing in the north-west corner, on the Pentonville principle, known as the 'Porridge Wing', is almost the only concession to standard prison architecture. It was added in the 1840s. Other additions were concerned with punishment (a treadwheel), execution (alterations for private hangings inside the Castle precinct after 1865) and dependants (a hall for prisoners' visitors).

The prison function continued throughout the 19th century, and numbers reached a peak in 1841-2, with some 350 crown prisoners and about half as many debtors. The 'Small Debts' Act of 1844 effectively changed the position of the latter, and a further Act of 1868 vastly reduced the total being held for debt. In 1846 the prison was reclassified as a female one, although some male prisoners continued to be held here. This situation continued until 1865, when the prison reverted to its former status, becoming in 1877 the responsibility of the Home Office instead of the County Gaol. In 1916 the prison was closed for what was perhaps the first time in seven centuries. The Castle was used to house German POWs, but the County Council opened parts of it to the public and later trained police cadets there until the new Police College was opened in 1937 near Preston. During the Second World War it was occupied by armed forces and by the Royal Observer Corps. Traumatised ex-POWs from Japanese camps were rehabilitated here in 1945-6 but in 1954 the County Council once more sub-let the Castle to the Home Office as a prison, and so it has remained to date, despite various hopeful signs in the 1990s that it might become completely accessible as a tourist attraction.

Nearly a thousand years on, Castle and Priory church still stand side by side on Castle Hill, representing the twin powers of church and state, although what vicissitudes both have passed through on the way!

Ten

The Majesty of the Law

The law has impacted upon Lancaster in a big way, and no history of the town can ignore its significance.

The Borough Court was held weekly from time immemorial to resolve disputes between freemen. Early records are disappointing, since they are formulaic and, up until the early 18th century, in very abbreviated Latin. From that time onwards they provide two interesting sets of evidence well into the 19th century. One is a cross-section of the misdemeanours committed by the townsfolk against the public good, ranging from allowing privies to overflow (John Gardner, 1752) to keeping a dangerous bear (William Hall, 1756), or even being a procuress or bawd (Margaret Heaton, alias 'Kendale Pegg', 1764). The other is a quite remarkable list of goods belonging to the defendant, covering virtually all trades, just at a time when probate inventories, so useful up to the end of the 17th century, cease to be used. The goods were enumerated by bailiffs so that in the event of the defendant's non-appearance in court they could be sold. These lists are to be found in the dull-sounding Rule Books, which should remind us never to judge a source by its name.

In some cases townsfolk were taken into custody pending their court appearance. The Town Hall of 1671 had small prisons for ordinary people and 'those of the better sort', the latter enjoying more space and an attic location. The 1783 building had a 'Black Hole' under the main stairs, where drunkards were detained.

Summary justice could also be dispensed, usually for drunkenness but also for tradesmen giving short weight, in the stocks or the pillory in Market Square. For instance, a vagrant was publicly whipped in Market Square in 1803, while James Morris was pilloried there

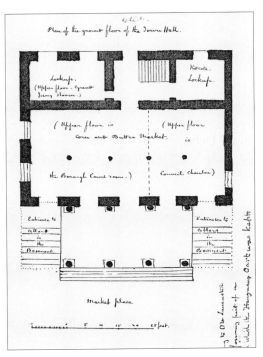

109 Drawing by J. S. Slinger showing the lockups in the old Town Hall. Both have now disappeared due to the moving of the stairs in the late 19th century.

110 The High Sheriff and javelin men ready to meet the Judge at the Castle. This postcard was posted in 1904.

in the same year for fraud – he was found dead in bed the next morning. Joshua Newsham was also pilloried in 1807. The ecclesiastical courts had their own sort of punishment. Hannah Clough, a prisoner in the Castle, did penance in the Priory church as late as 1824, dressed in a white sheet. This sort of shaming probably worked in a salutary fashion in a small town where everyone knew each other. Another device available to the local townsfolk was the 'cuckstoole', or ducking stool, which stood on the Green Ayre at the riverside. It is referred to in the earliest set of bye-laws dated 1562 but said to date from 1362, and is mentioned again in 1688 and 1726. At the latter date a new one was installed at a cost of £2 18s. 3d. The old stocks were probably fixed in place in the Market Square, as can be seen on a watercolour of about 1770 in the Whitworth Art Gallery, but portable wooden stocks were substituted in the mid-19th century. They are still preserved in the City Museum.

Quite distinct from the Borough Court was the court of Quarter Sessions, where all manner of smaller civil and criminal cases were held from Tudor times until 1889. The range of Quarter Sessions work was amazing, from the preliminary trial of suspected witches through to things like the management of roads and bridges.

At the top of the legal tree were the Assizes, where the principal criminal and civil cases were heard. Lancaster's position as county town from the Middle Ages gave it a significance far beyond its size as it resulted in the holding here, at the Castle, of the County Assizes twice each year, in spring and autumn. The Assizes were the result of a distinctively English centralist move in the 12th century which saw the dispatch of pairs of judges on a series of six circuits covering the country. The circuits themselves were made up of groups of counties, so judges proceeded from county town to county town, dispensing justice which, by definition, was more uniform in character and interpretation than that offered by other European countries. In effect, the justice of Westminster was available throughout the country.

The effect was that all criminal and many civil cases in the county were brought to Lancaster for trial. Other towns, particularly those in the far south of the county, might complain that their citizens had to travel inconvenient distances for justice, but they simply had to live with it until much later, when Assizes started to be held elsewhere by adjournment, and later still by right. The economic benefits to Lancaster were considerable, and it is not surprising it held on vigorously to its privilege reinforced by various charters. The arrival of the judges was accompanied by lawyers and their clerks and the county gentry, all of whom needed accommodation, or acquired town houses here. It was also an opportunity to transact business and for social occasions.

The Lancaster Assizes followed those at York, and one of the duties of the Sheriff was to meet the circuit judges at the county boundary, originally with an armed escort. As the route from York seems in the Middle Ages to have been via the desolate Trough of Bowland road, this may well have been a wise precaution. Later Sheriffs played up to the role by providing an escort of javelin-men, usually drawn from their tenantry, to meet the judges at the pre-Assizes church service. A number of these javelins still survive. The dates of the Assizes varied from year to year, and depended upon how many and how serious the cases were at the earlier Assizes in each circuit.

Because of the serious nature of cases brought to the Assizes it meant that most executions in the county occurred at Lancaster, with all the public excitement or forboding that entailed. As a significant town with royal connections, Lancaster was also the site for political executions, and display of heads and quarters of rebel leaders executed elsewhere. Also executed here were some caught up in the Pilgrimage of Grace in 1537, and a whole series of Catholic priests, as well as a few lay-men. Treason, either for rebellion or religious heresy, which became synonymous, was subject to the most gruesome and horrific forms of death, by hanging, drawing and quartering, and often attracted huge crowds upon Lancaster

THE
WONDERFVLL
DISCOVERIE OF
WITCHES IN THE COVN-
TIE OF LAN-
CASTER.

With the Arraignment and Triall of
Nineteene notorious WITCHES, at the Assizes and
generall Gaole deliuerie, holden at the Castle of
LANCASTER, vpon Munday, the se-
uenteenth of August last,
1612.

Before Sir I A M E S A L T H A M, and
Sir EDWARD BROMLEY, Knights; BARONS of his
Maiesties Court of EXCHEQVER: And Iustices
of Assize, Oyer and Terminor, and generall
Gaole deliuerie in the circuit of the
North Parts.

Together with the Arraignment and Triall of I E N N E T
PRESTON, at the Assizes holden at the Castle of Yorke,
the seuen and twentieth day of Iulie last past,
with her Execution for the murther
of Master LISTER
by Witchcraft.

Published and set forth by commandement of his Maiesties
Iustices of Assize in the North Parts.

By THOMAS POTTS Esquier.

LONDON,
Printed by W. Stansby for Iohn Barnes, dwelling neare
Holborne Conduit. 1613.

Title page of Thomas Potts'
account of the Pendle Witches.

111 Title page of Potts' 'Wonderfull Discoverie'. This contemporary account of the Pendle Witches of 1612 is far from being the only such account in the country but it has exercised a strange fascination since its publication, leading to a veritable mass of literature on these alleged witches. As a consequence little attention has been paid to other examples in Lancashire.

Moor, where all public execution took place until 1800. The crowds were not always sympathetic to the official line, in an area where Catholics and Protestants in general lived at peace with each other.

Other victims of the official process were so-called 'witches'. The Pendle Witches of 1612 have dominated the region's history and been considered from a great many angles, to the exclusion of a number of other cases. This is largely because the clerk of the court, Thomas Potts, wrote an account of the proceedings. Members of three families and a few other individuals, totalling 19 in all, from the poor and remote Pendle area were brought to court in April, accused of using various charms and curses. Among them were two old women, Elizabeth Southernes, known as 'Old Demdike', and Alice Whittle, or 'Chattox'. The former, aged eighty or so, and alleged to have been a witch for fifty years, described as 'a general Agent for the Devill in those parts', died in prison before she came to trial. An alleged plan to blow up Lancaster Castle and kill the Keeper, Thomas Covell, added to the seriousness of the charges. Ultimately eight women and two men were found guilty of witchcraft and hanged at the August Assizes, largely on the evidence of a nine-year-old girl. A sequel was played out in 1633 when 17 more from Pendle were accused of witchcraft on the evidence of a boy, Edward Robinson. Again they were tried at Lancaster and sentenced, but luckily for them the case came to the attention of the king, who examined and subsequently reprieved them.

These cases were not isolated. In 1629 Jennet Wilkinson of Ellel was accused of bewitching cattle and examined before Thomas Covell. We do not know what transpired, but from his actions during the 1612 proceedings we know Covell was no sceptic, so we must fear for Jennet. In 1634, 1635, and in 1654-5 trials for witchcraft took place in Lancaster of which no details survive, and in 1666 Isabel Rigby of Hindley was executed there, the last in the county to be hanged for witchcraft. Popular belief in witchcraft continued, however. As late as 1810 a calf was burnt alive on a farm in the district, in order to break a 'bewitchment', on the advice of a 'cunning woman'.

Between 1583 and 1646, when to be a Catholic was dangerous and to be a priest was regarded as treason, 11 priests and four laymen were horrifically executed on Lancaster Moor. A memorial now marks the fact of their martyrdom, but the actual site is unknown. It may well be that the gallows were set up each time somewhere fresh, to avoid creating a focus for pilgrimage.

Imprisonment could also be very unpleasant and dangerous. In 1664 George Fox, founder of the Society of Friends, or Quakers, was brought to Lancaster Castle to await trial, an inevitable consequence of his determined and head-on approach to the civil and religious establishment.

> Then I was put into a tower, where the smoke of the other prisoners came up so thick that it stood as dew upon the walls, and sometimes it was so thick that I could hardly see the candle when it burned; and I being locked under three locks, the under-jailer, when the smoke was great, would hardly be persuaded to come up to unlock one of the uppermost doors, for fear of the smoke, so that I was almost smothered. Besides, it rained in upon my bed, and many times, when I went to stop out the rain in the cold winter season, my shirt was wet through with the rain that came in upon me while I was labouring to stop it out. And the place being high and open to the wind, sometimes as fast as I stopped it, the wind blew it out again. In this manner did I lie all that long, cold winter till the next assize; in which time I was so starved with cold and rain that my body was greatly swelled, and my limbs much benumbed.

112   Engraving of life in the debtors' prison by Edward Slack, *c.*1836. This view of the Quakers', one of the best of the debtors' rooms in Lancaster Castle, shows that life, for some, was not all that bad. On arrival a debtor would pay 'entry money' which would determine which of the many rooms about the Castle he would occupy. Boredom and despair were the main problems. Many debtors pursued or learnt a trade while inside, including several who became artists.

The Castle and its prison became a place for sightseeing in the 18th century, especially as the prison was gradually rebuilt. The Rev. W. MacRitchie came here in 1795:

> Take a guide and go up to the Castle, as well worth seeing as anything of the kind I have ever seen. The new apartments for the State prisoners lately erected by Harrison on a plan that would highly please the benevolent Howard himself. Sixty-four neat apartments for them, with enclosed ground without for air and exercise. Go up to Johns of Gaunt's Tower, and enjoy an amazingly fine prospect of the town, the bridge, the windings of the Lune, the sea, and the distant mountains, etc …

A German visitor, Johanna Schopenhauer, mother of the philosopher, came here between 1803 and 1805:

> The prison in Lancaster owes its excellent arrangements to the noble philanthropist, John Howard. It is a large building, a little Bastille-like from the outside, surrounded by high walls with four corner towers which serve as dormitories for the prisoners. Inside are a number of small courtyards separated by walls, which are constantly guarded. Prisoners spend their days in these courts, able to enjoy the sunlight and fresh air, eat in a room adjoining the yard in which they can also employ themselves as they wish during the day, and at night are taken back to their dormitories.
>
> The whole institution seemed to us well suited to its purpose, while at the same time being as humane as possible … The prisoners are separated in the yards in accordance with the type and severity of their crime. In the first and largest courtyard, at the entrance, were the debtors, a great number of them, many quite cheerful, some playing a game with a ball. Others just stood around, lost in their misery, their misfortune obviously resting heavily on their minds.

113 'The Castle and Arrival of Prisoners'. This contemporary painting illustrates the arrival at the Castle of a gang of poachers caught after a gamekeeper was shot dead on the Fitzherbert Brockholes estates at Claughton near Garstang in 1827. The poachers are all shackled by the legs. The men in light greatcoats are the constables. All manner of mayhem is occurring among the watching crowd, such as picking of pockets.

In spite of the fact that blue sky and the bright light were able to penetrate this abode of suffering, we could not help finding the high walls, the narrow, low doors and the constant rattling of the bolts depressing. The building also contained two large courtrooms, well-furnished, the one for public hearings, in a rotunda, having seating arranged in the manner of a Roman amphitheatre. It must be an imposing sight when crowded with spectators.

Another foreign visitor in 1810-11 was the French American Louis Simond, whose journal of his trip to Great Britain was published in New York in 1815:

The old castle has been turned into a prison and court-house, the arrangement nearly on the plan of Chester, and owing likewise to the active humanity of Howard; it is even better than the one at Chester, as there is more room. The number of prisoners, however, we were sorry to see much greater, criminals as well as debtors. The jailor said he had under his lock and key debtors from £45,000 (a delinquent, collector of the customs) to seven shillings. Debtors for less than £10, we were told, are let out without cost, after as many days detention as there are shillings in the sum they owe; the creditor is obliged to pay for their maintenance. There are ten or twelve criminals executed every year, and a greater number transported to Botany Bay, who do not consider it as any punishment at all. Some are kept here at hard labour, something on the plan of our penitentiary prisons in America … This prison was perfectly clean in every part, to the very dungeons; - this again the fruit of Howard's labours.

A gentleman known only by the initials 'W. M.' saw prisoners arriving at the Castle in 1817:

> While I was in the castle yard a melancholy spectacle presented itself. Five unfortunate criminals arrived from Manchester, chained together by their legs, hands & necks, with heavy chains …

It is not often that we hear an account from the other side. In 1819 Samuel Bamford, the Radical and companion of 'Orator' Hunt of Peterloo fame, was brought to Lancaster Castle as a prisoner:

> Morning broke betwixt Garstang and Lancaster, and the first challenge of 'John-O-Gaunt's tower', as it stood out before us in the mild sun-light, excited our attention. It looked indeed like the stern and lordly keep of an old baron, and a small exercise of imagination was sufficient to place in our mind's eye, its powerful chieftain, waiting in helmet, cuirass and glaive, beneath its portcullis.
>
> We passed quickly along the streets of the town, and the clatter of our cavalcade aroused many from their peaceful slumbers. We dismounted at the foot of the castle steep, and walked up accompanied by our guards, and took our station beneath the arch of the grim old gate, the boldness and strength of its masonry attracting our admiration. A blow from the ponderous knocker made the place resound, and in a few minutes the wicket was opened, and we were prisoners in Lancaster Castle.

Anne Porter, who came here in 1849, saw evidence of the much tougher Victorian prison regime:

> Sept 5th Wednesday
> After breakfast this morning we went to see the Interior of the Castle which is now a Prison for Debtors & Criminals the former were playing & lounging idly in their exercising Court which we walked through to see the Prisoners confined there for theft & other crimes …
> We saw their food - & their sleeping apartments – everything beautifully clean – saw the Chapel and the Pew for the condemned criminals. Also the school - & the place where they picked Oakum & the Tread Mill (not at work) sad to see so many of our fellow creatures in this state degradation – I could only pray for their penitence & salvation …

Transportation

Although a large number of crimes in the 18th and early 19th centuries were regarded as capital, leading to the death penalty, in practice judges used a good deal of leniency. Where possible the accused were found guilty of a lesser crime, and even where the death penalty was recorded, the prisoners were often reprieved before the judges left town. This still left a horrific number of executions for crimes other than murder, but it is clear that the law as written and practised had grown a considerable distance apart by 1800. By the 1830s many crimes which had previously been regarded as capital were reclassified, and the number of executions diminished considerably.

An alternative to the death penalty or long custodial sentences (which were not common) was transportation. Initially this was to the American colonies, but their loss took away that option, which meant attention moved to Australia. The voyages of exploration of Captain Cook in the 1770s had led to the recognition that 'terra australis ignota' (the unknown southern land) was a continent. Its annexation by Britain and its remoteness led to the idea that it could become a penal colony. The First Fleet carrying nearly 780 convicts arrived in 1788 and the area around modern Sydney

('Botany Bay') quickly became a holding place for convicts transported for life, or for seven or 14 years. The most recalcitrant convicts were taken to Norfolk Island, far to the east of Australia. Transportation went on until 1868, by which time it was reckoned that 162,000 convicts had been taken to Australia. Some came back, legitimately or otherwise. Some did not survive the journey. Most probably settled down in what was to become a land of opportunity and made something of themselves.

Evidence at Lancaster for forcible transportation to America is at present slim, but for Australia the evidence increases dramatically. In practice there were three operations. The first was sentencing, and holding the prisoners. These were then selected (not all were thought able to make the journey) and taken in groups to the hulks of old ships moored in the Thames, awaiting a sailing. Finally groups of convicts were taken on to convict ships for the voyage to Australia. Local information from the Assizes occurs both in broadsheets issued at the time and in local newspapers. The further movement of convicts is largely covered by documents in the Public Record Office, while a book, *The Convict Ships*, usefully covers the voyages and complements of specific ships.

A few examples are worth considering. Thomas Robinson was tried at the Lancaster Spring Assizes of 1803 for highway robbery. He was found guilty and sentenced to death. This sentence was commuted to transportation for life 'to the eastern coast of New South Wales or some one or other of the Islands adjacent'. Before he could be sent, a royal pardon came through in June, conditional on him being imprisoned for 12 months. In March 1815 John Jones, aged 19, was found guilty of burglary in the house of Thomas Bolton in Liverpool. His death sentence was commuted to transportation for life before the judge left Lancaster and he was duly transported to Australia, where his descendants still live. John Smith of Dumfries was tried with two others at Lancaster Assizes in March 1830 for assaulting and robbing Joseph Sherwood at Walton-on-the-Hill (Liverpool) and robbing Joseph Bibby at West Derby. The death sentence for the latter crime was again commuted by the judge and, though nothing further is recorded locally, Smith is known to have been transported to Hobart, Tasmania.

This brief note describes the next stage, transfer to the hulks:

> Received this 21 February 1823 on board the *Retribution* hulk at Sheerness the Bodies of the undermentioned Male Convicts from the Custody of the Keeper of the Gaol of Lancaster, viz. Wm. Massey, James Garner, James Lomas, James Fielden. J Mears Overseer.

Executions

After 1800 executions moved from Lancaster Moor to the place called Hanging Corner at the rear of the Castle. Here a temporary scaffold would be erected outside the new round tower after each Assizes. The victims were given only a short drop, and generally died of strangulation. Rev. Joseph Rowley, master of the Free School for 23 years and prison chaplain for 54 from 1804, attended 168 executions. He thought it salutary for the boys of the school to see crime punished and gave them a half-holiday to watch.

From 1832 a number of crimes were removed from the capital list, and in 1835 the holding of Assizes ceased to be Lancaster's monopoly. This led to a great reduction in executions here. In 1868 executions ceased to be held in public, and a 'topping shed' was constructed within the prison. The last execution at Lancaster was that of Thomas Rawcliffe, in 1910, but the facilities remained here until 1965, just in case …

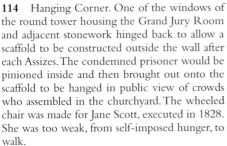

114 Hanging Corner. One of the windows of the round tower housing the Grand Jury Room and adjacent stonework hinged back to allow a scaffold to be constructed outside the wall after each Assizes. The condemned prisoner would be pinioned inside and then brought out onto the scaffold to be hanged in public view of crowds who assembled in the churchyard. The wheeled chair was made for Jane Scott, executed in 1828. She was too weak, from self-imposed hunger, to walk.

115 Portrait of Rev. J. Rowley in 1856, aged 86. As chaplain to the Gaol and master of the Free School he probably saw more public hangings than anyone else in Lancaster. The boys of the school were encouraged to watch, so that they might gain a respect for the law.

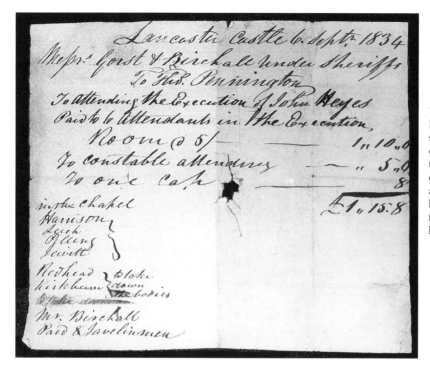

116 Bill for hanging John Heyes in 1834. This rare survival records some of the costs of attendants to watch the prisoner and to cut down the corpse afterwards, a cap or hood to cover his head, and accommodation for the under-sheriffs, who had to witness the hanging.

Executions at Lancaster Castle 1801-35

1801	September 12	Thos Walmsley	forged notes			Luke Lockard	forgery
		Arthur Garraghty	"			Peter Higgins	"
		William Gallant	seduction of soldier			James Yates	rape
		Isaac Slater	theft		September 27	T. Rix	sodomy
		Joseph)				Isaac Hitchen	"
		John) Mason	burglary	1807	April 11	Richard Reeves	uttering forged notes
		Simon)			September 5	James Callaghan	highway robbery
1802	September 2	Henry Hurst	murder			James Freeman	"
	September 18	Elias Gibson	forging will			Thomas Byrne	"
		Nicholas Sherlock	highway robbery	1808	April 9	Mary Charnley	robbery & arson
1803	April 9	Patrick Quigley	burglary	1809	April 22	Eli Lowe	uttering forged notes
		Henry Rice	"			John Richardson	"
		Thomas Ward	"			James Madden	"
		George Short	"			John Potts	"
1804	April 28	- Barker	burglary			Martin Goodhall	"
		- Chadwick	"			Charles Turner	"
	May 5	Joseph Brown	highway robbery			Thomas Barker	"
	September 8	James Ogilvie	forging	1810	April 21	Henry Cooper	highway robbery
		Thomas Smith	"			Thomas Hallpike	uttering forged notes
		Thos. Boadle	uttering forged notes			William Sandbach	forgery
		James Bridge	"			Adam Brooks	unnatural crime
		John Bradshaw Magee	"			Henry Young	wilful shooting
1805	April 1	John Lever	murder		October 13	Robert Welch	uttering forged notes
1806	April 19	Mary Jackson	felony	1811	April 27	William Cunliffe	burglary
		James Foxcroft	burglary			Nathaniel Dearden	"
		Christopher Simpson	highway robbery			Patrick McCourt	uttering forged notes
	September 13	Joseph Holland	sodomy	1812	June 13	James Smith	rioting
		S. Stockton	"			Thos. Kerfoot	"
		John Powell	"			Job Fletcher	"

Year	Date	Name	Offence
		Abraham Charlson	"
		John Howarth	"
		John Lee	"
		Thomas Hoyle	"
		Hannah Smith	"
	September 19	John Wright	forging & uttering
		James Cogan	highway robbery
		Henry McGleade	burglary
		Joseph McGleade	"
		Thomas Robinson	stabbing
1813	April 24	Thomas Dwyer	highway robbery
		John Davis	"
		Timothy O'Brien	"
		Tobias Tool	"
		James Rogers	"
		Robert Barber	uttering forged notes
	October 2	Robert Dewhurst	"
		John Thorpe	highway robbery
1814	March 19	John Buckley	murder
		George Ellwood	shooting
		Charles Taylor	burglary
		Benjamin Butterworth	"
		James Ashworth	"
	September 24	William Murphy	uttering forged notes
		John Brown	horse stealing
1815	April 22	George Lyon	burglary
		David Bennett	"
		William Houghton	"
		Moses Owen	horse stealing
		John Warburton	highway robbery
1816	September 16	Susannah Holroyd	murder
	September 28	John James	burglary
		John Jones	"
		Michael McGuire	"
		Peter Hughes	selling forged notes
		James McLean Boyd	"
1817	April 19	William Matthews	burglary
		John Hughes	highway robbery
		William Crabtree	"
		William Moore	"
		Hall Wylde	"
		T. McCullogh	"
		Joseph Bratt	"
		Peter Jones	"
		Edmund Lord	uttering forged notes
	September 6	John Nuttall	murder
		Henry Schofield	"
		James Ashcroft sen.	"
		James Ashcroft jnr.	"
		David Ashcroft	"
		William Holden	"
	September 20	Jenny Cheetham	uttering forged notes
		John Weld	"
		John Ashworth	"
		Patrick McManus	"
		Thomas Armstrong	arson
1818	April 18	Margaret Dowd	uttering forged notes
		William Stewart	uttering forged notes
		Robert Wardlow	"
		Thomas Curry	"
		George Hesketh	burglary
1819	April 17	Henry Entwistle	uttering forged notes
		John Kay	"
		John Horsman Drake	"
		John Clark	"
		Henry Moncrieffe	rape
		William Smith	highway robbery
	September 25	Thomas Price	highway robbery
		James Hagin	burglary
1820	March 27	John Dunn	murder
		J. Todd	uttering forged notes
		Philip Rogers	"
		Peter McCormick	"
		William Parker	highway robbery
		Charles Miller	"
	September 16	William Hall	highway robbery
		Henry Houghton	forgery
1821	April 21	Abraham Wade	uttering forged notes
		John Quin	"
	October 20	William Davis	shooting
		Joseph Jones	burglary
1822	April 20	George Farrow	"
		James Gallagher	"
		John Lawless	"
		John Duckworth	uttering forged bill
1823			no executions
1824	Mar. 22	Henry Griffiths	murder
	April 3	Kay Aspinall	burglary
		John Jolly	"
1825			no executions
1826	March 20	John Diggles	murder
	August 21	Alexander McKean	"
		Michael McKean	"
	September 9	Patrick Rafferty	highway robbery
		John Wainwright	stabbing
1827	March 26	Rachael Bradley	murder
	September 10	William Robinson	"
	September 29	William Heyworth	highway robbery
		Roger Heyworth	"
		George Heyworth	"
1828	March 22	Jane Scott	murder
1829	March 23	James Cliffe	"
1830	March 15	Alexander Gibbons	"
	April 3	Thomas Miller	murder
	September 18	Joseph Rowbottom	unnatural crime
1831	March 14	Moses Ferneley	murder
		Ashton Worrall	"
		William Worrall	"
	April 2	John Mulvay	highway robbery
		Thomas Mulvay	"
1832	March 12	William Heaton	murder
		John Thomas	"

At this time various offences ceased to be punishable by death, eg. coining or petty theft.

Year	Date	Name	Offence
1833	August 19	John Roach	murder
	August 31	Patrick McPartland	shooting
		John Howarth	wounding
1834	March 19	Mary Holden	murder
	September 6	John Heyes	rape
1835	March 23	Norman Welch	murder
	March 26	John Orrell	murder
1853	September 3	Richard Pedder	murder
1857	August 29	Richard Hardman	murder
1865	March 25	Stephen Burke	murder

The last public execution at Lancaster

Year	Date	Name	Offence
1875	August 16	Mark Fiddler	murder
		William McCullough	murder
1879	February 11	William McGuinness	murder
1886	February 9	Joseph Baines	murder
1887	August 1	Alfred Sowrey	murder
1910	November 15	Thomas Rawcliffe	murder

The last execution at Lancaster

Notes

Where do you come From?

Neolithic
G.D.B. Jones and D.C.A. Shotter, *Roman Lancaster: Rescue Archaeology in an Historic City 1970-75*, 1988, 77-9, 207 and Pl. 28

Iron Age and Roman
B.J.N. Edwards, 'Roman Finds from "Contrebis"', *C & WAAS*, ns LXXI, 1971, 17-34
D. Shotter and A. White, *Roman Fort and Town of Lancaster*, Lancaster University, Centre for North West Regional Studies, Occasional Paper no. 18, 1990
D. Shotter and A. White, *The Romans in Lunesdale*, Lancaster University, Centre for North West Regional Studies, Occasional Paper no. 31, 1995

Anglo-Saxon and Viking
W.G. Collingwood, *Northumbrian Crosses of the Pre-Norman Age*, 1927, 58, 126
B.J.N. Edwards, 'A Portion of an Inscribed Pre-Conquest Cross-Shaft from Lancaster', *Medieval Archaeology*, X, 1966, 146-9
E. Ekwall, *The Concise Oxford Dictionary of English Place-Names*, 1947
N.J. Higham, *The Northern Counties to AD 1000*, 1986
N.J. Higham, *The Kingdom of Northumbria AD 350-1100*, 1993

Normans
P. Morgan (ed.), *Domesday Book, 26, Cheshire*, 1978, 301c ff.
(Lancashire did not exist at the time of Domesday. Part of it is listed under Cheshire and part under Yorkshire)

Middle Ages
W. Farrer and J. Brownbill, *The Victoria History of the County of Lancashire*, II, 1908, 170ff

17th century
Lancaster Borough Records: Apprentice and Freemen's Rolls
Lancaster Borough Records, Minute Book B 1676-1702, f191; Book G 1709-36

Slavery
M. Elder, *The Slave Trade and the Economic Development of 18th Century Lancaster*, 1992
Parish Registers of Lancaster, Warton and Heysham

18th and 19th centuries
M. Hartley and J. Ingilby, *Yorkshire Album; Photos of Everyday Life 1900-1950*, 1988, 24

Holden: Rotherham Central Library 2/F1/1
Census Enumerators' Returns, 1881
Lancaster Central Library, Obituaries Scrapbook
Police Photograph Book, Lancaster City Museums, LM89.13

20th century
K. Chahal and S. Edwards, *A Survey of Minority Ethnic Communities and Services in Lancaster District*, 2002
1991 Census Analysis
I am grateful to Ruth Shaw who carried out some basic research on the Indian and Polish communities while on attachment to Lancaster City Museums in 1998

Development of the Townscape
Camden's *Britannia* (Philemon Holland's translation), 1610, 754
L. Toulmin Smith, *Leland's Itinerary in England and Wales*, vol. IV, 1910, 11
W. Stukeley, *Itinerarium Curiosum*, 1776, ii, 38

Fields
M. Derbyshire, 'Reconstructing the layout of the Town Fields of Lancaster', *Contrebis*, XXVI, 2001-2, 21-31
J. Field, *English Field Names*, 1972, 211, 213
Deeds of Marton property among those of 76 Church Street
Lancaster Central Library, MS3706 (1796)

Georgian development
J.J. Cartwright (ed.), *The Travels through England of Dr. Richard Pococke*, I, 1888, 14
A. White, *The Buildings of Georgian Lancaster*, Lancaster University, Centre for North West Regional Studies, Occasional Paper no. 39, 2000
Anon. 1747: Wiltshire Record Office WRO 1742/5144
'W.M.': Cheshire Record Office DDX 224

Victorian development
R. Owen, *Report on the Sanitary Condition of the Town of Lancaster*, Health of Towns Commission, 1845
A. White and M. Winstanley, *Victorian Terraced Houses in Lancaster*, Lancaster University, Centre for North West Regional Studies, Occasional Paper no. 31, 1996

Streets
S.H. Penney, *Lancaster: The Evolution of its Townscape to 1800*, Lancaster University, Centre for North West Regional Studies, Occasional Paper no. 9, 1981
A. White (ed.), *A History of Lancaster*, 2001, 50-3

House and Home

Roman

D. Shotter and A. White, *Roman Fort and Town of Lancaster*, Lancaster University, Centre for North West Regional Studies, Occasional Paper no. 18, 1990

D. Shotter and A. White, *The Romans in Lunesdale*, Lancaster University, Centre for North West Regional Studies, Occasional Paper no. 31, 1995

Middle Ages

J. Brownbill, *The Coucher Book of Furness Abbey*, II, I, 1915, 200-11

W. Farrer (ed.), *The Chartulary of Cockersand Abbey of the Premonstratensian Order*, III, I, 1905, 823-5

W. Farrer, *Lancashire Inquests, Extents and Feudal Aids*, II, L & C R S, 54, 1907, 27, 75ff, 167ff

S.H. Penney, *Lancaster: The Evolution of its Townscape to 1800*, Lancaster University, Centre for North West Regional Studies, Occasional Paper no. 9, 1981

W.O. Roper, *Materials for the History of the Church of Lancaster*, 2, passim

R. Cunliffe Shaw, *The Royal Forest of Lancaster*, 1956, 140

16th century

Col. W.H. Chipindall, *A Sixteenth Century Survey and Year's Accounts of the Estates of Hornby Castle, Lancashire*, Chetham Society, 102, 1939, 93

Capt. Howard: L.G. Wickham Legg (ed.), *A Relation of a Short Survey of 26 Counties*, 1904, 43-4

Lancaster Central Library, MS5553

17th century

E. Garnett, *Dated Buildings of South Lonsdale*, Lancaster University, Centre for North West Regional Studies, 1994

Georgian period

A. White, *The Buildings of Georgian Lancaster*, Lancaster University, Centre for North West Regional Studies, Occasional Paper no. 39, 2000

A. White (ed.), *Beauties of the North: Lancaster in 1820*, 1989

Victorian period

A. White and M. Winstanley, *Victorian Terraced Housing in Lancaster*, Lancaster University, Centre for North West Regional Studies, Occasional Paper no. 33, 1996

Oral history tapes and transcripts in the Centre for North West Studies, Lancaster University

Modern period

I am grateful to Deborah Dobby for the work she did on council housing in Lancaster while on attachment to Lancaster City Museums in 2001.

J.B. Cullingworth, *Housing in Transition: a case study of the City of Lancaster, 1958-62*, 1963

E. Roberts, *Working Class Barrow and Lancaster 1890 to 1930*, Lancaster University, Centre for North West Regional Studies, Occasional Paper no. 2, 1976

Lancaster on the Map

General

J.J. Bagley and A. G. Hodgkiss, *Lancashire: A History of the County Palatine in Early Maps*, 1985

G. Boulton, *Lancaster Maps; a Description of Maps published before 1900*, Lancaster City Museums, Local Studies 13, 1991

M.R.G. Conzen, 'The use of town plans in the study of urban history', in H. J. Dyos (ed.), *The Study of Urban History*, 1968, 113-30

1684

K.H. Docton, 'Lancaster 1684', *Historic Society of Lancashire and Cheshire*, 109, 1957, 125-42

1821

Lancaster Central Library; MS7055 (Binns family including extracts from Jonathan Binns' Commonplace Book 1785-1871), ff. 53-4

Working for a Living

John Lawson

C.M. Brooks, 'Aspects of the sugar-refining industry from the 16th to the 19th century', *Post-Medieval Archaeology*, 17, 1983, 1-14

George Fox's journal quoted in M. Mullett (ed.), *Early Lancaster Friends*, University of Lancaster, Centre for North West Regional Studies, Occasional Paper no. 5, 1978, 22

Towneley Hall Map, 1684

William Stout

J.D. Marshall (ed.), *The Autobiography of William Stout of Lancaster 1665-1752*, 1967

John Holland

A.J. White, 'Lancaster Clay Tobacco-Pipes', *Contrebis*, 3, 2, 1975, 58-68

Lancaster Borough Records; Stallenge Rolls 1737-55

Robert Gillow

Lancaster Borough Records; Apprentice and Freedom Rolls

M. Burkett *et al.*, *A History of Gillow of Lancaster*, 1984

Dodshon Foster

M. Elder, 'Dodshon Foster of Lancaster', *Lancaster Maritime Journal*, I, 1997, 14-18

Portrait and diary in Lancaster Maritime Museum

Richard Fisher

A. White, *The Buildings of Georgian Lancaster*, University of Lancaster, Centre for North West Regional Studies, Occasional Paper no.39, 2000, 13

Lancaster Borough Records; Apprentice and Freedom Rolls

Lancaster Borough Records; Rule Book 1784-1822

Richard Dilworth

Lancaster Borough Records; Apprentice, Stallenge and Freedom Rolls

Universal British Directory, 1794

Georgiana Trusler

Lancaster Borough Records; Rule Book 1784-1822

Lancaster Central Library; MS3706, (1796)

Correspondence with Emmeline Leary (descendant)

Thomas Standen
R.N. Billington and J. Brownbill, *St. Peter's, Lancaster: A History*, 1910, 215, 237
A.White, *The Buildings of Georgian Lancaster*, Lancaster University, Centre for North West Regional Studies, Occasional Paper no. 39, 2000, 12

Dorothy Bentham
Lancaster Gazette 8/7/1803
Lancaster Central Library; MS3706 (1796)
Deeds of 6 Castle Park

Jane Noon
'Cross Fleury', *Time-Honoured Lancaster*, 1891, 429
Trade Directories
Lancaster Central Library; MS8783
Soulby Collection of handbills, Cumbria Record Office, Barrow-in-Furness; ZS49 & 63

Gideon Yates
Lancaster Borough Records; Rule Book 1784-1822, ff. 63, 93
Lancaster Gazette 5/3/1803, 4/2/1804, 11/8/1804, 5/1/1805
Lancashire Record Office, QJB/53/45

Malcolm Wright
Lancaster Guardian 8/11/1845
Lancaster Central Library; Hewitson Memoranda, 2, 14
Illuminated Address in Lancaster City Museums, LMA235
Poem in Lancaster Central Library; PT1481

The Washerwomen of Golgotha
'Cross-Fleury', *Time-Honoured Lancaster*, 1891, 581
Census Enumerators' Returns, 1841, 1851, 1881

Robert Threlfall
Census Enumerators' Returns, 1871, 1891, 1901
Billheads in Lancaster City Museums; LM81.36/1-26
Grave Records, Lancaster Cemetery, Lancaster City Council
Lancaster Guardian 19/5/1928
Lancaster Central Library; Obituaries Press-Cutting Book 1923-32

More recent lives
E. Roberts, *Working-Class Barrow and Lancaster 1890 to 1930*, University of Lancaster, Centre for North West Regional Studies, Occasional Paper no. 2, 1976 (and oral history archive at Lancaster University)
D. Stocker, *Potted Tales; Recollections and Views of Morecambe Bay Fishermen*, Lancaster City Museums Local Studies, 8, 1988 (and oral history archive at Lancaster City Museums)

Entertainment
Middle Ages to 17th century
Cross Fleury, *Time-Honoured Lancaster*, 1891, 48-9
M. Mullett (ed.), *Early Lancaster Friends*, Lancaster University, Centre for North West Regional Studies, Occasional Paper no. 5, 1978
T. Pape, *The Charters of the City of Lancaster*, 1952, 20-1
J. Parker (ed.), *Calendar of Lancashire Assize Rolls*, RSLC, 47, 1904, 113
R. Simpson, *The History and Antiquities of the Town of Lancaster*, 1852

Boundary Ridings
W.O. Roper, *Materials for a History of Lancaster*, 1907, 321-62

Theatre
A.G. Betjemann, *The Grand Theatre, Lancaster: Two Centuries of Entertainment*, Centre for North West Regional Studies, Occasional Paper no.11, 1982
Rev. W. MacRitchie, *Diary of a Tour through Great Britain in 1795*, 1897, 35-6

Raree Shows
Lancaster Gazette, 8/10/1802, 3/5/1819, 11/10/1828
Lancaster Central Library, Sessions Book 1737-66, MS102, f. 99

Circus
Lancaster Borough Records, Rule Book 1784-1822, ff. 96-7
Lancaster Gazette, 5/5/1804, 19/3/1808, 30/11/1821

Balloons
S.E. Stuart and W. T. W. Potts, 'Richard Gillow and Vincent Lunardi: Early Balloon Flights and the Lancaster Balloon Mystery', *Contrebis*, XXIV, 1999, 26-33
Lancaster Gazette 31/7/1832 and 16/7/1832

Club Walks
C. Clark, *An Historical and Descriptive Account of the Town of Lancaster*, 1807, 51-2

Racing, Wagers and Cock-fights
K.H. Docton, 'The Lancaster Races', *On Lancaster*, 1971
Lancaster Gazette 6/6/1813, 15/2/1812, 9/4/1821, 31/3/1823
Plan of racecourse in 1720 by Rev. Holme, in J. S. Slinger's annotated copy of Clark's *History*, Lancaster Central Library, MS8687

Speeding
Lancaster Central Library, Sessions Book 1802-35, MS3333, 14/10/1802
Lancaster Borough Records, Rule Book 1784-1822, f. 165

Sport
Cross Fleury, *Time-Honoured Lancaster*, 1891, 546
N. Wigglesworth, *A History of Rowing in Lancaster*, Lancaster City Museums, Local Studies no. 17, 1992
Lancaster Gazette 12/5/1821, 22/11/1823

Cycling
S. Dawson, *Incidents in the Course of a Long Cycling Career* (n.d.)
(Anon) *Graphic Description of Lancaster and Morecambe*, 1894, 44, 47

Music Hall
A.G. Betjemann, *The Grand Theatre, Lancaster: Two Centuries of Entertainment*, Centre for North West Regional Studies, Occasional Paper no. 11, 1982

Cinema
Lancaster Official Guide (n.d., but 1936)

Old Lancaster Exhibition
Old Lancaster Historical, Antiquarian & Picture Exhibition (catalogue), 1908

Pageants
Souvenir Guides and Books of Words for 1913 and 1930 Pageants
Official photographs of 1937 City Celebrations in Lancaster Central Library

Getting There
General
A. Crosby (ed.), *Leading the Way; a History of Lancashire's Roads*, 1998
P.J.G. Ransom, *The Archaeology of the Transport Revolution 1750-1850*, 1984

Roman roads
D. Shotter and A. White, *The Romans in Lunesdale*, Lancaster University, Centre for North West Regional Studies, Occasional Paper no. 31, 1995

State of roads
E. Bowen, *Britannia Depicta or Ogilby Improv'd*, 1720 (reprinted 1970)

Transport of goods
Baines' Directory, 1825
Mannex & Co. Directory, 1881
Universal British Directory, 1794
Lancaster Borough Records; Rule Book 1784-1822

By Sea
J.D. Marshall, *The Autobiography of William Stout of Lancaster 1665-1752*, Chetham Soc., 3rd ser., 14, 1967
Baines' Directory, 1825
Universal British Directory, 1794

Over the Sands
H.C. Collins, *Lancashire Plain and Seaboard*, 1953, 162-85
J.C. Dickinson, *The Land of Cartmel; a History*, 1980, 41-53
Lancaster Borough Records, Bailiffs' Book H 1772-96, f.3

Turnpikes
W. Albert, *The Turnpike Road System in England 1663-1840*, 1972
R. Freethy, *Turnpikes and Toll Houses of Lancashire*, 1986
M. Hartley, J. Ingilby, D. S. Hall and L. P. Wenham, *Alexander Fothergill and the Richmond to Lancaster Turnpike Road*, 1985
J. Cary, *Cary's New Itinerary*, 1798, 232, 317, 600
Lancaster Borough Records, Bailiffs' Accounts, Rentals 1736-71, *sub* 1749
Plans of the toll-houses at Fowler Hill, Scotforth and Beaumont are in Lancaster Central Library, PL 53/5-7

Canal
C. Hadfield and G. Biddle, *The Canals of North West England*, 2 vols., 1970
A. White, *Fast Packet Boats on the Lancaster Canal*, Lancaster City Museums Local Studies, No. 1, 1987

Coaching
A. Bates, *Directory of Stage Coach Services 1836*, 1969
C. Clark, *A Historical and Descriptive Account of the Town of Lancaster*, 1807, 60
The Lonsdale Magazine, 1, 1820, 383
Lancaster Central Library, Obituary Scrapbook 1906-23 for Canon Grenside

Railways
D. Binns, *The 'Little' North Western Railway*, 1994
M.D. Greville and G.O. Holt, *The Lancaster & Preston Junction Railway*, 1961
A. Hewitson, *Northwards between Preston and Lancaster*, 1900
K. Nuttall and T. Rawlings, *Railways around Lancaster*, 1980
The *Lancaster Gazette* and *Lancaster Guardian* files, railway ephemera and catalogues are now in Lancaster Central Library
Objects and illustrations in Lancaster City Museum

Motorway
H. Yeadon, 'The Motorway Era' in A. Crosby (ed.), *Leading the Way; a History of Lancashire's Roads*, 1998, 240-81

'Alarums and Excursions'
1322
W. Farrer, *Lancashire Inquests, Extents and Feudal Aids*, II, 1907, 115ff
Farrer and Brownbill, *Victoria County History Lancashire*, Vol. 2, 199; Vol. 8, 12
J. Johnson *et al.*, *Holinshed's Chronicles of England, Scotland and Ireland in Six Volumes*, 1808, V, 355
R. Cunliffe Shaw, *The Royal Forest of Lancaster*, 1956, 363
A. White (ed.), *A History of Lancaster*, 2001, 66-7

1389
Farrer and Brownbill, *Victoria County History Lancashire*, Vol. 2, 210
T. Pape, *The Charters of the City of Lancaster*, 1952, 26-7

1643, 1648, 1651
W. Beaumont (ed.), *A Discourse of the Warr in Lancashire*, Chetham Soc., 1864, 29
S. Bull, *The Civil War in Lancashire*, 1991, 18-19, 27, 29
W.O. Roper, *Materials for a History of Lancaster*, 1907, 38-41
A. White (ed.), *A History of Lancaster*, 2001, 95-7

1698
E.L. Jones, 'The Reduction of Fire Damage in Southern England, 1650-1850', *Post-Medieval Archaeology*, 2, 1968, 140-9
J.D. Marshall (ed.), *The Autobiography of William Stout of Lancaster 1665-1752*, Chetham Soc., 3rd ser., 14, 1967, 120
Lancashire Record Office, QSP/809/1

1715
Marshall, *Autobiography*, 173
Roper, *Materials*, 56-79
White, *History*, 133-4
Lancaster Borough Records, Book C, Orders and Elections 1679-1736, ff. 263, 267
Parish Registers

1745
I.G. Brown and H. Cheape, *Witness to Rebellion; John Maclean's Journal of the 'Forty-Five and the Penicuik Drawings*, 1996, 26
F. McLynn, *The Jacobite Army in England 1745; The Final Campaign*, 1998, 67-76, 158-73
Roper, *Materials*, 80-99
White, *History*, 134-5
Lancaster Borough Records, Book F, Bailiffs' Accounts 1736-71, ff. 306, 297
Parish Registers

Priory and Castle
W.G. Collingwood, *Northumbrian Crosses of the Pre-Norman Age*, 1927
N. Heywood, 'A Find of Anglo-Saxon Stycas at Lancaster', *British Numismatic Journal*, ser. 2, vol. 1, 1914, 1-2
S.E. Rigold, 'Litus Saxonicum – The Shore Forts as Mission Stations', in D. E. Johnston (ed.), *The Saxon Shore*, CBA Research Report no. 18, 1977, 70-5
D. Shotter and A. White, *Roman Fort and Town of Lancaster*, Lancaster University, Centre for North West Regional Studies, Occasional Paper no. 18, 1990
D. Shotter and A. White, *The Romans in Lunesdale*, Lancaster University, Centre for North West Regional Studies, Occasional Paper no. 31, 1995

Priory
Anon., 'Lancaster Jottings', *Historic Soc. of Lancs. & Chesh.*, LXV, 1914, 190-3; 'Lancaster Jottings, II', *HSLC*, LXVI, 1915, 265-71
H.J. Austin, 'Notes on the Discovery of an Apse at St Mary's Church, Lancaster, in 1911, and of other Discoveries', *Trans. Lancs. & Chesh. Antiq. Soc.*, XXXI, 1913, 1-6
C.P. Fendall and E.A. Crutchley, *The Diary of Benjamin Newton Rector of Wath 1816-1818*, 1933, 203-4
E.M. Grafton, 'Notes on the Benedictine Abbey of Seez: Its English Lands and Charters', *Hist. Soc. of Lancs. & Chesh.*, ns 23, 1907, 119-31
W.O. Roper, *Materials for the History of the Church of Lancaster*, 4 vols., Chetham Society, 1892-1906

Other churches
Cross Fleury, *Time-Honoured Lancaster*, 1891, 331-74
J. Price, *Sharpe, Paley and Austin; A Lancaster Architectural Practice 1836-1942*, Lancaster University, Centre for North West Regional Studies, Occasional Paper 35, 1998
M. Winstanley, 'The Town Transformed, 1815-1914', in A. White (ed.), *A History of Lancaster*, 2001, esp. 204-6

Castle
R.A. Brown, *English Castles*, 1970, 190
R.A. Brown, H. M. Colvin & A. J. Taylor (eds.), *The History of the King's Works. 2. The Middle Ages*, 1963, 692-3
C. Chalklin, 'Quarter-Sessions Building in Lancashire, 1770-1830', *The Georgian Group Journal*, X, 2000, 92-121
J. Champness, *Lancaster Castle: A Brief History*, 1993
W. Farrer, *The Lancashire Pipe Rolls*, 1902
C. Foster *et al.*, *Lancaster Castle as a 19th century Prison*, Lancaster City Museums, Local Studies no. 20, 1994

M. de Lacy, *Prison Reform in Lancashire, 1700-1850*, Chetham Society, 33, 1986
Essex Record Office, Diary of Millicent Bant, 1804 (D/DFr F1)
Dr S.H. Spiker, *Travels through England, Wales and Scotland*, 1820, 283ff

The Majesty of the Law
Borough Courts
Records of the Borough Courts are contained in a number of Rule Books and Sessions Books, divided between the Central Library and the City Museum

Summary Justice
Lancaster Gazette 16/2/1803, 9/4/1803, 18/7/1807, 2/3/1824
Lancaster Borough Records, Orders & Elections (D), 1708-30

Quarter Sessions
These records are all in the Lancashire Record Office and have a very extensive card index.

The Assizes
The Catholic Martyrs are covered by M. Mullett, 'Reformation and Renewal 1450-1690', in A. White (ed.), *A History of Lancaster*, 2001, 82-7
The bibliography of the Pendle Witches is very extensive, but highly repetitive. For other incidents see E. Baines, *The History of the County Palatine and Duchy of Lancashire* (Harland's edition), 1868, 198-208; A. White, *Two Encounters with the Supernatural in 17th century Lancashire*, Lancaster University, Centre for North West Regional Studies Bulletin, 15, 2001, 55-62

Prison
T. Hilton (ed.), *Samuel Bamford: Passages in the Life of a Radical*, 1984, 198
W. MacRitchie, *Diary of a Tour through Great Britain in 1795*, 1897, 35-6
R. Michaelis-Jena and W. Merson (eds. and trans.), *A Lady Travels; Journeys in England and Scotland from the Diaries of Johanna Schopenhauer*, 1988, 91-4
P.L. Parker (ed.), *George Fox's Journal*, 1905, 381-2
Anon. [Louis Simond], *Journal of a Tour and Residence in Great Britain during the years 1810 and 1811 by a French Traveller*, 1815, 256
Anne Porter: Worcester Record Office, BA3940/66(1)
'W.M.': Cheshire Record Office DDX 224

Transportation
C. Bateson, *The Convict Ships*, 1959
Robinson: papers in Lancaster City Museum LM2000.38/1
Jones: *Lancaster Gazette* 25/3/1815, 8/4/1815, 15/4/1815
Smith: *Lancaster Gazette* 13/3/1830, 20/3/1830

Executions
J. Champness, *Lancaster Castle: A Brief History*, 1993, 34-5
D. Sailor, *The County 'Hanging Town'; Trials, Executions and Imprisonment at Lancaster Castle* (n.d. but 1994)
Lancaster Gazette, passim

Index

Note: page numbers are in ordinary type; illustration numbers appear in **bold** type.

Abraham Heights, 43
Ala Augusta, 2
Ala Sebosiana, 2
Anon 1747, 19
Apollinaris, Lucius Julius, 2, **3**
Asclepius and Hygeia, 3
Ashton, Lord (James Williamson), 85, 86, 134
Assembly Rooms, 52, 64
Assizes, 146-7

Bailen, Rabbi Jacob, 10
Baldreston, Agnes de, 116
Balloon ascents, **66**, 82
Bamford, Samuel, 151
banks, 52; Dilworth, Arthington & Birkett, 37;
    Lancaster Banking Co., 37-8; Thomas
    Worswick, Sons & Co., 37
Bant, Millicent, 97, 143-4
Bare Hall, 7
Bath House, 53
Bentham, Dorothy, 67, 70
Black Friars (Dominicans), 13, 21, **21**, 45, 50
black servants (*see also* slaves), 6-9
Bland, James, **28**
Bonnie Prince Charlie, **90**, 123
Borough Courts, 146
Boundary Ridings, **63**, 77-8
Bowerham Barracks, **50**, 55-6
Bowling, **69**, 84-5
Bracken, Dr Henry, 123-4
Brigantes, 1
Brockbanks, 8, 53, **59**
Buck, Samuel and Nathaniel, **1**, 141
building bye-laws, 39
building techniques: brick, 33, 42; cruck
    construction, **26**, 30; reed and plaster, **31**;
    stone, 31-3; timber framing, 28ff
buses, **86**, 112; Battery bus, **85**, 112
Bus Station, 22, 36, 112

Camden, William, 13
canal, 53, **77**, **83**, 101-2, 107, 110
Castle, **1**, 9, 13, 49, 52, 53, 70, 125-6, 136-44,
    102-8, **110**; Adrian's Tower, 138, 141; in Civil
    War, 117-18; Crown Court, 142; damage
    (1322), 116; debtors in, 70, **112**, 144;
    demilitarised after Civil War, 141; Dungeon
    Tower, 139, 143; Joseph Gandy at, 142;
    Governor's House, 142; Hanging Corner, **114**,
    152; Thomas Harrison at, 142; John O'Gaunt
    Gatehouse, **105**, 139; Lungess Tower or Keep,
    107, 137, 138, 140; Norman layout, **102**, 136-
    7; prisoners, **113**, 120-1, 124, 142, 143, 144,
    148, 149-51; round towers, 138; Shire Hall,
    141, 142; Well Tower, **104**, 139
Castle Hill, **20**, 125
Castle Station, 18, 111
Cauponae, 76
Central Library, **28**
Church St. (76), 31, **90**, 123
cinema, 88
circus, 80-2
City Museum, **28**
Clayton, Rimmon, 86
Club walks, 82
coaching, 103-6
coal mines, **76**, 96
cockfighting, **68**, 84
'Contrebis', 1
Corporation Charter of 1193, **88**, 118
Corporation in Church, **100**, 131
Corporation Police, 70-1
Corporation Rule Books, 65-6, 95, 145
council housing, **39**, 40ff; Bowerham, 41; Ridge,
    41; Ryelands, **39**, 41
County Lunatic Asylum (Moor Hospital), 53, 55,
    57, 67, 142
Covell, Thomas, 28, 29, 47
'Cromwell's Mound', 118-19

Crosfields, 9
Cuckstoole, 146
Custom House, 64
cycling, **70-1**, 86
Cynibad, 3, **5**
Cynibald, son of Cuthberect, 3, **6**

Dalton, John, **33**, 37, 52
Darque, J. S., 86
Dawson, S., **70**, 86
Derby, Earl of, 50, 115, 117-18
Dickens, Charles, **81**, 106
Dilworth, Richard, **56**, 64-5
Dixon, John, 6, 7, **8**
Dunn, Jonathan, 103

Ellel, Hulle de, 77
Emery, John, **9**
emigration: to Virginia, 6; to West Indies, 6
executions, 77, 143, 144, 147, 152-5

fairs, 76-7
Fell, John and James, 6
fields, 16-18, **17**; early names, 5; Bolrum, 17;
    Deep Carr, 18; Edenbreck, 5, 17; Fenham
    Carr, 18; Greenfield, 17; Haverbreaks, 5, 17;
    Head Haw (Haugh), 17, 36, 50; Highfield, 17;
    Kellet Croft, 18; Marsh, **16**, 17, 18; Mawdale,
    17; Moor, 17, 18; Oatlands, 17; Sowerholme,
    17, 18; Summer Pasture, **32**, 36, 50; Usher's
    Meadow, 18; Vicarage Fields, 18, **20**, 50
Fiennes, Celia, 93-4
Fire, **29**, 30, 31, **88**, 118, 119-20
Fish Market, 45
Fish Stones, **28**
Fisher, Richard, 63-4
Foster, Dodshon, **55**, 62-3
Fox, George, 57, 148
Free School, 18, 45, 129, 152
Freebairn, Robert, **108**
Freehold, 39, **49**, 54
Freeman's Wood, **63**
Freemen, 6, **16**
Freemen's Rolls, **54**, 64
French Priors, 5
Fryerage, **33**, 52, 54
Furness, Michael de, 98

Gallows, 47, 143, 144
Gardyner's Almshouses, 47
Gaskell, Mrs, 97

Georgiana Trusler's School, 65-6
Gild of St Leonard and Holy Trinity, 76
Gillow family, 135
Gillow, Robert, 6, **54**, 60-2
Glasson Dock, 64
Golgotha, **72**
Great Bonifont (or Bamfant) Hall, **25**, 28, 47
Greaves, **18**, 54
Green Ayre, **1**, **9**, 24, 34, 45, 47, 50, 57, 62
Green Ayre Station, 111
Grippenhearl, Heartwick, 9

Hardwine, 3, **5**
Harrison, Robert and Margaret, 98
Head, Sir George, 102, 106
Hearne, Thomas, **107**
Herber House, 28, 50
Heyes, John, **116**
Holand, Sir Robert de, **24**, 25, 27; house, **24**, 25,
    27, 47
Holden, Richard, 9
Holland, John, **53**, 60
Holthusen, Johann Hinrich, 9
Howard, Captain, 28

inns *see* public houses
Invasions: of 1322, 115-16; of 1389, 116; of 1643,
    116-19; of 1715, 120-1; of 1745, 121-4

Jamea (Islamic) School, 11
Javelin-men, **110**, 147
Jelle Beck, 49
John O'Gaunt car, 111
John O'Gaunt locomotive, **82**, 109
'John Threlfall's old house', **30**
Johnson, Francis Elisabeth, 7, 8
Judges Lodging, 28, 47

King's Own Royal Regiment, **50**, 55
Kuhnle family, 10

Ladies' Walk, 129
Lancaster, Thomas, Earl of, 27, 115
Lancaster & Carlisle Railway, 110-11
Lancaster & Preston Railway, **82-4**, 107-10
Lancaster Royal Grammar School, 45
Lancaster Wagon Co., 56
Launoy, Sir Guilbert de, 91
Lawson, John, **51**, 57-8
Leland, John, 13
Leper Hospital (St Leonard), 24

'Little' North Western Railway, 111
Lune Bridge (Old Bridge), 13, 47, 93
Lune, river, 1, 36

M6 Motorway, 20, **87**, 113-14
Maclean, John, 122
MacRitchie, Rev. W., 79, 149
maps: John Speed 1610, 20, **43**, 45-6; Towneley
    Hall 1684 (Docton), **25**, **44**, **45**, 47-50, 57;
    Stephen Mackreth 1778, **46**, 50-2; Clark
    1807, **34**, 37; Jonathan Binns 1821, **47**, 52-4;
    Harrison and Hall 1877, **18**, **48-50**, 54-6
Market Cross, **28**, 45, 64, 76, 118
Masonic Hall, **29**, 31
medieval townsfolk, 26
Mercia, 3, 125
Militia Barracks, 55
Mill, 45
Mill-dam, 23-4, 45, 47, 50
Mitchell's Brewery, **26**, 30
monasteries: Cockersand Abbey, 26, **74**, 91, 92;
    Furness Abbey, **24**, 26, 27; Seez, Normandy,
    127; Sion Abbey, 47, 129
Monson, 106
Moorlands, 20, **38**, 40
'Mr Hornby's Great House', **28**, 33
Music Hall, 87

Newton, Rev. Benjamin, 131-2
Nigroe, Richard, 6
Noon, Jane, **58**, 67-8
Northumbria, 3, 125

Old Hall/New Hall, 28, 45, 47
Old Town Hall, 21, **28**, 34, 49, 88, **109**
origins: Anglo-Saxon, 3; French, 5, 9; German, 3,
    9, **10**, 10, 11, 58; Greek, 2, 3, **4**; Indian, 11,
    12; Irish, 10, 11; Jewish, 10; Norman, 5;
    Polish, 11, **12**, 12; Roman, 1-3; Viking, 4, 5
Owen, Richard, 20

packhorse tracks, 94
pageants, **72**, 88-9
Paley & Austin, 85, 135
Pandolfini, Rodolphe, 10
Penance in church, 146
Penny's Hospital, 52
Penny St. Station, **84**, 109
Phoenix Foundry, 86
pillory, 145-6
Pinfolde, 46

place-names, 4, 5
Places of Worship: Baptists, 135; Black Friars, **21**,
    24, 45, 116; Cathedral RC (St Peter's), 12, 56,
    133, 135; Catholic Chapel, Dalton Sq., 62, 66,
    135; Christ Church, 56, 135; Friends Meeting
    House, 21, 52, 57, 59, 134; High St. chapel,
    134; Mason St. chapel (RC), 62; Methodists,
    134-5; Mosque, **11**, 11, 134; Our Lady Queen
    of Poland (RC), 12; Presbyterian chapel, 52;
    St Anne's, 53, 134, 136; St John's, 36, 52, 134,
    136; St Joseph (RC) Skerton, **101**, 135; St
    Thomas, 56, 135
'Playhouse Fields', 18, 38, 55
poachers, **113**
Pococke, Dr Richard, 19
Pointer, **18**
Poitou, Roger de, 5, 127
Port Commission, 63, 64
Porter, Anne, 151
Pothouse, 52
pre-fabs, 43
Primrose, 20, **38**
Priory Church, **1**, 13, 18, **20**, 26, **91-100**, 116,
    125-34; Anglian crosses, 3, **5**, **6**; bells, 131,
    133-4; chantries in, 129; choir-stalls, **95**, **97**,
    99, 129, 133; conventual buildings, **93**, 127-8;
    music at, 131-2; 'Noah's Ark' (pew), **95**, 131;
    Regimental Chapel, 128, 134; Tower, 131
public houses: *Bear & Staff*, 95; *Black Bull*, 95;
    Black Horse, 67; *Blue Anchor*, 26, **28**; *Bowling
    Green*, 85; *Bull Hotel* (Morecambe), 103; *Bull's
    Head*, 79; *Commercial*, **28**, 33, 103, 104;
    Corporation Arms, 95; *Cross Keys*, 80, 95, 103;
    George, 47, 104; *George & Dragon*, **28**; *Golden
    Fleece*, 95; *Horse & Farrier*, **64**, 78-9; *King's
    Arms*, **81**, 103, 104, 106; *King's Arms*
    (Morecambe), 74; *Mare Maid*, 47; *Mitre*, 85;
    Naked Taylor, 47; *New*, 29, 30; *Old Sir Simon's*,
    80, 95, 104, 106; *Queen's Head*, 67; *Red Lion*,
    30; *Royal Oak*, **28**, **58**, 67-8, 103, 104; *Sun*,
    28, 45, 47, 52, **69**, 85, 104, 106; *Three Mariners*,
    23; *White Hart*, 95; *White Lion* (Penny St.), 94;
    White Lion (St Leonardgate), 95

Quarter Sessions, 146
Quernmore, 90-1

race courses, **67**, 82-3
railways, 102, 106, 107-11
Redman, Bishop Richard, 91-2
Ripley Hospital, 55

roads, 91-5, 111-13
Sir Robert de Holand's house, **24**, 25, 27, 47
Robinson, Francis, 6
Roman town: archaeological evidence, 13; fort,
    13-16, 18, **20**, 125-6; Greek doctors, 2, **4**;
    houses, **23**, 25; inscriptions, 1, **2**; layout, **15**;
    reconstruction, **14**; roads, **73**, 90-1
Rowley, Rev. J., **115**, 152
Royal Albert Asylum, 55

St Martin's College, **50**
'Salt' roads, 94-5
'Sambo', 6, **7**, 7
Saturninus, Julius, 2
Scale Hall, **40**, 41
Schoolboy 1786, 97
Schopenhauer, Johanna, 149
Scotforth, 20, 75
Scott, Jane, **114**
Shambles, 52
Sharp, William, **28**
Sharpe, Edmund, 10, 85, 86, 87
Sheriff, **110**, 147
ships and boats: *Barlborough*, 63; *Edward & Jane*,
    96; *Flora*, 96; *Imployment*, 96; *Laurel*, 96; *Myrtle*,
    96; *Prince Frederick*, 62; *Rose*, 96; *Swallow*, 102;
    Swiftsure, 102; *Trafalgar*, 9; *Waterwitch*, 102;
    Waterwitch II (Crewdson), **77**, 102
shipyards, **9**, 52-3, **59**
Siddons, Mrs, 79
Simond, Louis, 150
Skerton, **1**, 20, **42**, 43
Skerton Bridge, 37, 52
slavers, 33, 63
slaves, 6-8
slum clearance, 42
Sly, Joseph, 106
Spiker, Dr, 144
Stallenge Rolls, 60, 64
Standen, Thomas, **57**, 66-7
Standen Park, 44
Stewp (or Stoop) Hall, **25**, 28, 45, 47
stocks, 146
Storeys, 6, 10, 46
Stout, William, 33, **52**, 58-60, 119-20, 120-1
streets: Albert Terrace, **35**, 38; Anchor Lane, **19**,
    21; Ashton Rd, **41**, 43; Bath Mill Lane, 38;
    Belle Vue Terrace, **18**, 38; Bridge Lane, 22, 47;
    Cable St., 37; Calkeld Lane, 5, 21, 45;
    Chancery Lane, **19**; Chapel St., **31**, 34;
Cheapside (Butcher St./Pudding Lane), **3**, **22**,
    23; China Lane (St.), 22, 45, 47; Church St.
    (St Mary St./St Marygate), 1, 20, **23**, 25, **29**,
    30, 47, **89**, 119-20; Common Garden St., 23,
    50; Dalton Sq., 19, **21**, **33**, 33, 37, 52;
    Damside St., 23; Fenton St., **11**, 11, 52;
    High St., 19, 36, 50; King St., 22, 50;
    'Markahastrete', 26; Market Sq., **28**, 33, 45,
    49, **58**, 67-8; Market St., 21, 45, 50;
    Middle St., 36; Moor Lane, **1**, 17, 24; New
    Rd, 36, 50; New St., 36, **45**, 45, 50; Penny
    St., **1**, **15**, **21**, 23, 25, 50, 70, 118; Queen Sq.,
    37, 50; Queen St., 19, 33, 37, 50, 52; Ridge
    Lane, **59;** Ross Yard, **22**; St George's Quay, **9**,
    32, **36**, 36, 39, 50, 52, **59**; St Leonardgate, **1**,
    9, 24, 45, 49, 57; St Nicholas St., 45; Spring
    Garden St., 23, 50; Stonewell, **27**, 45;
    Thornfield, **62;** Westbourne Rd, 40
Stukeley, William, 14
Sugar House, 49, 57-8

Theatre, 53, 78-9, 80, 87, 134
Threlfall, Robert, **62**, 74-5
'Tiburn', 47
Toulnson's Almshouses, 50
Town Hall, **37**; prisons, 145
traders: cheese and bacon factor, 74-5; landlady,
    67; licensee, 67-8; pipemaker, **53**, 60;
    shopkeeper, 58-60; slater and plasterer, 66-7;
    stonemason, 63-4; sugarboiler, 57-8; tallow-
    chandler, **56**, 64-5; washerwoman, **60**, **61**, 73
trams, 112
transport over sands, **78**, 96-9
Transportation to Australia, 151-2
Trusler, Georgiana, 65-6
Turnpikes, **79**, 99-101

velocipede, 84

Wery Wall, **13**, 45
West Indies, 33, 57, 59; Jamaica, 60
White Cross, 45, 118
Williamsons, 6, 56
'WM' 1817, 20, 151
Windmill Hill, 63
witch trials, **111**, 148
Workhouse, 53, 55
Wright, Malcolm, 70-1

Yates, Gideon, **27**, **59**, 67, 67-8

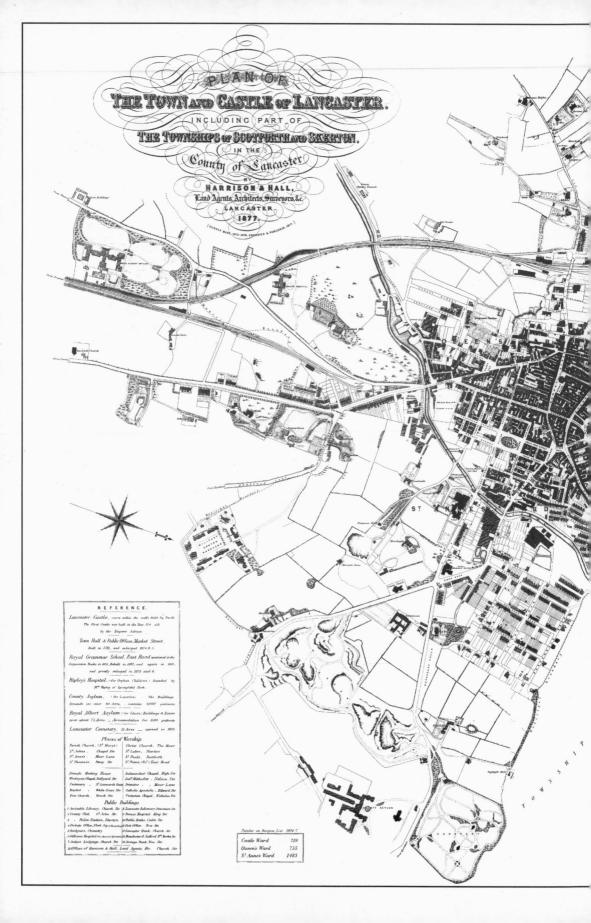

PLAN OF
THE TOWN AND CASTLE OF LANCASTER.
INCLUDING PART OF
THE TOWNSHIPS OF SCOTFORTH AND SKERTON.
IN THE
County of Lancaster
BY
HARRISON & HALL,
Land Agents, Architects, Surveyors, &c.
LANCASTER
1877.
(SURVEY MADE 1875-1876, ENGRAVED & PUBLISHED 1877.)

REFERENCE.

Lancaster Castle, covers within the walls 10,115 Sq. Yards
The First Castle was built in the Year 374 A.D.
by the Emperor Adrian.

Town Hall & Public Offices, Market Street.
Built in 1781, and enlarged 1874 & 5.

Royal Grammar School, East Road mentioned in the
Corporation Books in 1472, Rebuilt in 1682, and again in 1851,
and greatly enlarged in 1875 and 6.

Ripley's Hospital, (for Orphan Children) founded by
Mrs Ripley of Springfield Park.

County Asylum, (for Lunatics); The Buildings
Grounds etc cover over 80 Acres, contains 1,000 patients

Royal Albert Asylum (for Idiots) Buildings & Estate
cover about 75 Acres. Accommodation for 600 patients

Lancaster Cemetery, 21 Acres opened in 1855

Places of Worship
Parish Church, (St Marys)   Christ Church, The Moor
St Johns, Chapel Str   St Lukes, Skerton
St Annes, Moor Lane   St Pauls, Scotforth
St Thomas's, Penny Str   St Peters, (R.C.) East Road

Friends Meeting House   Independent Chapel, High Str
Wesleyan Chapel, Sulyard Str   Ind.t Methodist, Nelson Str
Centenary   St Leonards Gate   Primitive   Moor Lane
Baptist   White Cross Str   Catholic Apostolic, Edward Str
Free Church, Brock Str   Unitarian Chapel, Nicholas Str

Public Buildings
1 Amicable Library, Church Str   12 Lancaster Infirmary, Thurnham Str
2 County Club,   6 St John Str   13 Pennys Hospital, King Str
3 .   Police Station, Skerton   14 Public Baths, Cable Str
4 Probate Office, Fleet Sq   15 Post Office, New Str
5 Gas&?works, Chemistry   16 Lancaster Bank, Church Str
6 Gillisons Hospital   17 Manchester & Salford B's Market Str
7 Judges Lodgings, Church Str   18 Savings Bank, New Str
8 Offices of Harrison & Hall, Land Agents, Etc. Church Str

Number on Burgess List 1876/7
Castle Ward   719
Queen's Ward   755
St Anne's Ward   1483